Praise for Abigail Pogrebin's

ONE *AND THE* SAME

"[An] enchanting, fascinating book."

—Lesley Stahl of *60 Minutes* and
The Women on the Web

"A goldmine of information and insight into the twin experience. . . . *One and the Same* is not just for twins or parents of twins. It's a study of everyone's individuality. It looks at what makes us who we are and what shapes our identity. It's a fascinating look at the world of twinship, as well as a compelling read about the search for one's 'self.'" —Twins Talk

"*One and the Same* is a touching, funny, smart book, written with considerable flair. Though it contains medical, social, political, and historical perspectives, it is at its core a book about love and intimacy."

—Andrew Solomon, author of *The Noonday Demon*

"A witty and compassionate guide to the myths and science of twinship."

—Honor Moore, author of *The Bishop's Daughter*

"Pogrebin's candor about her own twinship [is] endearing. . . . A juicy read." —Bookslut.com

ABIGAIL POGREBIN

ONE *AND THE* SAME

Abigail Pogrebin is the author of *Stars of David: Prominent Jews Talk About Being Jewish*. A Yale graduate, she has written for many national publications and has produced for Mike Wallace at *60 Minutes*, Charlie Rose, Bill Moyers, and Fred Friendly. She lives with her husband and two children in Manhattan—as does her identical twin, *New York Times* reporter Robin Pogrebin.

www.abigailpogrebin.com

ALSO BY ABIGAIL POGREBIN

Stars of David

ONE *AND THE* SAME

My Life as an Identical Twin
and What I've Learned About
Everyone's Struggle to Be Singular

ABIGAIL POGREBIN

* *

ANCHOR BOOKS

A Division of Random House, Inc.

New York

The Library of Congress has cataloged the Doubleday edition as follows:
Pogrebin, Abigail.
One and the same : my life as an identical twin and what I've learned about
everyone's struggle to be singular / Abigail Pogrebin.—1st ed.
p. cm.
Includes bibliographical references.
1. Twins—Psychology. 2. Twins—Biography. I. Title.
BF723.T9.P64 2009
155.44'4—dc22 2009011195

Anchor ISBN: 978-0-307-27962-0

www.anchorbooks.com

For Robin, for everything

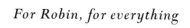

I wouldn't be myself without her.

—ALLEN SHAWN, *WISH I COULD BE THERE*

❋ ❋

CONTENTS

∗ ∗

INTRODUCTION

* ◈

A year after my first book was published, my editors called me in to talk about ideas for my next project. I remember they asked me what I found myself thinking most about, which subject had always preoccupied me. I blurted out, "Twins."

And then I immediately regretted it. Because writing about twins felt like I was volunteering to do a public striptease. Because being a twin goes to the core of who I am and I was wary of examining that. Because I knew that my twin sister, Robin, would be both supportive and hesitant; not only is she more private than I am but she writes for the *New York Times* and always wants to maintain a reporter's remove. Because I knew that as exhilarating as our twinship was growing up, its impact on Robin's sense of self was more complicated than mine. Because I knew that for me to be honest about my twinship and ask others to be honest about theirs was not to tell the perfect quaint story of how we all dressed alike, tricked people, or swapped boyfriends.

Being an identical twin—I can't speak for fraternals—is intense. It's all the clichés: feeling like you have an unwavering partner in life, knowing exactly what another person feels, wanting to tell her a story before anyone else, confiding with unrestrained—sometimes shocking—candor, valuing her opinion above anyone else's, taking on someone else's pain to the point of vicarious depression, being incapacitated by any minor dispute.

To say that someone's "always been there for me" was never meant so literally. Robin was there while I was taking shape in the dark muck of our mother's belly, before I took my first breath of air, when I was lolling in the crib, learning to grab and chew, teetering on two feet. I have never been alone in the world. I've always had someone to tell, someone checking in. Though I'm our parents' firstborn, I've never been an only child. I arrived as a package—the kind that's self-contained and comes with its own handy playmate, sidekick, advocate, therapist, fan, mentor, and accomplice.

I can't count the number of people who have asked us, "What was it like growing up as a twin?" The question lost its meaning over the years because we heard it so much and answered so often automatically: "It was great." "It was great."

I never mention that my twinship helped me meet people when I wasn't bold, kept me from ever feeling idle or rootless, confirmed I was deeply known when others misunderstood me, allowed me to dive into theater because I had an automatic "sister act", and to bypass the normal freshman-year anxiety in college because Robin was in a dorm across the street. It's hard to explain to people that we never felt competitive, though we constantly compared ourselves; that we couldn't hate each other, though we could argue bitterly; that we tacitly forbid anyone else to criticize one of us, even though *we* can be ruthlessly critical of each other; how it is that we never lusted after each other's boyfriends, though we adopted them affectionately; that we always want to talk to each other, though we don't always make time to see each other; that we love each other's children, though not as our own; that we admire each other's work, yet would never want to switch places.

I never explain that we tell each other everything but that there are things we don't say.

Or that Robin has spent the last five years pulling away from me.

Or that I want more of her.

I don't talk about how perfect our twinship was in childhood, why it isn't perfect anymore, yet that I still believe it's the best twinship I know.

Though Robin's and my story is not the focus of this book, it is, undeniably, its spine. It's the prism through which I listened to every other twin's experience, the test case with which I tried to deconstruct the elements of individuality, the emotional puzzle I set about taking apart and piecing together.

Our facts, bare bones, are these:

We were born May 17, 1965, at Doctor's Hospital in New York City. Robin had a lot of hair; I had none.

My mother recalls the names my father was mulling before we arrived: Troilus and Cressida, Anthony and Cleopatra, Julius and Ethel. I was named after my father's father, Abraham, who was a hat blocker. Robin was named after my father's cousin, Robert, who died in a car crash at twenty-two.

I came out one minute ahead, but only because we were delivered by C-section—Robin would have exited first in a normal birth, and she constantly reminds me of that fact.

I stood, crawled, and walked ahead of Robin; I don't constantly remind her of that fact.

We spent our first five years living on the ground floor of a Greenwich Village brownstone; each of us had our own crib; then we shared a bunk bed (Robin was on top and once rolled out, thudding to the floor). Later we moved to the Upper West Side and got our own bedrooms at age fourteen.

Mom dressed Robin in red (like the bird) and me in blue so that people not constantly ask "Which is which?" But we still often ended up in the same outfit—fluffy winter coats, yellow slickers, and OshKosh B'Gosh overalls.

Both of us were instantly outgoing, cheerful, and hammy. We performed constantly, without prompting. No one can say why; my parents weren't theatrical. They were exuberant, yes (Dad, a labor lawyer, is funny at dinner parties; Mom, a writer, is politically impassioned), but they weren't performers.

Robin and I had more dress-up clothes than real clothes and our main activity—with friends or more often just with each other—was to dress up and "act." We used British accents and a lot of flea-market costume jewelry.

We sang and choreographed by ourselves, almost daily. We were each other's taskmasters, quick to chastise when one of us missed a step or flubbed a lyric.

Our parents were summoned night after night to "buy" tickets to our makeshift show, and in front of the scratchy green blanket we hung between closets, we belted out our latest numbers.

We choreographed a "ballet" routine to Aaron Copland's *Rodeo*, complete with pantomimed lassos; we wrote a medley for our annual family Hanukkah party, with lyrics set to Broadway show tunes. (For example, "Don't cry for me Antiochus; the truth is I burned the latkes!")

For the annual Labor Day Show on Fire Island, where we spent childhood summers, Robin and I painted on too much red lipstick (the photographs are almost clownish, and I can't believe no adult saved us from ourselves) and sang duets like "Downtown." We fronted for the cute Weber brothers, who played guitar and drums while Robin and I slapped tambourines against our nonexistent hips.

When we were nine, we were interviewed by Marlo Thomas on the TV version of *Free To Be . . . You and Me*, because our mom was an editorial consultant on the project. I got more air time. At one point on-camera, I tell Marlo that I love being a twin because when you have a lot of feelings, "It's good that I can have somebody to bring it out to—who's my age."

When we were ten, we auditioned together in polka-dot shirts for the role of an orphan in the original production of *Annie*. The casting directors said they would take one of us; we had to choose which. Neither of us took the role.

That same year, a producer chose us to be in a TV show called *Call It Macaroni*, which filmed kids learning an interesting profession. Robin and I were taken to Tucson, Arizona, to watch how a movie is made, and the camera made much of our likeness. I was surprised, when I recently dredged up my diary from that trip, to discover that Robin and I had chosen to sleep in the same bed in our hotel room, leaving the other bed empty. On my crude diagram of room 112 at the Desert Inn, I scrawled on one of the double beds, "Robin and I slept in this one together."

When we were thirteen, we were asked by Channel 13 to shoot a promo for something with Erik Estrada—I can't remember what. We were dressed alike, and the gambit was that Robin punched herself in the arm and I yelled, "Ouch!"

We wanted to do more professional acting, but our parents didn't like the idea; they wanted us to have a normal childhood.

Robin and I always shared birthday parties. My mother created elaborate themes—a French party with berets and paper Eiffel Towers, a baseball party with personalized jerseys, et cetera. We always shared one cake.

We made sure we ate the same number of Oreos after school.

We always got the same cavities in the same teeth.

Our brother, David, was born when we were almost three. We were loving to him and cast him in the role of the dog or passenger in our skits, but we also left him out. My aunt tells me we were mean to him. I don't remember it that way and neither does he, but it's possible. Today David and I are close: We take an annual ski trip together (he's divorced), I'll stop in at whichever restaurant he's currently managing just to say hello, and I adore his two boys, Zev and Arlo. But we don't speak a fraction as often as Robin and I do, nor do we rely on each other as much.

Robin and I didn't think we wanted to go to the same college, but we ended up liking Yale best, and were fortunate enough to get in. We requested to room in separate residential colleges, and made separate friends. We often met for lunch or dinner in each other's dining halls and spoke on the phone every day (no e-mail back then).

We lived together after graduation in a two-room apartment with a shaky spiral staircase on West Eighty-sixth Street; we alternated who got the bed in the basement and who slept in the living room upstairs.

Both of us ended up choosing journalism. Robin went to the *New York Times*, then the *New York Observer*, then back to the *Times*. I produced television—for Fred Friendly, Charlie Rose, Bill Moyers, and then for Ed Bradley and Mike Wallace at *60 Minutes*. One year Robin decided to try television too and left the *Times* to produce for Peter Jennings's documentary unit at ABC News. She pined for the daily deadlines and returned to the paper. I switched to print journalism when I had my first child, and started writing for magazines. Robin asked that I not seek an assignment for the *Times*, so we could keep that territory separate. I said I understood.

We're physically similar except that Robin is half an inch taller, wears her hair shorter, and prefers more sedate colors. My voice is permanently hoarse and I can no longer sing because I developed cysts inside my vocal cords at age thirty-seven, which, my throat doctor tells me, were probably caused by "vocal abuse"—a nice way of saying I talk too much and too forcefully. Robin's voice is still intact (she's less voluble) and I sometimes make her sing to remind me of what I used to sound like.

Robin dated Edward for four years and then married him in January 1993.

I dated David for eight months and then married him in December 1993.

Robin gave birth to Ethan in February 1997.

I gave birth to Benjamin in April 1997.

We shared a baby-sitter for the infant boys until we discovered she was taking them to McDonald's instead of to the playground.

Robin had Maya in December 1998.

I had Molly in July 1999.

We live exactly twenty blocks—one mile—apart on the Upper West Side.

It's difficult to describe the depth and distance of this friendship.

We have been adjacent for so long, there's a fluency to our coupling, an elemental delight we don't necessarily let others see. When we're across a dinner table alone, we never have enough time to cover everything we want to talk about. When we're on the subway together, I don't want to get off at my stop. When we're sitting side by side at a Broadway show and one song swells in a particular way, we know exactly when the other feels moved. She's vitality to me; I have never in forty-three years been bored by her.

We are in constant communication; not a day passes without a phone call (or four), and too many e-mails and text messages. We'll impart the tiniest news—a TV episode we insist the other should watch, a newspaper photograph that made us cry, a dessert we regret, a great book we just finished, a clothing purchase we need the other to assess, something hilarious one of our children said. We're stirred by the same things, annoyed by the same people, tempted by the same vices.

I admire her from a distance—as a journalist, a parent, a wife, a hostess, as someone who, when she does confide, does so with a frankness and intelligence that feels rare to me. She is the person with whom I laugh the hardest: it sometimes escalates to the point where we can't breathe or utter a sound, and only we know exactly what's so funny. I look forward to our lunch dates as if they were parties; we dress up for each other, compliment excessively. I seek her advice before most major decisions, before I submit any piece of writing to an editor. Her approval matters because I just think she's smart and I trust her.

The fact that our kids are buddies seems too good to be true. She'll take mine for a weekend; I'll take hers. There's a private thrill when we see the four of them put on a show together, when our husbands play a good tennis match, when our families sit down to a big summer meal. The three years that we all went on Christmas vacation together felt idyllic to me.

Why do I love Robin so fiercely? Because on some level, we're fused; because I take enormous pride in her; because she listens, lifts, and surprises me even now; because I have a certainty that she wants the best for me; because, at the risk of cliché, we'd do anything for each other; because of the enormity of our history; because we know each other to the bone. And for all those reasons, I miss her now, the way we used to be together.

I wanted to try to write the twins book I couldn't find on any shelf: one that strips bare what it's *really* like to grow up as a matched set. I knew that meant I would have to unpack my private memories as truthfully as I could, but also to listen closely to other twins in my life and some I hadn't met before. So I tracked down the Langner twins, whom Robin and I were friends with in fifth grade and haven't seen since. And the Lord twins, one of whom went to college with us.

I interviewed the debonair Barber twins, football stars Tiki and Ronde, who exemplify twin symbiosis, and former *Baywatch* regular Alexandra Paul, who grew up competing athletically with her identical twin, Caroline, who ultimately became a firefighter.

I spoke to virtually all the twins thrown in my path, embracing the "I know a twin" approach. If someone heard I was writing a book on the subject and proffered a pair, I usually interviewed them, on the grounds that every set would shed some light. If they were willing to excavate their personal twin psyche, it would tell me something about twinship. It would help explain my own experience to me. It would answer the widespread curiosity—and prevailing fantasies—about growing up with a doppelganger. It would instruct the countless new parents of twins about what to avoid or aspire to when raising their pairs—or at least offer an insight into how "the twin thing" (as many of us call it) plays out over a lifetime.

I wanted, above all, to explore identity: how it's forged or hamstrung in the face of doubleness; how you go about finding singularity when you are both unique and alike, your own person and someone's other half. I believed before I started—and now that I'm finished, I believe it even more strongly—that twins put into high relief *the* central challenge for all of us: self-definition. How do we each plant our stake in the ground, decide how sensitive, callous, ambitious, conciliatory, or cautious we want to be every day? Do we even *get* to decide those traits? Are we actually at the mercy of our genetic predispositions to be combative, shy, addictive, antsy, or intelligent? Twins come with a built-in constant comparison, but defining oneself against one's twin is just an amped-up version of every person's lifelong challenge: to individuate—to create a distinctive persona in the world.

In addition to meeting twins, I also sought out "the experts"—the eclectic roster of psychologists, geneticists, obstetricians, behavioralists, social workers, artists, and philosophers who make twins their life's work. They include the ponytailed obstetrician who, with his brother—an army veteran—created the first Center for the Study of Multiple Birth; the plastic surgeon who believes he started life as a twin and who takes photographs of naked identical twins to home in on their parallel anatomy; the cultural historian who wrote a five-hundred-plus-page book about copies; the lactation nurse who, after having her own IVF twins, decided to specialize in preparing parents—bluntly and bossily—for twins chaos; the fertility specialist trying to reduce the number of multiples he creates; the biologist trying to determine if homosexuality is imprinted in utero; and the woman who lost one of her twins at birth and created a national resource for grieving parents of twins.

In September 2007, I was working on my laptop when an e-mail popped up in my AOL account from Proactive Genetics, a California lab that provides DNA testing for two hundred dollars a pop. My heart leaped. "The *results*," I whispered to myself. "The moment of truth."

I had asked Robin, a few months before, to swab her inner cheek with a Q-tip, as I had done, and then mailed in our DNA samples so we could finally know for sure if we were identical. People had always assumed so—most couldn't tell us apart—but there was no biological proof: Mom's obstetrician had died, his medical records were lost, and since we were a C-section birth and delivered in an emergency "Get these babies out now" situation, no one seemed to have noticed placenta differentiation (the mark of two eggs).

I thought I should know, before I started this book, my official twin status. The dirty little secret of identicals is that we all feel slightly superior to the fraternal brand. *We're* the gold standard: rarer, more identifiable, more mysterious. We happen only by accident. We are exact DNA replicas of each other—facsimiles, clones. I have always felt that my closeness to Robin is authenticated by our sameness. I didn't want it to be otherwise. And I also worried that after a lifetime of presenting ourselves as the genuine article, we'd be exposed as a fake.

"We are pleased to report to you the results of the twin zygosity test that you requested. Analysis of the DNA indicates that Abigail Sara Pogrebin and Robin Jennifer Pogrebin are monozygotic, or more commonly referred to as identical twins."

Staring at my computer, tears filled my eyes. How ridiculous. To be moved by an answer you already knew. Yet I was. Something about seeing our two full names there side by side—as they appeared on our birth certificates, the two Pogrebin babies, born on May 17, 1965, in a dead heat, one minute apart: 6:18 P.M. (me), 6:19 P.M. (Robin)—reminded me of what a run we've had side by side. After four decades, it was nice to have our intimacy confirmed. What a relief, I thought. We're the same. I didn't want to be *sort of* the same; I wanted to be fully the same. Because it represented a communion I'd already claimed and boasted of. Because it was how we'd been perceived. Because I didn't want our connection to be just emotional; I wanted it to be factual. Psychology professor (and fraternal twin) Dr. Nancy Segal states plainly in her book, *Entwined Lives,* what all of us identical twins already know: We're more connected. "Fraternal twins are not as close, nor are their lives as intimately entwined."

✧ ✧

Whom is this book for? Anyone who is a twin, has a twin, might have twins, married a twin, knows a twin, or is simply curious to get deep inside this extreme intimacy. It's for anyone who wants to understand why twins serve as scientists' ultimate petri dish, why twins' infancy can be so uniquely demanding, why their quest for individuality can be thwarted by the person closest to them. It's for anyone—all of us—trying to hammer out a separate, clear sense of self.

I think I started this book to get inside my own twinship. Or maybe to get outside of it—to approach it as a reporter, trying to untangle all the intricacies of being born two. I spoke to twins who cherish each other, resent each other, advise, prod, and protect each other; I spoke to parents who wanted twins, fertility doctors who make them, obstetricians who birth them, artists who photograph or are inspired by them, psychiatrists who study and counsel them, scientists who deconstruct them, coaches who prepare for them.

What did I come away with? Confirmation that twins, despite their recent ubiquity, still fascinate and confound. Evidence that twins will always play a key role in decoding what differentiates all of us—emotionally, temperamentally, and physically.

I envied some pairs and judged others. I met twins who had let go of each other, others who hold on, twins who exult in their twinship, others who wouldn't wish it on their own children. Along the way, I listened for the recipe for healthy twinship—to guide not just me but also the countless parents now raising two. Why do some twins end up feeling confined by doubleness, while others wear it like a medal? How does one start as a set and end up successfully single? Not just single meaning solo but single meaning singular: differentiated, distinct, particular, confident in one's separateness. How had Robin and I each become One when we started out as the Same?

1 THE MECCA: TWINSBURG

I'm twinless in Twinsburg, Ohio.

I've come to this little Cleveland suburb on a perfect sunny weekend in August for the annual twins convention. Thousands of sets of twins fly or drive from all over the world for a three-day twins party; imagine hundreds of identically dressed pairs milling around, stealing glances at one another, snapping furtive photographs of one another, eating funnel cakes, and buying buttons that say things like IT TAKES TWO TO DO TWINSBURG, or I'M THE ORIGINAL. SHE'S THE COPY, or MOM LIKES ME BEST.

Twinsburg was named by the Wilcox twins, Moses and Aaron, who founded the village in 1819 and succeeded in changing its name from Millsville to Twinsburg. In exchange, they paid the township twenty dollars and donated property to build the first school. The Wilcoxes were not only indistinguishably identical; according to the municipal Web site, they "married sisters; had the same number of children; contracted the same fatal ailment; died within hours of each other and are buried in the same grave."

Twins Days was started in 1976 as a way to celebrate the Bicentennial and boost tourism; in that first year, thirty-seven sets of twins attended. Today, it's a multinational swarm of thousands; in the year I attended—2006—there were twins from Germany, Switzerland,

Spain, and Great Britain, along with twins from all over the United States. Two thousand sixty-four sets—*sets*—descended on Twinsburg in matching plaids, stripes, and polka dots to meet and marvel at one another. Every generation was represented—from stroller to wheelchair—with every age in between.

It feels odd to be solo on the registration line. But it's also a relief, because the idea of having my twin here is unthinkable. Robin would squirm at the spectacle: pair after pair—copy after copy—in matching straw hats, matching suspenders, matching lime green dresses. This is a self-selected group: the Gung-Ho Twins, the kind who are game to welcome the novelty, the public curiosity, the party, and each other.

Robin isn't that kind of twin. Which means we're not among those who spent hours on the phone coordinating outfits and travel plans for this occasion, who designated this weekend as their annual escape from spouses and children. Robin didn't cosign my Enterprise rental car at the Cleveland airport earlier that morning, she won't be sleeping in the double bed next to mine at the Courtyard Marriott, and she isn't here to pick up her name tag, which I'm nevertheless accepting now on her behalf at the registration desk. (I'd given both our names in advance, because we were asked to, and because I felt illegitimate without it.)

"I think Twinsburg attracts a subset of identical twins," says Nancy Segal, who has studied and written about twins for thirty years, created the Twin Studies Center at the University of Fullerton, and also happens to be an avid swing dancer. "I think Twinsburg serves a useful purpose for those twins who always get stared at and feel uncomfortable about it. In Twinsburg, they're in perfect company and nothing's unusual."

"Obviously there's a need for it," says Sandy Miller, cofounder of the Twins Days festival. "It's somewhere where twins can be in the majority, where they can be themselves and enjoy other twins. We have a real family here. It's amazing what this means to them. This is their day. Their weekend."

There are other twins festivals—in Canada and Japan, for example—but Twinsburg trumps them all for its annual numbers. "That's according to the *Guinness Book*," Miller says. Her fraternal twin sons grew up going to Twins Days; one met his wife here, an identical twin. "When I had my twins years ago, it was novel," Sandy recalls. "Now it's almost an everyday occurrence. And then, with all the fertility drugs, you get the Super Twins." She says that accidental twins still feel like the genuine article. "It's a joke between some of the twins that have been coming to Twins Days for a long time: 'We're real twins. You're not.'"

Jean Labaugh, fifty-one, and her identical twin, Joanie Warner, whom I meet early on, are wearing halter-top dresses and red rubber clogs. They tell me they happened to buy exactly the same Clairol hair color, even though they live in different states. And they feel each other's pain.

"One time I had a deep throbbing in my leg all night," Jean recounts. "It went all the way to the bone. And Joanie called me the next day and told me she broke her ankle."

After marveling, I ask why they come to Twinsburg.

"Oh, it's so nice just to see other twins here," Jean enthuses, "to see what they're like, and hear what their lives are like."

I venture that some people might be overwhelmed by such a concentration of doubles.

Joanie shakes her head. "It's beautiful. Especially to see the guys be able to celebrate their uniqueness. To see them be so close together."

I go through the charade of actually accepting Robin's ID on a string from the woman behind the registration table, pretending I'll be giving it to my sister later when she "arrives." The truth is: I don't want to admit that my twin isn't coming. That would be an admission that I've arrived under false pretenses. I came to report on twins, but I also belong here because I am one. If Robin isn't beside me, I might be an imposter.

But Robin isn't here, because I didn't invite her. I couldn't bring myself to say, "Come see other twins with me." She's never been innately curious about other pairs simply because we happen to *be* twins, and until recently, neither have I. Growing up, we never sought out twin friends. When you're a twin, who needs more twins?

We've never been passionate about our twinship for its own sake. We're passionate about *each other*. I know we both feel lucky to be twins together, but that hasn't made us seek out other twosomes, or twin events.

So I came to Twinsburg on my own. But I didn't expect to feel so unmoored without Robin.

At the welcome desk, I notice two elderly men with exactly the same overgrown eyebrows, dressed in matching blue-striped shorts, blue-striped shirts, and newly purchased sneakers, which they later tell me were a fifteen-dollar bargain at Kmart.

"This is our twenty-third year!" one of them boasts to the woman at the check-in.

When they've received their registration packets and stepped away from the table, I approach the stooped duo and ask their age. "Seventy and three-quarters!" says one, who introduces himself as David. "Walter's older by eight minutes."

David and Walter Oliver still live together—in the same house they grew up in, in Lincoln Park, Michigan. David is clearly the talker. "Walter was too small and they had to keep him in the hospital for three weeks." He seems gleeful about this.

"I was under five pounds," Walter adds morosely.

"We both have keratoconus in the left eye," David reports. "We've both got neuropathy in our feet."

"And we both have diabetes," Walter pipes up.

And they always dress alike?

"We wear the same clothes every time we go to a twins gathering," David explains. "It's sort of an unwritten thing that all twins do."

The Olivers are suddenly joined by Janet and Joyce, seventy-six, in matching blue tops, who also hail from Michigan.

"We met Joyce and Janet at the International Twins Convention in Toronto, Canada," David explains. "Nineteen eighty-two."

Janet and Joyce, who have different last names by marriage, are distinguishable only because Joyce seems more frail.

"I'm the young one," announces Janet, who wears her white hair cropped exactly like her sister's. "We're five minutes apart. She's older. I'm married fifty-five years. She's divorced."

Joyce pipes in: "When you're that close to your twin, you have to make sure that the husbands are into the twin thing. Otherwise, the marriages will not work."

They went to their first twins convention in 1946 in Muncie, Indiana, and they've been coming to Twinsburg for decades. When I admit it's my first time, they tell me what to look forward to, including the research tents in which twins sign up for studies comparing twins' teeth, skin, sense of taste, and hearing.

Janet: "Last year, one of the tents offered us twenty dollars to smell things."

Joyce: "It took too long."

I ask these four elderly twins why they keep coming back.

"IT'S FASCINATING TO MEET TWINS!" David almost shouts. "And we've been trying to find females for the last fifty years."

So they've never been married?

"Never." David shakes his head. The smile vanishes.

I ask if they think they never married *because* they are twins; maybe their unique intimacy prevented other kinds.

"No," David says, dismissing my armchair analysis. "Females have ignored both of us all our life." (I notice his use of the singular: "life.")

I ask David why he thinks women take no notice. "I have no idea," he says. "It's *very* painful. To live an entire lifetime without having a loving relationship." He seems abruptly bereft. "Every year we come here to find twins for us to marry."

David asks me where my twin is and I fumble a quick explanation.

"It's hard to be a twin here without your twin," he declares, reading my mind.

I make my way out to the fairgrounds, which are set up for those families with young twins: there's a bouncy castle, a beanbag toss, and monster basketball. The toddler twins look more at ease than the adult pairs, who meander awkwardly in their matching ensembles, not saying much to each other, just being twins, side by side, observing other specimens. It's as if they'd gotten into costume too early, and now that they've walked out onstage, they're impatient for the show to start.

More twins arrive. They're everywhere now: twins on benches, twins on bleachers, twins on blankets, twins sitting under trees, standing in the sun, flipping absentmindedly through their welcome booklets. At first, it diminishes the rareness, frankly, this twin saturation. I thought the whole point of us is that we're unique, that there are so few of us. But I begin to see that saturation is exactly the point: when else, and where else, can twins find each other in such large numbers, revel in their unusualness, swap war stories? This is a refuge, a mecca, a commemoration of difference (the oddity of twinship) and sameness, too (even the fraternals dress alike).

So why do I mulishly seem to see the underside of a happy scene? What's wrong with a little kitsch, a little revelry? These multitudes aren't overthinking the coordinated outfits, the clever slogans on matching T-shirts (IT'S NOT YOU; IT'S ME.), the inherent randomness of strangers thrown together just because they share one anomaly: They were born alongside someone else. For these folks, concurrent birth confers an unspoken fellowship. It's not only that these twins want to *see* other twins; they really want to *be* with them. As the evening progresses, I notice people seem to like one another without knowing one another, to be predisposed to warmth simply because they're pairs.

I think I feel alienated, in part, because of where my twinship sits these days. There's a closeness that's sui generis, but also a certain detachment. Robin doesn't seem to savor our twoness, nor is she particularly nostalgic about our history. I can't say I parade it, but for me, it's still potent, still a point of pride. I don't question her devotion; but I know now that a lifetime with a double made her feel less singular in the world.

When the line dancing kicks off with "Y.M.C.A.," I'm reminded of how simple our simultaneity used to be. We were always quick to enter the line dance at a party. During our family vacations, we aced the Hustle or whatever Silly Signs routine was being taught by the pool. People watched us because of the kick of seeing double—replicas moving exactly in time. I remember feeling a charge not only in the ease of our synchronicity but in the tangible comfort of having her near.

As kids, we often joined the joke on our twinship, performing "Anything You Can Do, I Can Do Better" from *Annie Get Your Gun*, and "Why Am I Me?" from *Shenandoah*. In the middle school musical—a revue of old vaudeville tunes—Robin and I feigned a quick-change act, quickly popping out from behind a screen in different costumes, each of us emerging to sing a song from a different culture (I warbled a Hawaiian "Hicky-Hoy" in a grass skirt; then I disappeared and Robin instantly materialized in a Chinese costume to belt out "Chong"). When I played Velma in a college production of *Chicago*, Robin made a brief appearance as my character's dead sister. We danced a duet to the song "I Can't Do It Alone."

We used to embrace collaboration. In college, Robin wrote the lyrics to a musical I directed. When I choreographed *Anything Goes*, Robin was one of my front-row dancers. We cowrote a song for the commencement musical and sang duets on cabaret nights. But I was actually the first one to back off from the sister act. It became clear to me that some people chafed at the Pogrebin Show. There is something redundant about performing twins. Being identical is already a performance—you're drawing attention to yourself before you open your mouth. To dance and sing is kind of milking the point; it left us open to eye rolls.

I learned in college that some saw Robin and me as too brash, too visible, too *much*. I'll always recall freshman year, when a junior who'd known me in high school had a "heart-to-heart" talk with me in the courtyard of my dorm. He suggested that my sister and I were too audacious, said we'd "taken over" the theater community and he resented it.

I was stung; it plagued me that we might be viewed as puffed-up. I told Robin we had to fix the perception, modulate ourselves somehow. Her response was, essentially, *screw them*. She has never cared what people think the way I do, and I'm sure it has saved her hours of torment. But I learned in that moment that our twinship can be intrinsically showy, even before we set foot on a literal stage.

"There were bumps in the road," my father recalls when I interview him, "but I think the twinship was like a golden thing. You were used to a world that adored you from the beginning. That might make it tougher later in life when everyone is not so adoring."

As the line dancing gathers steam (along with progressively loosened participants), I notice a pair of women who stand out, not easy to do in this crowd. They're dressed in pink sequined cowgirl hats and hot-pink tank tops that say I'M THE REAL MCCOY. People seem to recognize them—they're quickly surrounded, hugged, kissed, and photographed.

I'd heard about the Ganz twins—several people I'd called during my early research had asked, "Have you met the Ganz twins yet?" In Twinsland, it turns out, these sisters are legendary. Self-dubbed "ambassadors of twins," they run a twins talent agency out of New York. In the 1990s, they founded and operated Twins Restaurant on the Upper East Side of Manhattan, where all the waiters were twins and Debbie and Lisa Ganz were usually on hand to greet patrons. I introduce myself (it turns out they know my brother from the restaurant business), and they chastise me for not booking myself at the Holiday Inn, "where everyone stays."

"We come every summer," Debbie exults over a fitting song, " 'Same Time Next Year.' "

Lisa chimes in: "The great thing about it is, you could be coming here for twelve years, and you might know everything about the twin part of people's lives, but I wouldn't know if they live in a trailer park or a mansion. In Twinsburg, you can literally have two politicians sitting next to two pig farmers next to the prince of Saudi Arabia twins, and they're all having a blast. Now in normal society, outside of this weekend, they wouldn't be together. In Twinsburg, it's our *identity* that's actually in common. Not our demographics or our careers . . . I know twins that I've been spending weekends with for twelve years and I still, to this day, don't know how many kids they have, don't know if they're married. But I can tell you everything about the two of them together."

Debbie adds, "I also think that people are fascinated by twins because they don't realize they grow up. They think twins are little, and then we grow up and go to another planet."

"We're like Disney films," Lisa says. "We're timeless!"

That night, back in my Courtyard Marriott, I flip through the hotel's movie menu and one description catches my eye in the "Adult" selections: "Nympho Twins." I tell myself it's a valuable research tool and click "purchase." The hotel's summary of the film shows up on the screen, and it's priceless: "Over 90 minutes long, this title is a great value. They're real twins and they love to screw the same guy at the same time. Light story line."

"Light story line." (Not like some porn movies, known for their complex narratives.)

Lacey and Lyndsey Love (actual twins—I checked later) play the nympho twins; one is more sexually inhibited than the other, and the shier twin has a crush on her coworker. The more confident twin offers to get him warmed up while her twin waits in the bathroom; after a dose of foreplay, the twins switch places. As can be expected, there's the inevitable confusion: When the timid twin replaces her sex-savvy counterpart, she asks the man to give her oral sex. "But I already ate you!" he says, confused—and then obliges.

Believe it or not, I didn't watch the whole film.

By nine the next morning, a brilliant Sunday, the village green is crammed with cars and onlookers waiting to see the Doubletake Parade. Twins in sunglasses, flip-flops, even large butterfly wings, gather on the dew-damp grass. The smell of the soil reminds me again of Robin: how we used to gather on the muddy baseball field on Fire Island for day camp on summer mornings, how she and I always won the three-legged races on that field because we instinctively knew how to move as one person.

So many photographs from my mother's scrapbooks remind me of Robin's and my physical proximity, and how natural it was. One image shows us at eight years old, in a summer costume festival: We're in bright clown makeup and identical red shirts, each of us stuffed into one leg of a pair of oversized yellow overalls. Another shot shows us making an arch with our arms, in matching white tutus before a ballet recital.

As the Twinsburg parade assembles, twins climb into vintage roadsters, pickup trucks, and an El Dorado convertible. Some carry parasols for the sun. One mom proudly wears a button: GOD GAVE ME TWINS.

A male pair in their fifties, Dana and Greg, are dressed in custom T-shirts that say NATURALLY CLONED IN 1956. Greg points at the wives. "They're still mixing us up!" He smiles. "Yesterday my wife grabbed my brother's butt in Wal-Mart!" Greg says that despite his perfect health, when Dana had a heart attack four years ago, Greg went immediately to the doctor. "The doctor said, 'You look fine, but because of your brother's heart issues, we're going to CAT you.' " It turned out that Greg had exactly the same blockage. "I ended up getting four stents!" he marvels.

Dana and Greg drive off to join the parade line.

There are maybe twenty twins under age five in matching T-shirts and black masks on a float meant to evoke the movie *The Incredibles*. A large sign on the front blares OUR TWINS ARE TWINCREDIBLE!

The pageant proceeds down Main Street, which is lined with spectators along the curb or sitting on porches. Some marchers toss candy to the waving children. Some sing "When the Twins Go Marching In."

The two-mile route ends at the fairgrounds, which are set up with food booths featuring frozen bananas and chicken teriyaki on a stick. Nearby the science tents advertise their research projects: Genetic Basis of Skin Disease in Twins Pairs; Twins Day Gum Study; Facial Changes in Identical Twins.

I wander over to the crafts tables and start to interview random twins among the displays of bandannas, wind chimes, sandstone coasters, and crocheted hats.

Jessica and Jennifer, from New Orleans, are twenty-three and ebullient about Twinsburg. "It's INSANE!" Jessica exclaims. "I LOVE it! All the TWINS! It's just the COOLEST thing. I'm like a big ol' tourist!"

"I was thinking, I feel less odd now," says Jennifer, "because there's so many others like us. You immediately have something in common with someone else. You're huggin' someone, and you don't even know them. You say, 'Hey I'm a twin! Where you from?' "

I ask them to try to describe their closeness. Jessica says, "I feel like *that*"—she points at her sister—"is just an extension of me. That's *me* over there, experiencing something different. Like astral projection, kind of."

"She's my other half, you know," Jennifer chimes in. "If something happened to her, I don't know what I'd do. It's like slicing part of you in half. No one can make me madder; no one can make me happier."

What about the perennial twins question: Were they competitive? "Oh definitely," says Jennifer. "I had to be better at it all, man." She looks at Jessica. "I couldn't let you beat me."

They even liked the same boy, and Jessica ended up marrying him. "We were freshmen in high school," Jessica recalls. "He flirted with a lot of girls."

"He did," Jennifer confirms. "He was flirting with me and he was flirting with her and I got mad that he picked her, but I was happy for her. The Lord brought them together."

Complicating matters, Jennifer had to chaperone her sister and the boyfriend she'd lost on every one of their dates. "The poor thing had to be the third wheel," Jessica recalls. "Because we were only fifteen when me and him started dating, and my Mom and Dad wouldn't let us be separated. It was like, 'No, she's got to go with you.' "

Every date?

"Pretty much," Jessica says, a little embarrassed.

"That wasn't fun," Jennifer says grimly.

I wonder if it was wrenching for Jennifer to watch her sister end up with her crush. "No, not at all," she insists. "As soon as he asked her out, I'm like, 'Okay, y'all were meant to be.' I was the maid of honor."

These sisters seem to be lucky enough to have found romantic relationships (Jennifer has a boyfriend) despite their twinship. But for some reason, Twinsburg seems to draw a number of twins—predominantly male—who have never been married.

"I almost married once," says Sam Zarante, fifty-one, dressed neatly in a button-down shirt. "Marie, my fiancée, didn't understand my being a twin. She thought my twin brother, Dave, and I were too close."

"I'd be over, visiting, a lot," Dave acknowledges.

"So it would be the three of us, not two," Sam adds. "He'd be competition for her."

Because she was never going to match their closeness?

"She didn't understand it," Dave says.

"I loved her," Sam states.

"I liked her," Dave chimes in. "I liked Marie. She was a good one."

"We did things together, the three of us," Sam recalls. "But after awhile, it came out: a little resentment. She wanted me to be her number one, you see. And I understand that. But I liked having him around."

I ask when Sam and Marie broke up. "Oh, it's been awhile now," Sam says.

Nineteen eighty-four. That was the last big relationship either twin had. For years, they've lived together in an Illinois suburb.

"Now, Abigail," Dave says, addressing me suddenly. "I have to admit: I'm looking for someone to marry."

"Maybe you'll find her here," I venture.

"Maybe." Sam laughs a little too hard.

"We came here for the first time years ago," Dave explains. "And my ma was thinking we'd be meeting some twins, you know!" He has the same laugh.

"Maybe that's what you need," I suggest. "Other twins."

"Maybe they'll understand." Dave nods. "As a matter of fact, one year, we got the address of two girls, and they were in North Carolina: Bridget and Ingrid—I still remember their names. And we wrote them and they never wrote back!"

There are no data on whether identical twins are more or less likely to marry, but when it comes to divorce, research shows that identical twins are more alike in their patterns than fraternal twins. A 2001 Boston University survey looked at eight thousand identical and fraternal male twins (all Vietnam veterans) and concluded that genetics play a role in divorce, based on the finding that identical twins mirrored each other more often (that is, if one identical twin got divorced, chances are so did the other).

The survey's author, psychology professor Michael Lyons, explained that identical twins might make similar relationship choices because they share traits that inform their romantic interactions. For instance, depression, alcoholism, or belligerence (all inheritable) can contribute to conflict in a relationship, which, in turn, can lead to a split.

Sandy Miller has her own theory: "A lot of times being a twin causes divorce because spouses don't understand the closeness."

There are clearly many happily married twins at this fiesta, but for some reason, the lonelier ones—the more twin-entwined twins—make a stronger impression. They're reminders that the idealization of twinship, so common in our culture, can have chinks. The intense intimacy can saddle a twin at the end of the day, because he or she isn't equipped for single life, because no one else has ever come first, because for so long, having each other felt like enough. Of course it's possible for twins' interdependence to morph smoothly into independence, but this was only my first hint of many that the transition is rarely uncomplicated, let alone smooth.

There are exceptions, like the Ganz twins, who make twin fusion seem not only joyous but profitable: They've made a business out of their impassioned twoness. Other twins similarly appear utterly grateful and unambivalent about having a built-in best friend. But some others remind me that, to varying degrees, twinship can cost a twin his or her self-sufficiency, and even his or her singularity.

After milling about the fairgrounds for hours in the heat, I feel queasy. It could just be the smell of Italian sausage, the sight of so many Doublemint pairs, or the simple truth that I don't see myself in a sea of people like me. Maybe I envy their jollity; maybe I'm baffled by it. For whatever reason, I'm aware of a certain claustrophobia, unsure whether to stay for the twins talent show or head for the airport early. I call Robin, out of habit, not explicitly to seek her advice. She gives it to me anyway. "Come home," she tells me. "Just come home."

ABIGAIL: Do you remember Becky Greenberg's Halloween party?

ROBIN: No.

ABIGAIL: Are you kidding? That was a major event for me: She invited you and not me.

ROBIN: Really?

ABIGAIL: You don't remember feeling sorry for me?

ROBIN: No.

ABIGAIL: I don't think you went to the party in the end.

ROBIN: Really? I boycotted?

ABIGAIL: I think you did. Thank you for that.

ROBIN: You're welcome.

✦ ✧

GEE WHIZ

In January 2008, a British married couple discovers they are actually fraternal twins who were separated at birth. They are forced to annul their marriage.

In 2006, Lech and Jaroslaw Kaczynski make history as identical twin leaders of one country: They are president and prime minister, respectively, of Poland. The brothers avoid joint appearances so that people don't focus primarily on their twinship.

In 1955, studies show that a tracking dog can find one identical twin once he has sniffed the other.

In April 2008, a biracial British couple gives birth to fraternal twins one black, one white, the odds of which, doctors say, are a million to one.

Elvis Presley's twin, named Jesse, was stillborn. Presley never discussed it in public.

Identical twins Mike and Bob Bryan, age thirty in 2008, are doubles tennis champions known for chest-bumping each other after winning shots. They were NCAA champions at Stanford and have won every Grand Slam tournament at least once.

Identical German twins Oskar and Jack were separated at birth in 1933; Oskar had been raised Catholic in Nazi Europe, Jack as a Jew in the Caribbean. When they were reunited twenty-five years later in 1979, they found they had the same speech patterns and had the same habit of flushing the toilet before using it.

Mothers of twin pandas often reject one infant, which means the favored twin survives.

In May 2005, Minnesota becomes the first state to pass legislation guaranteeing parents the right to say whether their twins should be in separate classrooms or together. Kathy Dolan, a Queens mother whose twins were forcibly separated, leads the charge to make sure other states follow suit.

Identical twin sisters meet identical twin brothers at Twinsburg in 1998, get engaged the same day, marry in a joint ceremony, and one couple gives birth to identical twin boys.

Becky and Birdie Jo Hoaks of Hoopeston, Illinois, who used their identical twinness and their youthful, androgynous appearance to commit crime sprees in small towns, are finally arrested at age thirty-three after sixteen years of swindling.

As of 2009, Massachusetts boasts the highest twin rate in America because it requires its insurance carriers to cover infertility treatments more generously than do other states.

Twins from Erie, Pennsylvania, lose exactly the same amount of weight—160 pounds—after gastric bypass surgery in 2005.

In April 2008, New York twins Kent and Kevin Young perform "telepathy art," where they solve crossword puzzles onstage by one sending mental clues to the other.

Twin stars Mary-Kate and Ashley Olsen become millionaires at age ten.

In June 2008, ten sets of twins are born in one month at a Salt Lake City hospital, four of them within the same twenty-four-hour period. One doctor there compared the hospital to Noah's ark.

In 2007, identical twins Dan and Walter Christ, eighty-two, celebrate their sixtieth anniversary with their wives, identical twins Betty and Jane, seventy-five. The couples each have one daughter, live in the same house, dress alike, and walk everywhere, since none of them ever learned to drive.

Pop-rock duo Tegan and Sara, identical lesbian twins from Canada who have a cult following and have toured with Neil Young and Rufus Wainwright, say they need to live on different Canadian coasts to stand working so closely with each other.

In 1979, identical twins separated at birth are reunited at age thirty-nine and discover that their adoptive parents each happened to name them James, that they both chose careers in law enforcement, married women named Linda, gave their first sons the same name (one spelled James Alan, the other James Allan), divorced their wives, married women named Betty, named their dogs Toy, drink the same beer (Miller Lite), smoke the same cigarette brand (Salem), and suffer the same migraines.

In 2002, seventy-year-old twin brothers are killed on their bicycles on the same road in northern Finland, two hours apart.

2 EMBRYO TO END ZONE:

TIKI AND RONDE BARBER

. . . we came into the world like brother and brother;
And now let's go hand in hand, not one before another.
—*The Comedy of Errors*, William Shakespeare

Tiki Barber, retired running back for the New York Giants, knows that he wouldn't be so famous if he wasn't an identical twin whose brother, Ronde, is a star cornerback for the Tampa Bay Buccaneers.

"Without even trying, people will take an extra look," says Tiki, sitting in his office at NBC News, where he is now a correspondent for the *Today* show. Dapperly dressed in a striped pink-and-white shirt with cuff links, Barber is syrup-voiced and affable. "No twins have been as successful in professional football as we have. In sports, or any kind of endeavor, part of the reason you do it is for recognition; we got that notice by default, just because there's two of us."

I tell him his and Ronde's looks don't hurt (they were *People* magazine's "Sexiest Athletes" in 2001).

"Yeah," he says, smiling that brilliant Barber smile. "We take care of ourselves. We got a good education, we don't get in trouble, and for many years we were both at the peak of our respective careers."

When I meet Tiki's brother, Ronde, a month later in Florida, he's in his twelfth year with Tampa Bay. He saunters up to the family restaurant he's recommended, dressed casually in jeans, a long-sleeved multicolored T-shirt, and aviator sunglasses. Both brothers are suave, obviously strong, and short for professional athletes—five ten. Both also appear guarded—a remnant, perhaps, of extreme childhood shyness, which they independently describe as paralyzing.

"We were very shy, to the point where, if I didn't know you, I wouldn't look at you, much less talk to you." Tiki smiles. "So Ronde was my comfort, you know? We were always right next to each other because it made us feel comfortable. My mom used to say that we had this 'twinspeak.' All it really was, was mumbling and talking very low and intimating certain things; he understood what I was saying, because we had the same thoughts."

"We wouldn't talk to anybody," Ronde confirms.

Which is not to suggest they're bashful today.

"There's one thing I know about myself and Tiki: We have a very distinctive charm about us," says Ronde. "I don't pretend that's not the case. I feel like I can charm anybody."

No argument there.

"Not intentionally," he continues. "It just kind of comes out—the Virginian in me, the politeness, the kind of person my mom raised us up to be. People love that."

But he's realistic about why he gets so much attention.

"I've said more than once, 'If I didn't have a successful twin as a running back for the New York Giants, how many people would really know about me?' There is not a city in America that I can go in and people not think that I'm Tiki."

Tiki doesn't correct strangers when they call him Ronde. "Unless people ask if they're mistaken, I let them think they got it right. They'll call out, 'Hey, Ronde, what's up?' I say, 'Good!' Unless it's someone who I know *knows* Ronde. Then I'll correct them. Otherwise, if they have no clue, I won't."

Ronde says his old timidity kicks in when he's walking through an airport or visiting Tiki in Manhattan. "Part of me just wants to hide," he tells me. "I just put my blinders on and walk fast."

Will he respond if someone calls out?

"I'll respond. But if someone's looking at me, trying to figure out which twin I am, I'll just keep walking."

Tiki is the Giants' all-time leader in rushing and receptions. He amassed more total yards in his last three seasons than any other player in the league, setting most offensive records for the Giants, which got him voted three times into the Pro Bowl, the NFL's annual all-star game. In 2005, Ronde became the first cornerback in NFL history to record twenty career interceptions and twenty career sacks. He was voted to the Pro Bowl four times and chosen by the Associated Press for five All-Pro Team rosters (essentially an honor roll, not an actual team).

I ask Tiki if, in the annals of football history, he or Ronde will be remembered as the bigger star. He pauses. "This is what Ronde likes to say, and it's very true: 'Tiki is the less-talented, more popular twin.' As far as pure accomplishments, far and away, he's better than me. He's always been a better athlete than me. But I was always faster, stronger, and I played the glory position. So people knew who I was, simply because I was a running back. I did an interview with Ronde for *Football Night in America* three weeks ago, and the last question I asked him was, 'Are you where you are because of me?' And he basically replied, 'If I *wasn't* your brother, I'd still have been a great cornerback, but I wouldn't have gotten any recognition. Because there are a ton of great cornerbacks that nobody knows.' So I say to him, 'You owe it all to me!' "

Ronde says, "I'm more diverse athletically. Tiki could never run hurdles; he's not coordinated enough. That sounds funny to say about a world-class athlete, but things are very specific with him, especially in his athletic ability. He couldn't play basketball."

And Ronde can?

"No, I can't either." He laughs. "But he *really* couldn't. I'd say I'm more agile. Put it that way."

What about strength?

"He was always stronger, always faster. He got all the good genes, man."

The Barbers' story is a classic sports fable: hardscrabble youth, a dad who walked out, a resilient mom who raised the boys alone, working three jobs and shuttling them to football practice and wrestling matches. Both boys were obedient, studious, and smart—Tiki made valedictorian—and both showed incredible athletic talent, although their height didn't bode well for professional sports. Their mom, Geraldine Barber, recalls how the junior high athletic director phoned to suggest gently that she was setting her sons up for disappointment. "She said, 'I just want you to think twice about letting your boys play football; you know, they're kind of *small*. . . .' For years after that, every time I saw her, she'd say, 'I know, I know! I was wrong!'"

Geraldine, a compact, sprightly breast cancer survivor who lives in Virginia, insists that her twins were tenacious and unbowed. "I've always known how determined they were from the day they were born. They fought for every breath they took." Her sons were born five weeks premature—Ronde seven minutes ahead of Tiki—and they spent their first two weeks of life in incubators. "I'd look down at them and Ronde would be sleeping peacefully, while Tiki would be screaming his head off. It was as if Tiki was yelling, 'I don't like this; I want to go!' and Ronde was like, 'Chill; we'll get out when we get out.' And they've always kind of been that way." Their names were chosen accordingly: Jamael Oronde (Ronde) means "firstborn son," and Atiim Kiambu (Tiki) translates as "fiery-tempered king."

Geraldine says when she finally took the boys home from the hospital, she'd put them on opposite ends of the crib at bedtime. "When they were old enough, they started scooting and squirming toward each other until they were touching. So I got smart: I started putting them in the same bed when it was nap time, and they would just go to sleep like that. I remember once, when they were two or three years old, they were still sucking their thumbs; it was naptime and I said, 'Go get on the couch.' One of them lay down; the other lay down right on top of him, put his head in the middle of his back, and they went to sleep. They just gravitated to each other. Maybe that was because they spent nine months—or in my case, eight—in the womb, hearing the other brother's heartbeat."

"We were always that way," Tiki recalls. "We *had* to be in the same room. Even when we were fifteen or sixteen years old, we had to be physically together. . . . Being with Ronde now is still a comfort that I haven't found anywhere else, that I don't think I'll ever find anywhere else. Just to be able to sit with someone and have absolutely no agenda. If there's something to talk about, we'll talk about it. If there's nothing to say, we don't. That level of ease doesn't exist in the world, that I've encountered, except with your twin."

I don't use the words *soul mates* anywhere else in this book, but it's required here; despite the geographic distance, there is no daylight between the Barbers. They admire, appreciate, and need each other; they constantly extol each other's gifts and characters; and they never argue—in fact, Ronde looks surprised when I tell him that my sister and I sometimes do. "Even now?" he asks, incredulous. "Come on."

Sitting with each Barber, it occurred to me, They're the paradigm. They actually have what so many mythologize about twins: an unqualified closeness they both view as primal and untouchable, careers they believe were honed in the crucible of their twinship because they egged each other on, and, at least from an outsider's perspective, thriving, separate adult family lives.

Maybe they're in denial about repressed "issues," maybe they've bought into a fantasy of twinship. But they seem to have the kind of twin relationship by which all others are measured—even mine. I find myself envying the Barbers as I listen to them, then reminding myself

I have what they have, then immediately wondering if I really do. My closeness with Robin resembles the Barbers', but I'm not sure we're as honest, nor as forgiving. I know we don't talk about the cosmic implications of having been in the womb together (they do) and I know we don't always tell the truth (Tiki and Ronde do) or hear criticism with the same certainty that it springs from the most loving, supportive place.

Their loyalty is reflexive. When Giants fans excoriated Tiki for quitting at the top of his game and for making disparaging remarks about his coach and some of his teammates, Ronde didn't waver. "Through none of it would I have said, 'You should have handled it differently,' " Ronde tells me. "He's my brother, man; I can't see him doing anything wrong. And if he does, I'll tell him. He had enough people ganging up on him; he didn't need me to do it, as well. Whenever anybody would do an interview with me, they'd invariably turn to that question, 'So your brother . . .' I'm like, 'Look, you guys know Tiki; he's going to say what he wants to say. He's an honest person. And if you want to vilify him in your mind for being wrong, then go ahead; that's your prerogative. . . . But I'm not going to *dislike* my brother because he states his opinion openly. You-all have every right to. But in the end of the day, fuck y'all.' "

During the eleven years when both Barbers were playing, they never missed each other's games—even if that meant watching later on tape—and they spoke on the phone immediately after coming off the field. "Sometimes even before the postgame press interview," says Geraldine.

Today they talk or text daily, but see each other rarely, thanks to separate cities, family commitments (Ronde has two girls, Tiki two boys), and constant work travel. Occasionally they'll reunite for a charity event or a book promotion. They've conceived five children's books based on their lives (they're not the actual authors), targeted to boys who might otherwise not be readers. And they take their role-model status seriously. "Boys like their sports stars," Tiki says, "and maybe if a sports star writes a book, they'll pick it up and read it. We can maybe influence kids to do the right thing. Whether we get involved in books, philanthropy, or education, we have a power and it's doubled."

Though they're now used to living apart, it was the NFL draft that separated them for the first time. "We spent every waking minute together till then," says Tiki.

The day of the NFL draft in April 1997, the brothers—at the time, both well-regarded players for the University of Virginia—distracted themselves by playing golf with friends. Tiki got the first phone call, when he was on the back nine: he was sixth pick in the second round. Ronde had to wait three more hours to learn his fate; he was sixth pick in the third round. By that time, they were kicking back with Mom and friends, ordering yards of beer at a restaurant in a Charlottesville mall. "Ronde had two or three cell phones in front of him," Geraldine recalls. "Tiki had a couple cell phones in front of him, and I'm sitting between the two of them; every time somebody's phone rang, they were all grabbing the phones." She laughs. "A few minutes later, one of Ronde's phones rang; he answered it, he was listening, and then he kind of sat back and I saw him grin that incredible grin he has when you know he's up to something—he kind of relaxes. I heard him say, 'Yeah, Coach. That would be great, Coach. Looking forward, Coach.' Finally he hung up and said, 'Well, I'm going to Florida. I'm a Buccaneer.' He and Tiki toasted each other and then they went off by themselves and had words, just brother to brother, and they came back, sat down, and Tiki put his arm around me and said, 'When you get back to Roanoke tomorrow, you quit your job. You don't have to work anymore. It's done.' I said, 'I'm not going to do that. What am I going to do?' And he said, 'Ronde and I just talked about it; you need to quit. Stay home and take care of yourself.' " She was due to finish chemotherapy the following week. (She's been healthy since—and she did defy her boys and went back to work in county government.)

I ask Ronde if it was hard to see Tiki favored markedly in the draft. "Not at all," he replies with a look that tells me I just don't get it. "Tiki *was* Virginia football. He was *it*, even though I'm the only three-time all-ACC first-team selection ever, I think." He keeps doing that—telling me how Tiki excels but then listing his own feats. "Tiki's always been more popular," he continues, "but I've had more accolades. Back to high school: Even though he was Player of the Year in football and whatever else, I won a national championship in track and field; he didn't—he finished second. I've been in more Pro Bowls and more All-Pros than him, and more first than him." (There are two tiers of All-Pro teams—first and second—each year.) "So if you were making those judgments based on that, then who's the more successful one? But we're not talking about that."

Tiki was paid more than Ronde. He says his Giants signing bonus was $800,000 and tells me Ronde's was $300,000 to $400,000. In 2001, Tiki signed a six-year $25.5 million deal and Ronde an $18.5 million six-year deal with the Buccaneers, with a $2.5 million guarantee. Ronde says he's never measured incomes. "Before Tiki got married, it was almost like, what he's got, I got. We shared everything forever. So if it had turned out that I was out of the league after just two years and he played for ten, he would have taken care of me. Or vice versa. I just know that to be a fact."

The thrill of that memorable draft night was tempered by the realization that the brothers would soon be more than a thousand miles apart. "There was anxiety," Tiki admits. "First, I worried, How am I going to survive in New York City? I'm a country boy. Two: How am I, for the first time in my life, going to be by myself?"

"It was a tough moment," Ronde affirms. "I remember when he finally left to drive to New York: I was still in Charlottesville because our training camp wasn't starting for another week. He got in the car, turned down I-29 at Charlottesville, and was gone." He pauses. "But I wasn't emotional."

Was he trying not to be?

"Probably. But there was nothing that we could do about it. I didn't get drafted by the Giants; he didn't get drafted by the Bucs."

It actually looked like they might end up on the same team until the final hour. Says Geraldine, "Jim Fassel, Tiki's first Giants coach, has said to me on a number of occasions, 'I really wanted Ronde, too. I had great plans for the two of them together.' But it was the luck of the draw."

"Of course we wanted it," Tiki says. "And there was a very good chance. I think if he had fallen two or three more spots, the Giants would have taken him."

"I'm glad it didn't happen," Ronde says now. "At some point—you understand this as a twin—you've got to stand on your own. . . . I was finally forced into it and I had to go make my name for myself. And that's kind of rewarding."

Their first year apart the Barbers bridged the gulf by running up their cell-phone bills ("I bet they single-handedly kept AT&T and Verizon in business," says Mom), and by buying a home together in Tampa, which they've since sold. But ultimately, living in different cities was more defining than they anticipated. "This question of nurture versus nature on how personalities are shaped," Tiki says, "I would have argued for nature until I was drafted to New York and he was drafted to Tampa. Because we completely changed. Our interests are now different: he's into all genres of music, primarily hip hop. I listen to jazz and rock music—not hard rock, but Pearl Jam. He plays golf almost every day, dresses casually, has seven tattoos; I have none, and I wear suits. We're just different now."

Ronde agrees. "New York shaped him and this culture shaped me. A perfect example: Neither one of us could play golf when we left Virginia, and now I have a four handicap and he still can't play the game."

Does Tiki try?

"He tries and he quits." Ronde laughs. "It's not something he can perfect on the Upper East Side."

Ronde says it wasn't just their tastes that changed but their dispositions, too. "I became real casual," Ronde says. "Just doing my thing. No guidelines, no real sense of urgency to do anything, other than my job. While Tiki turned into this structured guy who went by the minute on the clock. His second year on the Giants, he was already doing commentary in the morning with WCBS Sports, and I was like, 'What the hell are you doing? Don't you want to be a football player?' He was gaining interest in new things, stuff I had no exposure to, and eventually turned into who he is now. When we left Virginia, I wouldn't have predicted for anything in the world that he would have become this guy, but that's who he is. I think he took advantage of a good situation because he's an opportunist."

I ask Ronde if he'd describe himself the same way.

"Yes, but I don't know if that's translated in the ways that it has for him. I mean, he left football and went right to a great job at NBC News. I don't have that opportunity like he does. It's something I may do down the road, but I can't possibly set it up the way he's set himself up. That's just about being in the number-one market in the country. The opportunities to groom yourself here are not the same as they are there. . . . And he's good at what he does—for no reason! He never had any formal training other than jumping into the fire. I don't know if my jumping into the fire here would be as fruitful."

Is he surprised that Tiki's had such a smooth career-change? "No." He smiles. "He's good at everything."

Does he look at Tiki and say, "He has skills I don't"?

"Yes. He has learned skills that I don't have. Tiki is much more cerebral than I am. He's an intelligent dude, picks up things very quickly. It's been that way our entire lives. For the most part, I was the twin that was beating on his door, saying, 'I can't figure this homework out.' He was like, 'Come on, you're stupid; it's easy.' He's always been more above-the-neck than I've been. But I've got a tough standard to keep up, because one of us has got to be the short end of the stick."

I tell Ronde that his mom remembers his childhood response when she suggested that he study five minutes more each night: "You've already got one geek in the family; you don't need two."

"Exactly." Ronde nods. "And I don't know if that was self-conscious or intentional. I don't know if I was saying to myself, I don't want to be like him, or, I want to be *exactly* like him. Tiki always did everything so easily in school, and I felt like I was the one that had to work at it. Somewhere along the way, he became the smarter twin."

How many twins could say that without bristling? Very few. There's this odd sanguineness when the Barbers describe their flaws and strengths, while other twins I spoke to seem to dodge and weave about who does what better. Maybe professional sports breeds bluntness; there's no whitewashing whether you're good enough to make the team, good enough to play (at first neither Barber made the starting roster), average or exceptional. The Barbers fling their compliments and gibes without seeming worried that it will color the larger picture—that they think the world of each other. The only time Ronde recoils at an adjective is when I offer one that might sound negative.

I asked Ronde if he'd call Tiki more "ambitious," and he seemed to stiffen. "Depends on how you use the word," he cautioned, clearly protective of how I might label his brother.

I clarified that by "ambitious," I meant "itchy, always reaching for the next thing."

Ronde softened. "I could see that, yes; judging by the fact that I have absolutely no idea what I'm doing next, whereas he knew exactly what he was doing and he put a lot of thought toward it."

Tiki tells me why one day he was finished with football. "This wasn't about 'I hate my coach,' or this or that; this was about quality of life. The year before I retired, when my wife asked me to play with my kids, and I didn't want to, nor could I, I knew it was time to do something else. . . . I said, 'If I'm fifty-two, like Earl Campbell in a wheelchair, who's going to be cheering for me then?' "

"He didn't talk about quitting all the time," Ronde recalls, "but you could just feel it. Same way as when you play Ms. Pac-Man a thousand times and you've beaten it a thousand times and you're like, All right, either Ms. Pac-Man 2 is coming out or I'm going to put in Galactica. That's what it felt like. Not that he was bored by what he was doing, because our sport's unique: It's exciting when you play. But I think he was just bored with the routine of that part of his life and he was ready. He knew it wasn't going to last forever, so he made steps to move on. Whereas I'm more along the lines of 'It will end someday, and when it does, I'll decide what to do then.' Eventually your body just can't do it anymore and then you have to do something else."

"Physically I was much more beat-up than Ronde is," Tiki says. "Being a running back, I get hit forty times a day, where Ronde gets hit maybe four or five. It starts to take its toll."

"I feel great," Ronde tells me. "I swear to God, I would never know that I'm thirty-three if I didn't read it every day in the paper or in every magazine article written about me: 'He's thirty-three; he can't do it forever.' Eventually in the back of your head, you start thinking, Is this true?"

Why does he think he's still thriving at the older end of football age? "I think it's something in my makeup; I refuse not to be successful. Take that back to my youth: I refused to be a failure in comparison to Tiki. And I'm sure my mom told you this—last year she was thinking I felt guilty because I was still playing football when Tiki quit. And I don't know if I put that much thought on it, but I could see that being the case, because we always did everything together, and now, how do I judge my success? I never judged it against anybody else's. . . . That aspect of my motivation was suddenly lacking, and I honestly had used it a lot. It was definitely a void I had to fill, and I don't know if I did or not."

I ask if Tiki drove him in a competitive way or a motivational one. "More in a motivational way. I was just excited to see him be successful. . . . It made it worth doing, above anything else. Even if the game stank and our team stank, it was, 'Hey, we may have lost today, but I'm going to see how Tiki did.' And that element completely disappeared last year, and in my mind, it was all on me. I had to find a way to adapt to the new structure of it."

"There is no doubt in my mind," says Tiki, "that we are both successful because we refused to let the other one down. It was partly 'I have to keep up with him; he has to keep up with me.' But it was also 'Don't dare be a failure, because then you drag me down.' So we competed against each other's successes. And we were always fortunate— actually, it may have been intentional, even subconsciously—that we never did the same thing. So when we wrestled in seventh and eighth grade, he dropped weight so he could wrestle at one thirty-six, I wrestled at one forty-two. When we ran track, he learned the hurdles while I was a sprinter and did the long jump. When we played football, he was defensive back, wide receiver, and I was a running back. We never did the same thing, but we always had success. It was kind of like, 'If you're going to win, I'm going to win. If you're going to be good, I've got to be good.' "

Doesn't it bother Tiki that Ronde's the one with a Super Bowl ring? "It was probably the greatest moment of pride I've ever felt," says Tiki of Tampa's victory over Oakland in 2003. "Cynics will say, 'Oh, you're jealous.' But those same people have no idea what we have."

The press loved the twin versus twin angle whenever the Giants played the Bucs, but the Barbers viewed it as "more talk and hype." Ronde says, "At the end of it, he was just another opponent."

Tiki tells me Ronde was playful during those match-ups. "One time, I was getting tackled out of bounds and he wasn't even close to me, but he comes over and just elbows me like this." He shows me. "I'm like, 'What the hell are you doing?' He says, 'I'm just trying to make it look good.' " He especially loves one particular photograph of Ronde tackling him near the goal line in 2006, because he's enveloping Tiki just as he must have in utero.

"Someone told me this great quote yesterday," says Tiki. " 'Life is a crack of brightness between two eternities of darkness.' My first eternity of darkness with my brother was me on top of him—because he came out first. And when we were babies, my mom would put us on opposite ends of the bed and before you know it, we were lying on top of each other like we were in the womb. And here we are again in this photograph."

I wonder where the wives fit into this duet. Tiki's striking wife, Ginny, a former publicist who comes from Korean and Vietnamese lineage, has known the Barber twins since college, when she started dating Tiki. (They married in 1999.) Ronde's equally attractive wife, Claudia, who now works with Diabetic Charitable Services, is of Filipino descent and married Ronde in 2001. All three Barbers I spoke to tiptoe around the question of how the wives handle the twinship. "Let me answer it this way," says Geraldine. "Do they understand it? I'd say, 'Not totally.' Do they respect it? Definitely."

"When we're all together, it's a great foursome," Ronde says. "When we're not, it is what it is. . . ." He smiles, clearly not wanting to expand further, then takes a different tack. "You know what it is? And they'll never admit this: They're both control addicts; they want control. And neither one of them can have it, especially when Tiki and I are the ones who are really in control, if that makes any sense. It's not intentional; they have the *appearance* of control and they do a lot of things for us. But at the end of the day, we all know who's making the decisions. It will come down to what Tiki and I want to do, because that's the Relationship. So *you* figure out the psychodynamics of that. . . . When you're married to a twin, essentially, whether you like it or not, you're married to the other one, too. Tiki's as much involved in my life now as he was back when we were in college."

Does he think that bothers their spouses? "Of course. Absolutely. And they'll never talk about it; they probably don't even necessarily recognize it, but, yeah, that's what it is."

Tiki echoes him: "I think our bond is the strongest it's ever been and the strongest bond that there possibly is. Greater than marriage. I'm closer to Ronde, without a doubt. And that will never change."

So many married twins told me the same thing. And it always moved me to hear it, but it's not how Robin and I feel. Our husbands know us better. They get more of us now—not just in terms of time spent but in what we tell them and whose counsel we seek. When Ronde told me their spouses don't always embrace their closeness, I thought of my brother-in-law, Edward. He's accustomed to my relationship with Robin, but I wouldn't say he facilitates it. He and I have a warm friendship, but it's been clear over the years that he doesn't believe that a twin should get special treatment. When Robin first got pregnant, for example, Ed didn't think she should tell me the news ahead of his family or the rest of ours. She told me anyway, but it was hard to learn she'd had to overrule him to follow her impulse. It seemed self-evident to me that she would rush to share something so momentous. To thwart that reflex was to obstruct the normal blood flow of our relationship.

Days later, I asked Ed to meet for coffee to discuss it, and he explained matter-of-factly that he didn't see any reason why I should get particular consideration, any more than his younger brother or older sister. I was stymied; I couldn't sit across a table and make the case for the Twin Exception. It felt like if it wasn't obvious to him, it wasn't defensible—my argument for twin precedence was basically "It just is."

I tell each Barber that some twins' relationships have struck me as a kind of love story and I wonder if they find that's a fitting analogy. Ronde nods, "We see beyond who we pretend to be. I know who he really is, he knows who I really am, and if you were writing a love story, that's what it would be. All those romantic ideals—'conquers all,' 'stands the test of time'—yes. That's certainly the case with us."

Tiki agreed that twinship is "a perfect intimacy."

"It starts from the zygote splitting and one destined person becoming two," he continues. "And while we go our separate ways in life and our experiences vary, at the end of the day, we're still one."

ABIGAIL: Have you ever felt excluded by us?

LETTY POGREBIN (MOM): Always.

ABIGAIL: What makes you feel that way?

LETTY: You just talk to each other and you close everybody else out. You're not aware that people are there and listening and don't know what you're talking about, and feel sidelined. You still do it now and then.

ABIGAIL: Is it what we say to each other or how we look at each other?

LETTY: It's just that you don't see anybody else. You're just talking to each other and it's like no one else is there. And you don't care about anyone else.

ABIGAIL: And you think that we're aware of it?

LETTY: Obviously not, or I don't think you would do it.

* *

3 IDENTICALS: A LOVE STORY

Each is the other's soul and hears too much
The heartbeat of the other. . . .
—Karl Jay Shapiro, "The Twins," 1942

The model twinship of Ronde and Tiki Barber manages to combine an unquestioned primacy with a sturdy independence. Which is no easy feat. Two of the fundamental questions psychologists ask about adult twins are "When did they separate?" and "How did they individuate?"

So it's interesting to meet identical twins who haven't; twins who celebrate—and accentuate—their sameness nearly every day of their lives, or who have a kind of love that clearly defies the idea that twins must, in a sense, leave each other to grow up.

Debra and Lisa Ganz are the empresses of the Twins World. They're brassy, buoyant, foul-mouthed replicas who have made a career of their twinship. They amass twins on their Web site, Twinsworld.com, boast an international twins database, raise money for terminally ill twins and twins in tsunami-like disasters, and run a twins talent management company (child labor laws prevent infants from working more than two hours a week, so twins and triplets are essential to keep the cameras rolling). As mentioned earlier, they opened the first Twins Restaurant in 1994 in Manhattan (which employed only twin servers and closed after a successful run in 2000), and they have attended virtually every twins gathering, conference, or festival that exists around the world.

Soon after I arrive at Debbie's modest Manhattan apartment with its orange walls and no windows in the living room, Lisa bounds in the door, announcing, "I COULDN'T FIND THE RED SHIRT!" I get it. They had agreed beforehand on what they'd both wear, but Lisa fell short. Except for the red shirt, they are dressed exactly alike in jeans, black boots, black velvet jackets, high ponytails, and big sunglasses on the tops of their heads. It strikes me suddenly that here are two near-forty-year-olds playing dress-up, unapologetically cornball, and kind of joyous. Both have husky, assertive voices, both drink take-out coffee, and both constantly, ruthlessly interrupt each other—and me.

"Abby's not only here to get our expertise," Lisa tells Debbie. "She's getting *our* story."

Debbie looks at me. "Does Lisa not think I speak English?"

Lisa leans in to me. "Debbie's the slower half. She came out six minutes after me. I got six minutes more of the brain."

Lisa continues: "We say we are 'the ambassadors of twins.'"

I confirm to them that nearly every place I go, people say to me, "Have you met the Ganz twins?"

Lisa jumps in: "I have a question for you."

They both bellow, unprompted, in unison: "HAVE YOU MET THE GANZ TWINS?"

I tell them that their identical costumes at annual twins events (I saw them in Twinsburg in rhinestone cowboy hats), and their unreserved gregariousness, make them appear larger than life.

"She's not talking about our butts," Debbie says, clarifying for her sister. "She's talking about *us.*"

"To start from the beginning," Lisa says, "we always say—"

In stereo again: "WE'RE LIVING IN A 'WE' WORLD AND EVERYBODY ELSE IS LIVING IN AN 'I' WORLD!"

Lisa: "That's what set us apart from everyone else."

Debbie to Lisa: "Talk about the twinship first."

Lisa to Debbie: "Well, no. I'm talking about what *I* want to talk about."

The irony is that when they were growing up in Long Island, they stopped dressing alike as soon as they could dress themselves; but in their twenties, they decided to dress the same again. "Why do we do this as women?" Lisa asks the question for me.

"Because it's part of our business and that's part of our twinness," Debbie replies. "We're marketing ourselves. It's like airline flight attendants. They have a uniform; so do we."

"Everyone says, 'Don't you twins want your own identity?' " Lisa says.

"We *have* our own identity!" Debbie announces. She turns to Lisa. "What do we say?"

In unison again: "WE'RE TWO VERY INDIVIDUALS THAT MAKE ONE HECK OF A WHOLE TOGETHER!"

Oh my God. I feel like I'm watching a comedy routine. Is any of this unrehearsed?

"We mean that," Debbie insists, as if reading my skepticism.

Debbie clarifies that they're not joined at the hip. "We don't live together. We could *never* live together!"

Why not?

"We need to be alone," Debbie says without irony.

"That said," Lisa adds, "there are times when someone will walk into my apartment and I have the phone to my ear without talking, and they'll say, 'What are you doing?' And I say, 'I'm watching a movie with Debbie.' They'll say, 'Where's Debbie?' Debbie's on the phone. Neither of us have said a word for two hours. But we're watching a movie together. I know that's not normal."

But Debbie insists they're still separate beings. "People who don't know us think we're so twinny that we're one person. No. We're not like those twins out there that believe they're one person in two bodies. There are twins we know that have to live together, sleep together; they count how many rice pilafs are on the plate before they eat the same amount."

"We've seen old ladies who have never been married," Lisa says, without seeming to realize that might ultimately describe them. "They walk out to the mailbox together. They turn out the light at the same time. They're one person in two different bodies. We're two different people in one body."

But when I ask them *how* they're different, they seem stumped. Which Debbie doesn't apologize for. "If you ask our five best friends, including our younger sister, Lisi, 'Are Debbie and Lisa the same?' they will say, 'Absolutely not.' And then you ask them, 'How are they different?' They can't tell you." She doesn't accept the conventional wisdom about twins—that differentiation is always optimal. "We speak at all the state conventions, and parents often say to us, 'I have five-year-old twins and I just got them their first separate birthday cakes.' And we devastate them, because Lisa and I say, 'We're thirty-something years old. We have *never* had our own birthday cakes!'"

"Ever," Lisa confirms. "We celebrate the twin thing every day."

"Someone came up to us about eleven years ago," Debbie recalls, "and said, 'I knew you two in college. I now have my own twins and I sent them to different preschools, because I don't want them to be like you two.'"

"We laughed," Lisa says defiantly. "Parents who don't know what it's like try to do everything in their power to make their identical twins different, instead of celebrating their twinship."

"We don't tell parents to dress their twins alike or to treat them as one person," Debbie explains. "What we're saying is, 'It should be an individual decision.'"

The Ganzes shared friends growing up and still do. "It's come to the point now," Debbie says, "where if someone that Lisa knew better got married tomorrow—"

"They'd still invite Debbie," Lisa says, interrupting. "Do you know how sad it is that at thirty-nine years old, we get invited to wed-

dings together without dates?" Lisa laughs. "Like we're the twin enter-
tainment: Rent-a-Crowd. 'Let's invite the twins.' I'm like, 'Debbie.
They want a three-hundred-dollar wedding gift and I don't even
know the girl's damn last name!' "

"What about that wedding six months ago?" Debbie asks Lisa.
"Was it Kristen or Kirsten?"

"See! We don't even know!" More laughter.

Though they complain about being everybody's favorite mascots
or diversion, they clearly revel in their popularity. "We were blessed
with the gift of gab," Debbie says. "We're the icebreaker. Most people
may think that's overwhelming and exhausting, but the truth of the
matter is—"

"We're visionaries," Lisa says.

"We have an infectious enthusiasm for life," Debbie continues.
"We *infect* people. I can't name someone who's met us in our lives who
doesn't remember us. Not me alone—there's *plenty* of people who forget about me alone. But together, I don't know anybody that forgets
meeting us together. And that's a twin thing."

Lisa: "And that's our twin slogan. . . ."

In unison: "YOU CAN ONLY MAKE A FIRST IMPRESSION
ONCE: WE MAKE IT TWICE."

Debbie: "We exhaust ourselves."

And sometimes, despite their effusive intimacy, they come to
blows. "There's a lack of respect that goes on between twins," Lisa
explains. "Because it's like fighting with yourself. I could say curse
words—things that truck drivers would say—but we don't hold it
against each other."

"You know how you say the meanest things to those you love?"
Debbie asks me.

"Vicious," Lisa adds.

"It's worse than being married," Debbie says. "Because you—"

"Push buttons," Lisa says.

"You can say anything you want," Debbie says, "because we know
in our relationship, it's over in a second. If I say, 'F YOU! DROP

DEAD!' two seconds later it's like, 'Are you going to meet me in a half hour to go shopping?' "

Speaking of shopping, Lisa does it for both of them. "I buy two outfits of everything," she explains. "Debbie doesn't come with me. So unless a store has two, I won't buy it. I'll walk in the store and say, 'Can we try this on?' And I see the saleslady look around, like, 'Who are you referring to? Who is the *we?*' I'm the only one standing there."

How did Lisa become the designated shopper?

"Because I don't like it," Debbie says. "I haven't gone shopping in twelve years."

Do they relate to the many twins who have difficulty being seen as a set?

"They choose to be considered separate. We choose to share what we are."

Debbie: "To answer your question—"

Lisa: "Oh, I'm sorry. I thought I was."

Debbie: "We believe that the people who have a problem with it are not the twins themselves; it's society. Everybody our entire life"— she uses the singular—"since we were five years old, has been trying so hard to find the differences between us: Who's taller, who's skinnier, who's prettier, who's smarter, who's sexier, who's better. If everyone left twins alone, then you wouldn't see all these talk shows with twins who hate each other."

"Every day you're being picked apart," Lisa confirms. "Every day you're being compared. People feel the liberty to say whatever they want, like we're a circus."

"It's sort of like we always have to be *on,*" Debbie says.

"But you *are* always on," I point out.

"For us, it works," Lisa says simply. "We know we're always going to get attention and people are going to stop us on the street, and we use it to our advantage because our business is related to twins. But for a lot of people, the attention is just annoying. They think, Yeah, we're twins, whatever."

Lisa wants to make it clear that they have existed apart—once. "When I lived in Australia for a year in 1990." Debbie concedes that was the first time she got a serious boyfriend. "I ended up living with him, but it didn't last."

Has the twinship generally gotten in the way of romantic relationships?

"NO," they answer in unison, as if anticipating the question.

Lisa now has a long-term boyfriend, Bill, who, she says, "embraces our twinship. He gets it. He leaves us alone. My boyfriend is very quiet—obviously because he wouldn't have room to get a word in. So for him, he'd be happy sitting at home reading a book, while we want to be off doing our twins stuff and being *on*. Debbie and I had a fight in Paris on the Champs Elysées—a screaming fight in the middle of the street, while Bill's walking along, 'La, la, la,' and we're screaming, 'FUCK YOU!!!!!!' "

They agree that any man who dates one of them has to know that the twinship takes precedence—no matter what hour of the night. "Lisa would call me at one A.M.," Debbie says, "and after we spoke, my boyfriend would say, 'Why didn't you tell her it was too late to call?' I'd say, 'Because it was Lisa. She had to tell me something.' 'What did she have to tell you?' 'She wanted me to turn on Channel 2 because there was something on.' "

"*Willy Wonka and the Chocolate Factory*," Lisa remembers.

" 'Why does she need to tell you that?' " Debbie continues quoting her boyfriend. " 'Because it's important.' It's a twin thing."

Lisa tries to explain it with another anecdote: "We know a man who has been married for fifty years to an identical twin. He said to me, 'Let me put it to you this way: If, God forbid, I had to stand on a cliff with my wife and her twin, and make a decision which one of us was going to be pushed, I might as well jump.' "

Donald Keith, seventy-two, a former army major who cofounded the Center for the Study of Multiple Birth with his twin, OB-GYN Dr. Louis Keith, is unapologetic about the seniority of twinship. "I say to people, 'You as a mother or father are not going to get between those two people. You, as a spouse, will have your own place, but you're not going to get between those two people. However, if you get between the two, look out. Because you may lose.' My second wife couldn't stand the relationship. She was against my being that close to Louis and talking to him every day. I could talk to him from my office but not from home. It hurt me and he knew it, and he was hurt. I've now been married to my third wife twenty-two years, and we've tested our patience with each other on many occasions because of what I did *with* Louis or *for* Louis. Because it came before what *she* wanted."

"I think that anybody who marries a twin," Debbie says, "has to understand that they're marrying two people. Men who marry twins get all the disadvantages and none of the advantages of marrying two women." She says it can be unsettling. "Two years ago I went out with a gentleman who was forty-seven, single, never been married, an only child. And we had one of the best dates I ever had. But afterward, he never called. Okay, so that could be a typical girl story. My girlfriend looked into it—she happened to be dating his buddy—and she said, 'That's odd that Jim didn't call Debbie.' And Jim said, 'Yeah, I thought she was hot, but you know what? She's a twin.' "

Lisa sums it up gravely: "He couldn't handle that."

Debbie: "He couldn't handle the 'We' world."

Debbie admits that her confidence as a desirable woman is shaken when Lisa's not at her side. "I'm so used to being looked at, I could walk into a huge trendy restaurant with Lisa and I'd be fine. If I walk into that same restaurant and someone looks at me, and I'm by myself, I get very insecure. I think, What are they looking at? Sure, I could say to myself, Maybe they're looking because I'm pretty or something. But I can't. I am telling you, with Lisa next to me, I will dance on a bar; I can stand in front of a thousand people and give a speech. I could have stuff hanging out of my nose, or my zipper could be open, but when I'm with Lisa onstage, I'm in my element. Because they're not looking at *me*; they're looking at *us*. A guy once said to me, 'I don't want to know about your twin thing; what are *you* like?' I froze and started to feel upset. Because I couldn't answer him."

Lisa underscores this: "The twins business is what we do; it's also who we are. To divide the two is difficult."

And they feel lucky for it. "Why does *everybody* want to be a twin?" Debbie reminds me. "We're all looking for that relationship that twins were born with. Everybody wants to be loved that much."

"It's definitely a universal wish or aspiration," affirms psychologist Ricardo Ainslie, who has treated twins, is the author of *The Psychology of Twinship* (1997), and whose mother is an identical twin. A Mexican-born forty-eight-year-old who teaches at the University of Texas at Austin, Ainslie explains the idealized twin connection by invoking one of the prevailing theories about child development: that primary relationships are "symbiotic"—between baby and parent, or baby to baby in the case of twins. "There's an experience of self and other as being one," Ainslie tells me. "A complete closeness. A sense of immersion in another person that feels whole and complete and almost ideally satisfying. That's at least one reading of what early childhood development entails. It's a powerful experience that, in some ways, twins, because of the nature of their closeness, aspire to and sometimes feel: *We understand each other better than anyone else does. We are closer than other brothers and sisters are.* It's a kind of magical intimacy. And it's what we all look for in partners." In his book, he writes about the common "wish to return to a symbiotic relationship—that is, a relationship characterized by a lack of self-other differentiation in which one's needs are magically understood and met."

Twins researcher Nancy Segal, a fraternal twin who has studied twins for three decades, affirms the mythos of twins: "For singletons especially," she tells me, "I think you look into that world, and especially for people who are missing something vital in their relationship—you see a certain closeness and camaraderie. And you're envious of it. Some people might be put off by it because they see it as a claustrophobic closeness, almost too much, a lack of independence.

But I think that's basically what we all crave: We all want to have somebody who knows us as well as our identical twin *would* have if we'd had an identical twin."

Twins in love. It actually flashed through my mind more than once during my interviews—with the Barbers, the Ganzes, and with others: *These two have a romance.* Not in a queasy, freaky way, but in the sense of uncomplicated devotion and delight in each other. They weren't careful. They flaunted their identicalness like a trophy. They prioritized each other without reserve.

Liza and Jamie Persky, friends of my oldest friend, Jane, live in different states—when we meet, Jamie runs a bakery with her husband in Stowe, Vermont, and Liza is single and a television producer in Manhattan—but they are in touch in a way that makes the miles irrelevant. We talk in one of Manhattan's ubiquitous Pain Quotidien cafés one summer afternoon.

"We've never had a fight," Liza confesses sheepishly. "We've never screamed at each other."

Jamie says the only thing that maddens her about Liza is her lack of confidence. "It annoys me when she doubts herself. That gets so frustrating for me. Because for me to be happy, she needs to be happy. If I feel that she's in a bad place, it's hard for me to be in a good place. It never feels better to be doing better than she."

The only thing they don't tell each other is when they've been complimented.

"Like if someone says I'm pretty," Jamie says.

"She *is* prettier," Liza insists. (I stay neutral.)

Dr. Ainslie describes how twins recoil when people point out disparities: "There seems to be a feeling that the recognition of differences is experienced as a loss to oneself when one's twin is being acknowledged," he writes. "This sense of unequally distributed characteristics only exacerbates the feeling that one has lost something important. Recognition or demarcation of certain abilities or talents feels like a taking away."

"If someone compliments me in a way that will make her feel worse, I won't tell her," Jamie says.

Similarly, when seventy-three-year-old Larry Gordon, a childhood friend of my mother-in-law, tells me that he and his identical twin, Gerry, both applied to University of Michigan, he won't tell me which one didn't get in. "What you're asking is who didn't make it," he says without smiling, "and I don't want to answer that."

The Persky girls are often holding hands in childhood photographs. They shared one room, one best friend—"It was always awkward because this friend knew she could never be closer than we were to each other"—and they didn't reach out to other people. "To make friends, you need to be lonely," Liza explains. "There has to be a need. . . . We don't need anybody else." I notice she used the present tense. "Which is probably why we were single for so long."

They lived together both in college and after graduation, and they joke about being so protective of the other that they will suffer if necessary. Liza tells the hilarious example of when their expensive haircuts went awry. "Jamie sat in the chair first," Liza recounts. "The stylist says, 'What do you want?' We're like, 'WHATEVER!' I'm sitting behind her—she can see me in the mirror—and he cuts her long beautiful hair so it looks chopped off, like Stockard Channing's in *Grease*. It was awful. I'm sitting behind her and the tears are welling up, like, I can't believe this is happening!" She mock sobs. "I'm not saying a word. And then he's done; he styles her and he's like, 'So, what do you think?' I'm like"—she makes her voice meek—" '*It's great.*' And I get in the chair like I'm going to the gallows. He says, 'Same thing?' I'm like"—more stage sobs—" '*Yes, please.*' "

"She got the *same terrible haircut*," Jamie marvels.

"I couldn't let her go through life looking like that alone," Liza adds.

Their first real "individuation" was when Liza moved to New York. "We were twenty-six and I'd never been on a plane without her," Liza confesses. "Jamie wasn't even going to drive me to the airport, because we thought we might have panic attacks in the car. I said to people, 'I know what it's like to leave my parents; I know what it's like to leave home. I don't know what it's like to leave Jamie.'

"I will never forget saying good-bye. Oh my God! It was like Dead Twins Walking. We were both thinking, When are we going to actually say it? I remember getting out of the bathroom stall, looking at each other, and just crying."

I ask when that was, and they both blurt without hesitation, "September 20, 1992. 8:01 P.M."

Jamie says her marriage could only have happened because Liza left. "I wouldn't have met him if she'd still been living in the same city," she says.

"Jamie and I didn't date much before that," Liza admits.

"Because we didn't do anything apart!" Jamie explains. "No one knew us differently. We didn't know each other differently."

"I think there's something about being twins," Liza ventures, "where you stay younger longer in a weird way. It's infantilizing."

"Growing up, we didn't develop, boywise," Jamie adds.

"Nor did we want to," says Liza, clarifying. "We had no desire."

"My husband's only the second person I've slept with," Jamie admits. "Literally, if Liza had stayed in L.A., I wouldn't have dated my husband. I'd have rather spent time with her."

The hardest moment in their twin romance was when Jamie got engaged—on their birthday, no less. "I didn't even tell Liza right away when it happened," Jamie admits.

Liza remembers it was a blow. "I was trying to figure out what the feeling was; it wasn't jealousy. It was that this was the first thing that was so different between us, the first time there was something separating us. When I went to get fitted for my bridesmaid's gown, I sobbed in the Vera Wang dressing room. And then I said to myself, Pull it together. I didn't want to bring her down or have her be worried about me."

"Cut to my wedding." Jamie smiles. "It was literally like WE were getting married: Liza and I."

"I told my mom before her rehearsal-dinner toast," Liza recalls, " 'Mom, don't forget this is about *Mark* and Jamie. Not Jamie and me. Seriously, Mom, *you have to mention Mark.*' "

Jamie laughs. "There are more wedding pictures of Liza and me standing together than there are of me and Mark together. I swear."

"All the speeches became a roast of our relationship," Liza adds. "And it didn't even seem weird."

The Perskys are in Manhattan to celebrate their fortieth birthday the night after our interview. Jamie has flown in for the party, leaving her husband back in Vermont to tend to the bakery. (He ends up coming and surprising her.)

"When I travel, I don't have to pack anything," Jamie boasts.

"Her entire birthday outfit tomorrow night? All my clothes," Liza says proudly.

"Her moisturizer, her socks, whatever I need—" Jamie says.

"—I'm going to have it," Liza says, finishing for her. "And we can even sleep in the same bed. My apartment is small and I don't have a sleeper sofa."

"We play games," Jamie says. " 'Confessions.' We do ego boosts: 'You looked SO good the other night.' "

" 'Tell me what you love about me,' " Liza adds. They both laugh.

❋ ❋

Like the Perskys, my sisters-in-law, Fern and Sharon, have a twins romance, which they believe may have stunted their social life. Though they both ended up happily married, Fern didn't find someone till she was forty-six (thank you, Match.com), and she does believe their twin interdependence hindered her confidence and nerve.

"I remember in grade school not talking to other kids and actually *pretending* to talk to someone," Fern recalls as we sit in my parents-in-law's apartment in a Chicago suburb. "So if someone was looking at me from a distance, I wanted it to *look* like I was talking to someone, but I wasn't. It makes me sad just thinking about it. I remember not knowing what to say to anybody."

"I'm sure that somehow stems from the fact that we were never separated," Sharon ventures, "and didn't know how to be social on our own."

Sharon, in fact, says she "hated" the effort of talking to other kids. What about friends?

"What friends?" Sharon replies.

"Yeah, really," Fern affirms.

Ainslie writes that extreme twin dependency can entail "a degree of anxiety associated with functioning as a separate, autonomous individual." He elaborated on this in our interview, explaining that twins are socialized from infancy to need each other, partly because they're pushed together by two major forces: their parents and their twin. When parents are overwhelmed with exhaustion, as most parents of multiples are, they feel relieved when their twins can occupy and entertain each other, and they often plop the twins together to give themselves a break or because they think it's good for the twins. The twins meanwhile gravitate toward each other because of an instinctual familiarity and comfort. "So the world around twins may have a way of pushing them together and accentuating their connection," Ainslie says, "and twins themselves, because maturation is inherently stressful in some ways and anxiety-provoking, may turn to one another to ease that stress."

The result is that twins often grow up leaning on each other, reliant on the constant company, feeling at sea without the other. So when life throws the curves of adolescence, independent friendship, or romance, twins can worry about whether they're equipped. Ainslie gives an example: "Any kid is going to feel ambivalent about going away to college. That's a normal anxiety any adolescent may have. But for twins, it's compounded or made more complex because you're separating not only from your family but from your twin. So some twins manage that by trying to forestall the separation: 'Let's go to college together. Let's be roommates at college.' " (Fern and Sharon did both go to the University of Illinois and lived together their last two years.)

Dr. Michael Rothman, supervising psychologist at New York's Beth Israel Medical Center, has studied the psychological snags of having a double. "I think your social development probably is delayed," he tells me in his downtown office. "You're slower in some ways. You're probably better at the intimate stuff than you are at the 'Let me get to know you' phase, which isn't something you've had to do that often; you've always had your twin, who knows you. And you know how to connect to and relate to another human being in a very powerful, old, long-term relationship, but not necessarily in a new one."

Psychotherapist and fraternal twin Dr. Dale Ortmeyer, eighty-five, who wrote about twin psychology in the 1970s, said that twins are good at intimacy because they've had a lot of practice with each other. But Rothman says twins can be bad at intimacy because they haven't needed to find it elsewhere. In his paper on twins, Rothman says forging romantic relationships can be an extra challenge—not just because twins haven't sought outside intimacy before but also because they don't feel that anything's missing. "While twins can engage in their own 'chumship' much earlier than pre-adolescence," writes Rothman, "learning to seek objects outside of the twinship is, for obvious reasons, a crucial skill that should be developed but may not seem needed to the twin."

"If Fern and I were young today and I was our mother," Sharon says, "I would have been a little concerned that we were not social at all."

She tells me they fell in the awkward category in grade school, which was compounded by them having two of everything—skinniness, acne, and thick glasses.

"Had there been just one of us," Sharon offers, "there wouldn't be fuel or fodder."

"We were at the bus stop with this girl, Valerie," Fern recalls. "There we were, the Nerdy Twins, and she had this curly thick hair; she wasn't cute. We weren't cute. They'd call us 'Boobsy, Bobsy, and Brillo.' They were just mean."

Fern says it wasn't until she was twenty-five that she really gained confidence apart from Sharon. "It wasn't till I moved to New Jersey that I realized I can be social on my own," she says. Sharon, meanwhile, was much more proactive about finding a mate. "Sharon wanted to be married," Fern says. "More important, she believed it was going to happen."

As with the Perskys, there was some melancholy when Sharon actually did get engaged. "I felt for Fern," Sharon says; "I worried she might feel bad."

"I *did* feel bad," Fern confirms—partly because she sensed her family pitied her. "I didn't want people to feel sad for me," she said. "But there was also a part of me that thought, What's wrong with me that I can't find someone I feel comfortable with and fall in love with?"

And the twinship got in the way?

"Yes. That may be an excuse. But once you know Sharon, how do you find someone to match . . . ?" She doesn't finish the question. "There's a closeness that we have—even if it isn't spoken—that was hard to duplicate."

Sharon nods and smiles. "She completes me."

※ ※

Paul and George Kogan, Russian-Jewish identical twins who were orphaned at the age of fifteen and adopted by Orthodox Jewish parents in Manhattan, are archetypes of twins who felt married and then went through a tense divorce. When I meet the brothers—forty-two, five eleven, spirited, rosy-cheeked—at a noisy café in Manhattan, the fault line in their love affair emerges as our dinner progresses. But it all starts out cheerfully with descriptions of how their twinship used to be a powerful wooing tool. "It was a mark of distinction and it got me laid in college," George boasts.

"When we would go out together during college," Paul recalls (he went to Princeton, George to Penn, and they visited each other often), "typically we would be in some booth at a bar with some girls, and the banter and flirtation was very much driven by the twin thing."

George continues. "We'd be sitting there, and girls would say, 'Hey, are you two twins?' And we would literally have, I think, three or four witty repartee scenarios worked out."

They admit their interaction was alluring—or reassuring—to women. "George and I were very close," Paul says. "We would rub the backs of each other's heads; we were very affectionate with each other."

"It was exactly what the girls wanted to see," George marvels. "It's terrifying how much we played on that."

"We were shameless." Paul smiles.

Why do they think women were attracted to Twin PDA (public display of affection)?

"It was warm to watch," George ventures.

"I think they wanted to see men showing physical closeness," Paul adds.

I ask if they continue to act that way with each other. Paul answers yes immediately, but George is more equivocal.

"I think there's a recognition that at some point, there was a split in the road and we both went our own ways," George says. "When my brother found someone he was very serious about, it changed our relationship a lot."

He's referring to Paul's marriage to Deborah Copaken in 1992. (Deb, an author and photographer, is a close friend of mine, who happens to have identical twin sisters.) "Paul and I were not in the same place," George recalls. "There was some point, when I moved back to New York from working in Moscow, I realized we had very different social scenes and I had kind of *lost* my brother."

Paul looks surprised.

I ask George if he mourned that loss a bit.

"I think I mourned that privately and very quickly, but I did mourn that."

He didn't express it to his brother at the time. "I just sort of moved on."

And, in fact, he says that their threesome—he, Paul, and Deb—was felicitous while it lasted. "This whole *Jules and Jim* trilogy stuff worked very well," George admits. "I played the third wheel and it suited me perfectly."

Paul: "He was always very entertaining."

George: "Paul and Deb would just set me up with all of their friends."

Paul: "You shagged a lot of our friends."

George: "So everyone got their new roles: Paul was the Committed Guy and I was the Single Irresponsible Guy."

After thirteen years (and Paul becoming a father three times over), George married Irina in 2006, which wasn't as smooth going.

"You know . . . I *like* her," Paul says tentatively. "I certainly have my issues with George's choice."

"You don't like my wife at all!" George protests. He turns to me. "He was counseling me to leave her at the beginning."

"It's true," Paul concedes.

"He doesn't think she's worthy of me," George explains.

"It's not true to say that I don't like her at all," Paul insists.

"I thought we were going to be honest," George says.

"We're being very honest!" Paul objects.

"I think you're being a little defensive," George says. "You don't like my choice. You're willing to accept it, but you're not thrilled about it."

The fissure in their twin romance is exposed at the dinner table.

"I think, in the end, I found the woman who was right for me," George says somewhat defensively. "But when I met Irina, Paul was already married for ten years. We had grown apart; there's no question. We weren't nearly as close as we were at eighteen or twenty-two years old. . . . When he started having children, our lives and values became completely different."

"The thing that was upsetting to me was ultimately the lack of communication," Paul explains. "Certainly, after I was in the trenches of marriage and children, there was a real disconnect."

They now rarely see each other alone. To me, it appears that George misses Paul more than he admits—and, frankly, more than Paul misses him. "I understand that my brother's life structure is very heavy," George allows. "There are his kids' schools and other friends. He has a very extroverted, socially focused wife. So that world is very pulling for him."

I ask George if he sees Paul as much as he wants to.

"No. Of course not."

Same question to Paul.

"The simple answer is yes, I see him as much as I want to, in terms of what I can do right now."

I see myself in George: the jilted lover. I've had that dispiriting realization that my twin is satisfied with the amount of time we spend together. I am aware of wanting her to want more dates with me.

Paul thinks that Irina is primarily what's keeping them from spending more time together as couples. "Before George was married," Paul says, "I had a vision of the four of us sitting around having brunch, drinking coffee, and reading the *New York Times*."

"But I needed to marry a different person for us to do that," George interjects. "I needed to marry an East Coast, Ivy League–educated chick, who spoke the same language. Irina is a Russian émigré. She's been here for twelve years; she has completely different concerns. Her priorities are much more earthy: yoga, holistic medicine.

She's as far from the Upper West Side as you can get. So that was the big division. . . . I think my brother's house, or his family, generally makes Irina feel very intimidated, so she tries to drag me away from them."

"I think there are two divides," Paul interjects. "One is the divide of the woman who George married, and the other is the divide of my brother not having kids. So I hold out great hope that at the very least, when they have kids, we will enter a common—"

"I don't see it." George skewers the daydream. "I think our social circles are too different."

"But we'll speak the same language," Paul insists. "We'll speak the language of naps and diapers, at least for a few years."

"But I don't think we're going to socialize more because of it," George counters.

"I think that's up to Irina," Paul persists. "For instance, Deb helps run this music group that meets every Friday morning. . . . Irina and your future baby could join. I'd love to see a return to some sort of a more common conversation we might have."

"I think that could happen," George allows.

"It would be nice," Paul says. "It would make our lives easier."

I see that George doesn't buy the happy ending. "I think it's part of our character—this resignation," he says. "My brother and I never made the effort to get back closer. We look at time as sort of an inevitable process. We say, 'Well, if anyone's going to make the effort, it's going to be the other guy.' "

I relate to that—waiting for my twin to make the first move.

"If my brother made more of an effort, I would respond," George confesses. "But I don't see him making an effort, so I'm not going to do it."

I find myself wanting to nudge them to a more acute awareness of the preciousness of each other. Maybe because I wish someone would nudge Robin and me, or maybe because I've recently met Gregory Hoffman, who lost his twin on 9/11 and thus dramatized most painfully how twins can't be too casual about time together.

"I do think that my brother and I take each other for granted in a way that we expect the other one always to be there," George says in response. "If we were ever to admit the idea that he may not be there, you'd be touching on the idea that we're not permanent. The easier option is to take each other for granted."

Paul shakes his head. "Taking each other for granted is only part of it. The other part of it is the time pressure and how crazy our lives get. Part of it is the gap between us, from my perspective. Very honestly, to some degree, I see George falling behind me on certain levels. And my wish is that he would catch up."

What does he mean by "falling behind"?

"I think there is a movement forward in a life cycle," Paul says, clarifying. "So I feel like, in terms of maturity and getting to a certain place, even though we're twins, he's my younger brother. That he's about seven years behind me."

"Because I don't have kids," George says.

"Primarily because he doesn't have kids," Paul affirms. "In addition to my dream of sitting there together reading the *New York Times*, there is the other dream of us sitting and having our babies play together during a backyard barbecue as we talk about auto insurance. I consciously and actively miss that."

I ask Paul what would happen if he reached out to George more to ask to spend time together.

"No." Paul cuts me off. "No."

"See, it's a central and immovable denial on his part," George declares. "He never changes." He looks at his brother with a fearlessness I can't imagine showing Robin. "The truth is that it's really your insecurity, in the most fundamental sense, that is preventing you from, first, reaching out to me, and, second, from admitting the fact that it's not a passive thought like, Oh, I wish my brother had kids. Then it would all get fixed."

Paul is insecure?

"It's hard to define," says George. "If Paul was more at ease with himself, maybe he would appreciate what he had and he would be charitable enough to share it. But I think that he's not quite comfortable in it, so I think there's a sense of hoarding what he has for himself."

"I'm very at ease with myself," says Paul, disagreeing. "I'm surprised you say that."

"Part of it is, yes, him wishing I'd get to the same point," George continues. "But my guess is that when I have kids, there will be other reasons why we don't get closer."

"I agree with you," Paul agrees, sharing his pessimism. "Even when you have kids, I don't see much of a scenario where we get much closer."

Somehow the Kogans' sparring actually makes them appear *more* intimate, not less. Their exchange bespeaks an entrenched familiarity with each other, and safety in candor. They can say the toughest thing and survive it.

"I guess I do have visions of us, at some point, just doing a me-and-you trip," Paul says.

"That suggests your carving time out from your family," George challenges him.

"Yes—let's say, going on a trip to Moscow together," Paul replies.

"So the effort on your part would be carving time out from your family." George is pushing the point, it seems, to make sure he's hearing Paul correctly, or maybe to hold him to a promise.

"But we all know that that trip would be impossible right now." Paul appears to back down.

"It's not impossible; it just requires effort. People do it."

"They do."

"It just comes down to: What are your priorities?"

"It's true. In other words, would I like to do a trip with you to Moscow? I would fucking love it. I think it would be totally hilarious and fun."

"I see a more realistic scenario where my family could get closer to your family: I could bribe you with real estate." (George has been making more money.)

Paul smiles. "You could."

"For example, if I was to rent a house that would have room for your family, you would find time to spend with me, because of the functionality of making *your* kids happy."

"Done." Paul slaps the table. "In fact, you said you were going to get a ski house upstate. I'm all over that, baby."

Dr. Joan Friedman, an identical twin and mother of fraternal boys, who counsels twins in Los Angeles, published a book called *Emotionally Healthy Twins* in 2008. She says part of what backfires for twins is the idealization of their intimacy. "If you buy into the romance of twins, you don't give the twins any capacity to feel ambivalent about it. In my relationship with my sister, there was no room for us to articulate any negative feelings. We twins are supposed to have ESP, telepathy, be soul mates since birth. That's what people project on twins. It's almost like if you tell people you're not best friends, they're disappointed. If you don't have ESP, they're disappointed. When you're thrust into that kind of closeness with someone, in order to safeguard a sense of self, you can't be completely intimate. Because being open and honest would mean you'd be willing to be mad, or say 'I hate you,' or 'I don't want to take care of you.' Twins are socialized very early to get along. So you can't really be authentic. Parents are told that twins aren't supposed to fight, hate each other, get angry. Because they're twins. That label is so laden with all these stereotypic ideas."

Robin confirms this burden when I ask her how she feels when we argue. "I hate it. I feel like even as close as we are, we don't totally tell the truth. And that's really hard. You'd think we could say the hard, horrible thing, and we kind of can't. There's a protecting of each other. There's so much tiptoeing, and you'd think we wouldn't have any."

On the other hand, we go full throttle in our pep talks when one of us feels down or anxious. Nancy Segal explains this pattern in *Entwined Lives:* "An identical twin may be the best source for most types of assistance for which we would normally rely on other people, such as emotional sustenance. . . . This is because, genetically speaking, helping an identical twin is like helping oneself."

Even if my turning to Robin actually counts as self-help, it looked pathetically like overdependence when Robin pointed out that the pep talks typically go one way.

ROBIN: "I think I play that role for you more often."
ABIGAIL: "What do you think that's about?"
ROBIN: "You're still turning to me more. It's fine, though; I find it very easy. I know what I say will get you through it, because you're very much like me. It's not like I don't see myself in you. I know what will help."

[I felt silly and predictable. *Robin knows my fractures so well, she can simply plug in the right sermon and patch me up in a phone call.*]

ABIGAIL: "Do you see me as more childlike?"
ROBIN: "No. I just see you as more emotionally out there. I don't judge it."
ABIGAIL: "Do you see me as weaker?"
ROBIN: "No. More volatile. It makes you less even."

What struck me during that interview with Robin is that I may be in our love story by myself. Of course I know she loves me, but she doesn't sentimentalize us, while I'm still mushy about our history. I was surprised to watch her sit through three hours without once choking up. I outwardly maintained a reporter's neutrality, but I was waiting for emotion to get the best of her. When it didn't happen, I noticed something inside me switch off.

Writing this book forced me to confront the degree to which I retain a fantasy of our twinship, which is probably, on some level, immature. Some part of me is simply unwilling to accept the fact that our friendship today doesn't resemble its twelve-year-old version. Maybe it's not that Robin gives me too little; it's that I expect too much. What three-handkerchief movie am I living in?

The experts seem to believe that ardor logically cools—or that it *should*, in the interest of both twins' healthy development as adults. But when does the love story actually begin? Could it really start in utero? My gut says yes, just because it feels like it should be true. Robin and I were smushed together for nine months; I can't believe there's no emotional trace of that snug cohabitation. But there's no science yet to back up this theory.

There are, however, pictures: sonogram films that show twin fetuses bumping up against each other, kicking, touching, stroking, and what looks like kissing—their lips pressed together. The pioneering research came from German obstetrician Birgit Arabin, a serious-seeming fifty-five-year-old with bangs, who currently works in the Netherlands. In the late 1990s, Arabin studied twin behavior in the womb in the earliest weeks of a pregnancy, when the two fetuses were still small enough to be observed side by side in one video frame.

"She showed us twins kissing years ago," recalls OB-GYN Dr. Louis Keith, former president of the International Society for Twin Studies. "She also showed us twins punching each other. But to say that you could follow these twins for twenty years, and that twenty years later, they are going to be kissing or punching each other in the nose, I don't think she wants to say that. She won't go that far."

He's right. When I met her in the hotel room where she was staying before delivering a lecture in New York, she refused to draw any conclusions about whether inuterine activity predicts twins' interactions later in life. "Let's say I don't know, and I don't have the scientific proof," she said carefully in her quiet German accent. "I asked pediatricians to follow it, but they didn't. . . . In the videos, you're seeing incidental reactions of one twin toward the other when they touch each other," she said, sipping a beer she'd retrieved from the hotel kitchenette. "You can maybe observe and describe some kind of reactions to one twin's touch. The identical twins' reactions are definitely more similar than the fraternal twins'. And we found differences dependent on gender: In males, these kinds of reactions were faster; I wouldn't say 'aggressive,' because that's an interpretation, but the reactions were faster and they were more enduring in males."

Arabin's work was also groundbreaking because of the length of time she kept the camera trained on the twins' activity. Child psychotherapist Alessandra Piontelli had done similar studies earlier in the decade, but for shorter periods of time.

"The Italian studies from Piontelli," says Keith, "were more like a peep show than some scientific view. You make a scan: 'Oh, look! They're kissing. Oh! They're punching!' " Piontelli did conclude that twins, in their infancy and toddlerhood, exhibited similar behaviors to those shown in utero.

While Arabin is loath to read twin bonding into the fetal behavior she captured on her tapes, Israeli obstetrician Isaac Blickstein is not so reticent. When I talk to him and Keith together at the 2007 International Twins Conference in Belgium, Blickstein says Arabin's films changed his mind about early attachment. "When I saw the first images, I said, 'Birgit, this is rubbish. This is just a chance event. The faces of the babies are in front of one another and their lips come together for a second. And you happened to be there in the moment.' But if you follow her videos—and I have them at home, so I look at them from time to time—you *see the pattern.* . . . So maybe these weren't chance events. There is, for instance, one video when you see both twins and the membrane between them. They are sleeping like two fetuses. All of a sudden you see one twin wakes up and goes up to the membrane. And makes some vibrations with the membrane, and the membrane moves. And the other twin wakes up. And you see them coming closer to each other, face-to-face. And then they are happy. One of the twins makes a circle. The other twin does the same, turns the same. Like dancing. One moved, then the other moved. Sure, everything can be chance. But there is another explanation."

Which is what?

"Which is that there are some *connections.*"

Keith looks at me curiously. "Why do you question that for one second?"

Because it's such a touchy-feely, amorphous idea.

"No, it's not," he counters.

But Keith himself acknowledged, as did Blickstein, that there is no scientific foundation for it, no studies.

"You are telling us what you *feel,*" Keith says.

What's that worth?

Blickstein takes over this lesson. "Not everything can be evaluated scientifically by randomized controlled trials. They're good for medications, intervention. But not for things like this. We cannot prove it."

"And no one will ever prove it," Keith stresses. "What you have experienced with your sister is *yours.* None of us can argue with your feeling."

Keith regales me with stories about how he and his twin brother, Donald, have felt each other's pain, sent each other mental messages.

"We have been sending messages for years," Keith tells me. "Donald would go into some kind of self-trance and say repeatedly to himself, 'Louis, call me. Louis, call me. Louis, call me.' It had never worked outside of the United States before. But one time when I was driving from Berlin to Rostock, Donald had to get to me and he did."

(Two months later, when I'm back home in New York and Robin is on Shelter Island, I actually decide to try sending her a telepathic message. Up until that day, Robin and I had been sending each other e-mails daily, but not talking much on the phone, so it would have been unlike her to call me at noon on a summer weekday. But I tried to enter the focused, meditative state Keith had described, saying over and over, "Robin, call me. Robin, call me." The phone rang, and I jumped out of my chair. I asked Robin why she was calling me at that moment, and she said she wasn't sure herself, that she had been making lunch for her kids and she suddenly felt compelled to. Chalk it up to chance, but it freaked me out.)

"We are doctors," Keith summarizes. "And we are telling you these stories, knowing full well that you have a tape recorder on, that you can quote this in your book. And what do I care if you quote it? I'm not lying. I'm telling the truth. So your feelings with your sister: perfectly normal."

I tell them I just keep imagining the skeptics.

"There are always going to be skeptics," Keith says with a wave of his hand.

"Abigail." Blickstein smiles. "I am very well known. Louis is very well known. Suppose we stand up in a meeting like the one you saw today and we give a talk entitled 'Intrauterine Experience.' They'll start throwing tomatoes at us."

Were Robin and I ever in love? Before I started interviewing other twins for this book, I pored over old scrapbooks, and reread Robin's notes and cards to me, which were especially copious in college and then postgraduation, when we shared apartments. Taken together, they made me feel both tickled and wistful. Tickled because her affection was so open then; wistful because her expression hasn't felt that pure, that profuse in so long. It may be melodramatic to say that our romance couldn't survive adulthood, but it certainly isn't unbound anymore. Somewhere along the way, we buttoned it down.

> *You know you love someone when you look forward to them. I look forward to you. With affection everlasting. Robin.*
> WINTER 1987

> *Abigail—You are more loyal than any friend*
> *More loving than any lover*
> *More knowing than any sister*
> *And more valuable to me*
> *Than anyone else in my life.*

Thank you for everything
And happy Hanukkah. Yours, Robin
12/87 HANUKKAH CARD

In the days of the womb,
in our neat little room,
the couple was me and you.
But now there are many,
So I'm asking, "Abby—
Can I be your Valentine, too?"
Love <u>always,</u> Rob.
2/88 VALENTINE CARD

ABIGAIL: When I was going through my scrapbooks, I was
struck by the fact that we were together all the time as kids.
And I actually felt envious of it. Even though I wouldn't
want that literally in my life right now, that routine just
went away without my saying good-bye to it. You evolve
and grow up, but there's got to be something to that—how
much we were together. And then we weren't. I think I
kind of mourn that in a certain way, more than you do.

ROBIN: You can opt for our togetherness now and it's not a
zero-sum game for you. And for whatever reason, it *is* for
me. It's like, if I'm choosing you and I'm spending time
with you, then I'm not developing this other side of my life.
And my whole life was with you before. So I'm trying to
have some other life besides you. . . . I just feel like you
were able to carry me with you and still build something
else at the same time. And I didn't. You were all I had and
I sort of resented that on some level. I didn't prepare. And
I don't want you to be all there is.

ABIGAIL: Do you feel like I need you more than you need me?

ROBIN: I feel like you, for whatever reason, are more confident in your individuality. So that you can be more generous with me.

ABIGAIL: Or more demanding of you.

ROBIN: You can include me in your life and not feel like it compromises your individuality. You can have me there next to you at a party and you're not worried about whether people are seeing you individually. You're not worried about carving out your little section of the world. You're more grounded that way.

ABIGAIL: But do you also see that I probably want more of you?

ROBIN: But you want more of me because you feel a hole sometimes.

ABIGAIL: Whatever the reason, I'm saying I want more of you than you want to give right now.

ROBIN: Yes. I think we've had that tension.

ABIGAIL: Is that hard for you?

ROBIN: It's hard to distinguish it to you: that it's not saying, "I'm rejecting you"; it's saying, *"I'm claiming something."*

ABIGAIL: If you look back, can you trace when the twinship affected the way you approached people or friends?

ROBIN: I don't remember any of it, except for when we were on a family vacation—that I wanted to lose you a little bit.

[Robin would sometimes elude me on family vacations so she could get to know people without me constantly at her side.]

ROBIN: And I remember your being upset about it. I didn't really understand why I did it at the time, but in retrospect I think I do. People see the two of us and it becomes about *the two of us.* "Wow, look at the two of you." That sense of just being received *on my own*—I feel like I missed that.

And I feel like my parents didn't give it to me. Because they lumped us together so much as kids and they were so worried about parity that they never spent time with us separately. So I've always had this sense of, *Do Mom and Dad know me as distinct from you? Is there any way in which our connection is different than yours is with them? Would they miss me per se if they haven't been in touch with me, as opposed to you? Are we interchangeable?* This sense of being interchangeable really bothers me.

ABIGAIL: When did you become conscious of that feeling?

ROBIN: Pretty late. Like five years ago. . . . I remember running into a friend on the street and her talking to me for fifteen minutes and then calling me later and telling me, "The whole time I thought you were Abby." That just, to me, summarizes what I hate.

ABIGAIL: Why do you hate it?

ROBIN: Because it doesn't matter whom you're talking to, you could have been someone else. You could be *anyone*. It upsets me when people tell me the same thing twice. It's like they don't remember having told me. I did not make a mark. And I think that has to do with all of this.

ABIGAIL: "This"?

ROBIN: This twin thing.

ABIGAIL: What about being mistaken on the street, which constantly happens?

ROBIN: That doesn't really bother me, but it's not at all fun. Sometimes it's fun if I take you to my office and show you to people for the first time. There's always been a little bit of pride in that.

ABIGAIL: But do you like walking into a party together?

ROBIN: No.

ABIGAIL: Why not?

ROBIN: A party is hard enough. You're trying to make your own impression.

ABIGAIL: You don't feel like it gives you a strength to be together?

ROBIN: No. I don't like gimmick. Walking into a party together is, to me, leading with the gimmick. I guess I feel like it's my private given identity. It's not what I want to be publicizing or making prominent. Then you just become a phenomenon, not a person. . . . What's become very important to me, which some people don't necessarily understand and they take offense at, is that I just need my own thing. It's just become a theme of my life. And I think it has to do with being a twin, and I only came to it late. But I just need my own little world—a few things that are just mine. It's become almost excessively important to me. I want to carve out my own life. I feel like I just never really did.

ABIGAIL: Would you say that individuality requires a conscious effort if you're a twin?

ROBIN: Well, I think on the part of the parents, they could have done a much better job. They really should have.

ABIGAIL: How?

ROBIN: Just spending time with each of us alone. Making us feel like we were individual people, who had a presence in their lives.

ABIGAIL: Instead, they did what?

ROBIN: We did everything together. Or they made sure it was always equal. Which I kind of hate now. Like I hate when Mom evens out the grandchildren: "I've seen Ethan, so I have to see Ben." What if she got closer to Ben? What if she saw more of Ben? What's the worst that would happen?

ABIGAIL: Do you think that's informing the way you are raising your children?

ROBIN: Yes, a lot. I think it's why I was afraid to have a third kid. Because I just really felt like I wanted to make sure to have that time one-on-one with each of my children. It's so what I missed.

ABIGAIL: Do you feel there was any early consciousness of a difference in our friendships?

ROBIN: No. I think the first real memory I have of it is you just being happier at your high school, noticing that, and being aware that I was not as happy. I remember your being very socially active, and clearly at home, and I was having the opposite experience of feeling there was nobody there that I fit in with.

ABIGAIL: What about our relationship in high school?

ROBIN: I think it was fine. I think I have some memory of your including me in your social life a little bit, which was helpful. But I think it was the first time where I might have felt an inkling of resentment. Like you had it better.

ABIGAIL: Did you feel that in college, too?

ROBIN: No, only after college, when I realized that you had kept friends and I really hadn't. But when I was there, I think I was pretty fine. I had a hard senior year in college, but I don't remember connecting that with your having a better one.

ABIGAIL: Years later, as adults, when we invited some of our friends for a women's weekend in Connecticut, it wasn't really enjoyable for you?

ROBIN: You mean that I felt they were more your friends than mine? I think it's been hard that I don't have my own social life very much. I mean this issue of friends has also been a big thing for me, and I think that has to do with my having a twin. But it's confusing, because you didn't have the same issues. I think there is a sense that if you have a twin, you don't really need friends or a best friend, so it made me sort of lazy. All through my youth, I wasn't that open to close friendships. You were enough. Now I feel like my eggs are in one basket a little bit and I resist that. I just don't have a larger circle. On the other hand, I'm also someone who doesn't really necessarily want to hang out with friends all the time. So it might be more an intellectual thing that I miss having more friends. I also think I just don't really know *how* to do friendship. I don't know how to do the day-to-day tending of a friendship very well. I think that's partly because ours was a given.

ABIGAIL: So, if I were going to ask you who's more psyched to be a twin, I can assume the answer.

ROBIN: It's not that I'm not psyched to be a twin. I just don't need to be trumpeting that part of my identity. I just feel like it's my quiet foundation. And it doesn't make it any way less or less valued. It's just less overt. And it's not the thing that needs tending—for me. It's not at risk. It's there.

※ ※

4 YOU DEPLETE ME: COMPETITION

Competition and issues of power are embedded in the twin relation-ship by the sheer nature of it.
—Dr. Michael Rothman, psychologist

Tiki and Ronde Barber described their brand of competition as almost too good to be true: They've always driven each other to excel, but they've never felt an ounce of schadenfreude.

The more typical example of twins and competition is much less generous. And it seems to have its roots in ancient texts.

Rabbi David J. Wolpe of Sinai Temple in Los Angeles has taught classes about twins in the Bible. There are only two sets in the Torah: Jacob and Esau, born to Isaac and Rebecca, and Perez and Zerah, whose parents were Judah and Tamar. What their stories have in com-mon, Wolpe says, is one central idea: "They're all about who gets to come out first."

Jacob holds on to Esau's ankle as Esau exits Rebecca's womb—presumably to hold his brother back from being the firstborn. (The Hebrew root of Jacob's name, Yakov, actually means "heel.") Simi-larly, during Tamar's labor, her son Zerah sticks his hand out of the womb, and just as the midwife ties a red string around his wrist to signal that he'll be the firstborn, Zerah's hand suddenly retreats back inside and Perez actually comes out first; it's as if Perez pulled his brother back and charged ahead. His mother remarks, "You broke through," or "Wherefore hast thou made a breach for thyself?"— thus the origin of his name, Perez, which means "breaking" or "breach."

"The stories are both about the younger usurping the older," Wolpe says, pointing out that in each parable, the twins struggle, as if to suggest that they're born already in conflict. "In both cases, the natural order is overturned by deception or by force."

English professor Hillel Schwartz, in his book *The Culture of the Copy: Striking Likenesses, Unreasonable Facsimiles*, has a different take on why Zerah in Genesis began to surface, only to pull back and have Perez go first. "Commentators describe the two struggling for primogeniture," Hillel writes, "but the episode can also be read as expressing Zerah's reluctance to leave the perfect twinship of the womb."

Rabbi Wolpe echoes the same idea in discussing why Jacob grips his twin's ankle. "You actually could read it as saying that Jacob was frightened that Esau was leaving him, so he grabbed hold," Wolpe says. "Because he didn't want to be abandoned."

It reminds me immediately of the Yoruba tribe—the African clan I've been researching because it has such high rates of twinning. The Yoruba believe that the older twin is actually the one who emerges *second*. Their conviction is that the older twin protectively stays back, holding down the fort, as it were, while sending the younger twin out to safety.

I personally prefer this African interpretation to the biblical one, because it suggests the intimacy and gentleness of twins' first moments in the world, not the violence of grappling to be first or the notion that twinship, even in its incubation, is a clash. My twin experience has not been contentious like that.

The Yoruba give every second-born twin the same name, Kehinde, meaning "arriving after the other," while the first to come out is always named Taiwo, meaning "having the first taste of the world."

Birth order matters, according to Louis Keith and his identical brother, Donald, who together started the Center for the Study of Multiple Birth in 1977. ("We were the first to study twins academically in the United States," Louis tells me.) The Keiths are seventy-two and dressed all in black when I meet them. Donald wears his gray hair curly; Louis wears his slicked back in a short ponytail. Donald sports a silver bracelet, Louis a gold necklace. They're hip and they're ornery. Every response is offered somewhat begrudgingly, as if it should be obvious to me already, such as the fact that the firstborn will always be dominant.

"I was Twin A," Donald begins.

"It's a fact," Louis interjects, "that Twin B is Twin B, and Twin B will never become Twin A. No matter what. So Twin B better just adjust to that."

What does that mean?

"Well, were you Twin A or Twin B?" Louis asks me.

I came out first. (But I would have been second were it not for Mom's C-section.)

"You're Twin A," Louis pronounces. "Legally—"

"And emotionally," Donald adds.

"First born," Louis says solemnly. "You have the rights of the first-born. You're older; you're smarter; you're whatever society gives to the firstborn as opposed to the second-born. The second-born is always sucking on the hind tits, as they say."

Even if few people were even aware that I'm a minute older?

"This is between you and your sister," Louis says.

I tell them I don't feel like Robin defers to me—maybe because my taking the cesarean shortcut canceled out my advantage. "I'm not sure there's *deference*," says Donald. "But it's bragging rights."

That's nonsense, according to psychologist Joan Friedman, an identical twin and mother of fraternal twins, who counsels twins and their parents. "No one knew anything about me just because they knew I was two minutes older," she insists. "But they focused on it, made much of it, drew conclusions because of it. It was defining even though it was meaningless. That's why we did not tell my boys which one was older until their bar mitzvah date. Because I spent my entire life being asked and being differentiated by 'Who are you? Who is older?' My husband and I blocked out the time of birth on their birth certificates, and we told our sons, 'When you're thirteen, you can find out who is older.' Of course by the time they were thirteen, they didn't care. But at least they weren't organized their whole life by their stupid birth order. Because this is what I lived with, and I hated it: the presumption that someone understood me because I was born two minutes before my sister. God. That made me crazy."

I have always told people, much to their skepticism, that Robin and I were not competitive. It seems the first thing nontwins assume about twins is that we collide or try to outdo each other. But that misses the nuance. We saw each other's triumphs as reflective, if anything, and our stumbles were suffered vicariously.

It is true that, like the Barbers, Robin's feats prompted me to try harder—not just to match her but because she showed me it was physically possible. If she can do a tripod headstand in yoga, I should be able to. If she loses five pounds, I should be able to. When she gave birth naturally, just two months before I went into labor, damn if I was going to have a C-section, though my son was a whopping nine pounds, twelve ounces. I channeled Robin and pushed that baby out.

I did realize, however, during the interviews for this book, that the knee-jerk presumption of rivalry isn't entirely wrong. Crudely stated, I found there were two schools of twinship: the kind that begets a kind of interconnectedness that means one twin's success is shared, and the other kind, which yields a kind of zero-sum equation—one twin's trophy is the other's defeat. Either way, the simultaneity of twinship—always being in the same place at the same time, always fodder for endless comparisons and checking, like a mirror you can't help looking into—can spur twins either to great accomplishment or to massive frustration, to a firm confidence or to a pesky insecurity.

Twins Avi and Gil Weitzman, thirty when I meet them, are like poster twins for hyperachievement and hostility. Avi is now a federal prosecutor at the U.S. attorney's Manhattan office; Gil is, when I meet him, New York Presbyterian Hospital's chief resident for the Department of Medicine and an attending physician in gastroenterology. "I hope my kids aren't as bad to each other as we were," says Gil, having to shout to be heard in the loud seafood restaurant.

"I don't remember it being that bad, Gil," says Avi.

"Yeah, you do," Gil says, correcting him.

"Part of it," Avi tries to explain, "was because people would mix us up. So when Gil would do something, it would embarrass me. If something made him look bad, I felt it reflected poorly on me, because people would mistake me for him. It truly is the case that you are your brother's keeper when twins are together. The actions of your brother so pervade everyone's perception of you that it forces you into a box. We didn't have separate identities. From elementary school on, no one called us 'Avi and Gil.' They just called us 'Glavi.' "

The Weitzmans admit they weren't the hippest boys during their adolescence. But unlike today, where they're distinguishable because Gil has more girth and less hair—"I used Propecia in high school," Avi says, smiling; "it works"—they used to look exactly, maddeningly identical. "I was so much cooler than you." Gil smiles. "It was unfair that you were bringing me down." He tries to explain the Twin Trap: "It's like seeing yourself in a video throughout your entire life."

"We all have a skewed image of ourselves," Avi explains. "But for those of us who are twins, what our twin brothers or sisters do is bring truth to the reality. They shatter the hopeful misperceptions we have about ourselves."

Their father, an Israeli-born manufacturer, demanded high achievement, and their mother, a French-Israeli teacher at Manhattan's Lycée Français, did make an effort to keep them in separate school classes but couldn't help but compare them at home. "If one person's grade was better than the other's, they'd say, 'Your brother did better than you,'" Gil recounts. "I think they had some insight into the psyche of being a twin, but not the same that you or I would have had."

"My dad was a lot worse," Avi says. "He fostered a lot more competition between us."

"He's a pressure cooker," Gil affirms. "I don't know how many Israelis you know, but there is no such thing as 'You tried your best.' There is only perfection."

The friction between the twins detonated when they became debating partners in tenth grade.

"Our debate coach thought it would be a good idea," Gil recalls.

"We opposed it," Avi declares.

"It was good for our success as debaters, but not good for the success of our relationship," Gil says. "There's so much competition in debating as it is, even between debate partners, because every round involves a judge who ranks the various participants. Debaters even fight for which speech they're going to deliver—one is more prestigious or more fun. I would outrank my brother in a certain debate round, and then he would outrank me."

"We both had a strong drive to achieve, and every time we didn't, we would blame each other," Avi says. "It was completely obnoxious, because we would delicately curse each other out in Hebrew so that nobody else in the room would know we were calling each other idiots and morons."

Avi believes he had the harder road because Gil was slightly more impressive academically. "My dad desperately wanted us both to be doctors," Avi says. "Desperately. Undeniably. And Gil excelled in math and sciences in a way I never was able to. He was in all the AP classes and I was struggling to keep up, and at some point in time, I had to withdraw from the honors classes and go into the regular classes because I just didn't have that excellence. It was a real sore point for me."

It's hard to conceive of Avi's insecurity, since the differences between the brothers were minimal. "I was so proud of my SAT scores," Avi recalls, "because I did fairly well—I got six ninety math, six ninety verbal. Not bad. And I showed my scores to my dad, and he said"—Avi imitates his father's accent—" 'Theese is good.' And then Gil showed my dad *his* SAT scores, and Dad sees that Gil got an eight hundred in math, which is what he would have expected from us both, and he says, 'I don't understand why Gil, who has your genes, can get an eight hundred in math and you can't.' "

Tough love.

"I did get therapy." Avi smiles.

Gil jumps in to suggest that his father was not entirely to blame: "I think we're genetically driven to be highly competitive personalities."

"I don't know if I'd let Dad off the hook that easily," Avi counters. "I think there's clearly a level of competition that's *fostered* by parental treatment of twins. It's different with friends: the competition that friends foster is in things like sports, girls, who's the more fun twin. No one knows what grades you get. My father demands a high level of success, which trickled down to tremendous ambition. We would have been perfectionists whether we were twins or not, but what our twinness did was magnify that—in a way that hurt our relationship."

Gil again disagrees: "I think my parents tried to breed friendship and sharing and niceties between us, but I think we were very resistant to that. I don't think it stems from Dad's desire to make you better."

But Avi is less sanguine: "Our parents are really much prouder of Gil," he says simply. "He's the doctor. When I was in college in the nineties, my dad would tell me over and over again, 'You shouldn't go to law school. There's no recession for doctors; people always need doctors.' He sent me articles. It was always clear that there was medicine, and then there was law. There's nothing like being a doctor in my family."

Dr. Ricardo Ainslie, author of *The Psychology of Twinship*, describes how a twin's feeling of being underappreciated can be powerful, whether it's true or not. He writes, "The fact that each twin might have different areas of talent that are reinforced or acknowledged by the parents does not necessarily mitigate the feeling that the other is favored or that the other's characteristics are the preferred ones to have."

Francine Klagsbrun, who doesn't specialize in twins but wrote a 1992 book about siblings called *Mixed Feelings: Love, Hate, Rivalry and Reconciliation Among Brothers and Sisters*, found that "a whopping 84 percent" of the 120-plus people who answered her questionnaires felt that one parent had shown partiality. "Parental favoritism," Klagsbrun writes, "when it has been keenly felt . . . can remain not only a cause for underlying tensions, but an open sore, picked at again and again."

Gil refuses to let Avi disparage himself. "I think being a Harvard Law School graduate and now being a U.S. attorney—it doesn't get much better than that," he says. He goes further, describing Avi as a "BMOC" in college when Avi was at Kentucky and Gil was at SUNY-Binghamton. "I'd come visit him," Gil recalls, "and for a New York Jew to achieve such prominence in Kentucky—it's unheard of. It's the first time I felt such pride in my brother's achievements. Before that, any achievement he got meant that I was probably a little jealous because I didn't get it."

Gil recounts that when he was recently honored at a Manhattan dinner for his chief residency, he knew immediately whom he wanted to invite. "Aside from my wife, I wanted my brother there," he says.

"Because I always think that Avi's strengths are partially what drive me to achieve also. I think I am who I am today because of the competition that I had with my brother back then. And I want to make him proud of me."

A fraternal twin I'll call Daniel (he preferred a pseudonym) is clearly still bitter about being labeled the less smart one all his life. "When I told my brother that you were interviewing me, he said, 'Be kind.' Because he still thinks that I'm resentful, having always felt myself the vanquished."

He describes how the family's adulation of his brother colored everything. "You don't want to get rid of your twin, but you do want to get rid of your twin," he says, recalling the feeling. "There are all sorts of fantasies of killing them off or keeping them around. You go back and forth."

Even birthdays are tainted. "I always have to remember to get him a birthday card on my birthday. To this day, I can't just have *my* day, where I don't have a chore."

It was years of psychoanalysis after college that pulled Daniel out of the worst of it. "That's when I started to process what it was like to have this experience of constantly being under his thumb in some ways. And how difficult it was. It's funny, when I hear someone is having twins, my first thought is, Oh, I'm so sorry. Both for the twins and for the parents. For the parents because I know how hard it is, and for the twins because I think it's harder than not."

Hating one's twin is rare and definitely carries an extra stigma—as if it's particularly awful to loathe the person you're supposed to be closest to, or to spurn the friendship other people wish they had.

Gertrude (she preferred not to give her last name) is eighty-five years old and lives in a retirement village in Southern California. She doesn't hold back when it comes to her twin experience: "I feel like it ruined my life, very frankly," she says in a coarse, effortful voice on the phone. "I've had a hard time with it ever since we were born."

Gertrude and her sister grew up in a small town in upstate New York. "I know there are twins who bond as early as intrauterine," Gertrude says, "but I wasn't one of them. I was told that I pushed and pummeled and scratched her. She seemed like an appendage who clung to me her whole life. . . . I looked after her, even though my true feelings were to find a way to drop her in a hole somewhere. I had the sense that she wanted to become me—to crawl inside of me and be me. I had a real identity crisis at seventeen, started to punish myself, lost sleep, had symptoms of sickness."

Gertrude says there was no distance between them, hard as she tried to create some. "Oh, I could never shake her," she says bitterly. "We were always together. . . . She made me stay with her, walk with her. We slept together, went to college together. She was always there. I couldn't lose her."

Today, Gertrude's twin lives in a senior facility many hours away. "She calls me very often," Gertrude says, sounding drained by it. "She pushes me to tell her I love her, calls me 'sweetheart.' I try to return her affection, but I have trouble summoning up real feeling."

How much does she see her sister these days?

"As little as possible."

It's hard for me to get a handle on why being a twin was so suffocating for Gertrude.

"I was never my own person. I always had to consider my twin. I didn't belong to me. I can't see that there was anything positive about it. I feel as if I lived half my life. . . . And here I am; I got to be this old lady. Now I just take it easy, do a little sculpture, painting, and try to put it out of my mind."

But as soon as I chalk this story up to an anomalous case of twin disgust, Gertrude surprises me. "I care what happens to her," she announces suddenly. And then, even more incongruously: "I think I would feel devastated if I lost her."

Fraternal twins Sheila Lambert and Erica Frederick, sixty-one, who are both slim and olive-skinned in a way that suggests Middle Eastern blood or decades of tanning, didn't speak to each other for three years and now spend every summer weekend together. "It's almost like we had to have this separation," Sheila ventures, "to figure out how much we value each other. And to leave the baggage of 'Who do my parents prefer? Who's the smarter? Who's the better-looking? Who's this? Who's that?' Those three years helped us leave all that behind."

So their parents constantly compared them?

"I don't think they actually did, but it was our *perception* that they did, and certainly that others did," replies Sheila. "And we always thought the other came out ahead in that comparison. . . . Each of us thought our parents thought the other was smarter."

"And the favorite, too," Erica adds.

Their childhood loyalties were not to each other but to their separate friends.

"They delighted in putting a wedge between us," Erica recalls.

"And we let them do it." Sheila nods.

What precipitated the breach decades later was one misinterpretation on top of another. When neither called to sort it out, silence set in. "It was really just a horrible time," Erica says, sitting in her spacious office at Manhattan's Hebrew Union College, where she's executive vice president of development. "Such a huge hole in my life, in my heart."

Their grandmother's ninety-fifth birthday broke the stalemate. "We were sitting together," Erica recalls, "and I guess we just said, 'It's time.' "

"Since we reconnected," Sheila adds, "I don't think we've had even one fight. We never spoke about the period of estrangement. . . . To this moment we've never discussed those three years."

Dr. Michael Rothman, supervising psychologist at New York's Beth Israel Medical Center, says the groundwork for competition is laid before birth. "Twins are not favored equally in the womb," he writes in "The 'Twin-Self' System." "And thus one twin, by circumstance of biological randomness, is a weaker womb-dweller than the other." The notion that twins are battling in their earliest moments—

for nutrition in the womb, then to get out, then for mother's milk and attention—is explored in Rothman's review of the psychological literature on the subject. He cites psychoanalyst Dr. Susan Davison, who reported in 1992 on her observations of one set of twins, Luke and Mark. Davison "describes events that occurred in the twins' third and fourth months that reveal the beginnings of a rivalry as each twin developed a stronger awareness of the other. . . . As the mother would tend to one twin, the other would cry and bawl hysterically. . . . There appeared to be an intense competition brewing in which attention was the primary yet limited commodity. . . . Of particular distress for the boys was witnessing the other being breast-fed."

Rothman quotes Davison's article, "Mother, Other and Self—Love and Rivalry for Twins in Their First Year of Life": " 'By 3 months the twins were exquisitely aware of not being each other: Mark could tolerate mother attending to Luke, but not the sight of Luke breast-feeding. He "knew" he was not having something Luke was at that moment having and what's more he wanted it too. At 4 months it was slightly more complicated in that Luke began to protest when mother left the room, and it may not be too fanciful to think that for her to return with Mark seemed to him like a betrayal. His lovely squeals and shouts were not good enough, Mark had only to cry from the next room to steal their mother away from him, and then insult was added to injury when Mark was breast-fed despite Luke's insistence that he wanted mother for himself.' "

Rothman sums up the inborn strain between twins: "Born into an environment in which need-gratification is not a simple matter, twins must immediately engage in what remains one of their most salient relational patterns: They must both compete against and collaborate with each other in order to attain the sought-after nurturance from their parents."

It makes sense intuitively that, like any newborn mammals, there would be a fight for sustenance. But the fact that this congenital opposition is happening alongside a primal intimacy strikes me as somewhat contradictory. And, in fact, Rothman does emphasize that twins have an instinctive benevolence alongside their feuds: "As important as it is to acknowledge that competition is part of the twin relationship, as one will always achieve something before the other," Rothman writes, "they still function as intimate companions capable of soothing each other."

It reminds me of one of Klagsbrun's quotes, which I underlined when I read her book: "Both the rivalry and the closeness may be fueled by the same thing: alikeness." That to me encapsulates the tension of twinship. Klagsbrun elaborates on this when we talk. "You want to be treated the same and you want to be treated differently. You want to be alike and you want to distinguish yourself."

Journalist Lawrence Wright underscores the same idea in his 1997 book, *Twins: And What They Tell Us About Who We Are*: "There is one side of you that wants your twin to be exactly like you in every detail, a perfect replica, but another side of you is struggling for air. You feel like you are being smothered by the sameness."

Janet Lee Bachant had a heightened kind of rivalry in childhood, because she was the third wheel in a triplet set: Her two triplet sisters were genetically identical twins, while Janet was the odd fraternal sibling. Even though she was one of a threesome (still exceptional when they were born, in 1944, prior to the use of widespread fertility treatments), and even though they were all dressed alike till age twelve, the other two—Nancy and Karen—were the standouts: They were the identical twins and an inseparable team. "I'd say it was my first memory," Janet tells me. "That they wouldn't play with me. I played by myself."

The isolation was compounded by the attention the Bachant triplets received, not just due to the phenomenon of their birth but because their father didn't live to meet them—he died on the beaches of Normandy in August 1944. A news story several years later followed up on how the triplets were faring, and quoted Janet's mother, who'd remarried: "The twins stick together. And Janet gets pushed around. Sometimes they gang up on her—though she has learned to protect herself. She has to—with the two of them pushing her about. . . . They don't want her to play games with them."

Janet had the advantages of being seven minutes older, prettier, and a more deft musician. But she is always the one standing apart in photographs.

Now sixty-four years old and a psychologist, Janet lives in Manhattan and talks to her sisters more than she sees them, since Karen is in London and Nancy in Seattle. She's closer to them these days, but it's obvious her childhood exclusion left scars. "No question that it was the central, informing event in my life," Janet says flatly. "I did feel like a triplet because that's what I was always told that I was, but I never felt like a twin. In some way I felt outside of something."

She says it led to a necessary, healthy independence, but also a permanent extra-sensitivity. "Certainly in the present day, when things happen in which I feel left out, I get really triggered," she tells me. "It must be automatic. We all went to Normandy a few years ago to mark my father's death, and at one point we went to a flea market; Nancy and Karen were shopping up and down the rows of the market when all of a sudden they were just gone. I went back to the car, looked up and down the street, and it turned out that they'd decided that they were going to go to lunch; so they went to a little café. I was apoplectic."

The distrust she learned as a kid, Janet believes, later informed her romances. "I'm in my second marriage," she says, "and I would say that my earlier relationships were characterized by being involved with people who were not available to me."

Her social unease is similarly traceable. "Glibly, I say, 'I was born in a group, and that was enough groups for me.' I don't enjoy being in groups. I think that probably comes directly out of the whole situation."

When I spoke to Janet's triplet sister, Nancy, who runs a theater company outside Seattle, she said that the twin-plus-one dynamic didn't last: "I'm closer to Janet now than my twin. Maybe because Karen is away in London. Sometimes being as close as identical twins are can bring a lot of friction, as well. Maybe there's relief in having another one who isn't the same as you."

When I ask Rabbi Wolpe why he thinks the Bible renders its twins as mainly combative, he ventures that it reflects a fundamental need: to be distinct. He paraphrases an apt line from the W. H. Auden poem "September 1, 1939": "Auden says something about it being the struggle that's bred in the bone, not to be loved but to be loved alone. In other words, we don't want to be one of many; we want to be *the one*," Wolpe explains. "For nontwins, if you're the younger child, it's more clear: The older child has already been established and has been there awhile, so you come into a world in which there's a struggle for primacy, but it's already assumed that there's someone ahead of you, with all that that implies. But as a twin, it's got to be very hard. Because you can't even be unique. Not only can you not be the only one; you can't even be the unique one."

Caroline Paul, forty-one, said she and her twin gave up trying to be special or to surpass each other; they just wanted to keep up. "We didn't want to fall behind, because we were constantly judged against each other," she says, cuddling her cat, Femur, in a temporary apartment in San Francisco's Protero Hill District. "Somebody who is born single doesn't have a measuring stick next to them. But twins always do. So either you don't stand next to each other and you have totally different lives or when you do stand next to each other, you make sure you're just as good."

Caroline and Alexandra Paul were legendary beauties and athletes in their small town in northwest Connecticut; both are still striking, lithe, intelligent, and fit—and each often felt she was none of those things next to her sister. Both women have been rescue workers. Caroline actually *was* one—she was a firefighter for eight years—

while Alexandra *played* one for five years on TV: Lt. Stephanie Holden on *Baywatch*.

"I was only athletic because she was athletic," Alexandra says when I interview her in L.A. at the sun-filled condominium she shares with her husband. "I'm twice the person I would have been if I were a singleton because I strove to be more like her—my whole life. If she wrote a poem, I'd go write one. I never played with dolls because she didn't dig dolls and I didn't want to admit that I did. And I would practice and practice swimming, but I would never be as good as she."

That's not how Caroline remembers it: She recounts the story of how, when both girls were training in their hometown lake, Alexandra outdid her by doing the butterfly stroke across the entire two-mile expanse and back. "She probably didn't tell you that," Caroline says.

She didn't.

"Don't let her tell you I'm more athletic," Caroline continues. "We were very good swimmers, and part of it is we were ridiculously focused. We used to do extra laps. We used to have fights in the middle of the lake, because if she started zigzagging, it meant she was getting more of a workout, and I'd have a fit and scream, 'STOP! You're zigzagging!' Because that would mean I'd have to zigzag, too. And you were not allowed to stop; if you stopped, you were a total wimp. That's how highly competitive we were."

Psychologist Nancy Segal says twin competition is not so much about beating the other as matching her. "I see identical twins competing not to outdo one another but to stay abreast," she tells me. She has researched elite twin athletes who are born with comparable physical prowess and drive. "When I read about how they feel when the other one wins, it's such selfless behavior," Segal says. "It struck me the first time that this can't be real, but I've seen it repeated over and over again."

Dr. Ainslie writes that "competition can also be a source of differentiation." In other words, twins compete to stake out their own personas. And, he says, they know instinctively that by honing separate skills, they might be able to avoid going head-to-head in the same sphere. "Carving out different interests or areas of expertise," he says, can be "a means of avoiding competing directly with each other." So one twin decides he's going to be the math/science twin, the other, the English/history twin. "So I can get straight A's in my area, and you can get straight A's in your area," Ainslie says. "But if we're both in math together, one of us is going to get a better grade. If we're both in swimming together, one of us is going to be in first place, one of us will be in second. It's easier for me to be independent, to do something else, and just let you keep swimming. At least that's what you tell yourself. Although there will inevitably still be activities both of us do, and if I'm on the B team in tennis and you're on the A team, then I still feel like shit."

The Pauls were not particularly close when they went off to different boarding schools, and Alexandra wrestled with acute anorexia.

"I was devastated by it," Caroline recalls. "But we didn't confide in each other at the time. . . . It's funny, because I started mimicking anorexia later, while she was still struggling. I was losing weight and doing the same food issues. It almost felt like it was a learned thing, like, Woah, she's doing it; I'll try it."

Dr. Joan Friedman tells me she frequently sees anorexia in teenage twin girls, she believes, because identical twins are expected to be equal and harmonious, not encouraged, or allowed, to be overtly competitive the way normal siblings are. "That's the only way they can be competitive with each other: Who can get thinner than the other one? . . . It's this silent competition that filters through their relationship. But there's such a need to say, 'I want to beat you. I want to be first. I want you to find out I did this ahead of you or better than you.' That's what regular siblings do: They're overtly competitive and everyone knows that's the nature of the game. Parents are comfortable with that because it makes sense: Siblings are genetically different. But identical twins are forced into this perspective of being absolutely the same, and the way they keep their relationship stable is by having the competition and the comparison as a subterfuge, under the surface."

Alexandra admits she hid the worst of her illness from her twin, the same way the two never really discussed how they'd always privately measured their academic and athletic achievements by each other's. Caroline writes in her 1998 memoir, *Fighting Fire*, "What you could be walks right next to you all the time."

It wasn't until much later that they started to share the truth about themselves. In fact, Alexandra was not the first to learn that her twin was a lesbian.

"I told my brother before I told her," says Caroline, who came out at twenty-four. "I don't know why; because I wasn't settled in it. For me, it was just going to be a big secret, and then it kind of leaked out."

Was she nervous about Alexandra's reaction?

"Yes," Caroline replies. "It mattered a lot."

"She'd had boyfriends," Alexandra tells me. "But it turns out that in high school and college she also had girlfriends; I just didn't know it. So one day I called her in the morning in her dorm and her friend Simone answered the phone and sounded groggy, and I knew. Caroline got on the phone and I said, 'Are you gay?' And she said, 'Yup.' And I said, 'Oh,' trying to be incredibly open-minded. . . . I know I had a therapy session later that day, and I didn't talk about Caroline; I talked about *me*—because I've always had issues about whether I was feminine enough. And so I was equating the fact that if she's gay, I'm not feminine. It was all about me, of course." She chuckles.

Alexandra has since become a committed gay rights advocate and relishes the chance to play lesbians on camera. "Actually, I've played two gay parts and I'm hoping to play a third soon," she tells me. "I always tell people I'm half gay because my twin sister's gay, so I have gay genes."

These days, both Paul women get choked up when discussing each other—a far cry from when they were racing each other feverishly in their hometown lake. Talking to them individually, what comes through more than anything is how delighted they are to be so close at this point in their lives. "This is probably the most important thing about being a twin," Caroline says. "You have a confidence in the world that no one else does. And that's because you know you'll never be abandoned."

The Pauls no longer strive to distinguish themselves; in fact they are invested in the idea that officially, they're genetically the same, so much so that they were reluctant to find out they might not be. "We took the DNA test," Alexandra explains, "because people always asked us if we were identical, and my mother would say, 'No,' because she wanted us to be individuals, while Dad would say we were. A few years ago, we decided to offer ourselves up for sexuality studies, since she's gay and I'm straight—we thought it would be a help to figure out whether it's nature versus nurture—so we took the test by swabbing our cheeks, and the results were to be mailed to me, and we were so afraid that it was going to be fraternal, we didn't open the envelope for two and a half years. My sister said, 'If you open it and it says we're fraternal, don't tell me. Say you lost it.'"

What were they afraid of?

"That we wouldn't feel close," Alexandra replies. "That it would break a bond. But one night at midnight, my husband was away and I thought, You know, the truth is in that envelope and I'm going to open it up. And of course it said we were identical—seven out of seven markers. . . . We were thrilled and relieved. And we entered into twins studies. They've never called us, but they do send us a birthday card every year."

Jane Harnick is the only friend who has stayed friends equally with Robin and me since we were four years old and met on the bleachers of the baseball field on Fire Island.

ABIGAIL: Do you see Robin and me as competitive with each other?

JANE: I feel like each wanted the other to do so well—and that your competitiveness was with everybody else, not with each other.

ABIGAIL: Do you think that I am protective of her?

JANE: No. And when you guys were younger, she was the one who took control of the situation and got you through things. I don't see you as protective.

ABIGAIL: You're saying she was the adult in the twinship?

JANE: Yes. She was definitely the adult. Remember your trip to Greece, when she held the plane tickets and kept you from getting lost? Those stories were always hysterical. That's another thing I should mention—the way you two make each other laugh. When you're together and you're on some kind of roll, I'm crying, I'm laughing so hard.

ABIGAIL: Do you remember that dinner a few years ago when we made you angry because we were laughing so hard?

JANE: Maybe because that reminded me of childhood, when the three of us would be together and you two were onto something and laughing; I wasn't included. And here you did it again.

ABIGAIL: What was it like when we were younger—for you to be the third wheel?

JANE: Horrible. I remember when the three of us would plan to do something together, and I'd always be very excited ahead of time, but then I'd get into the situation and say to myself, Why do I keep putting myself in these situations? It's awful to be with the two of them. Because you guys would ignore me. You'd have your own private language. It was a feeling like, They don't need me here. Now it's better, but when we were younger, you were so tight; there was no room. I wanted to be the third Musketeer and you just wouldn't let me. I don't know if you let anybody.

ABIGAIL: And yet you stuck with us.

JANE: We've been friends since we were four. You don't give up on that.

ABIGAIL: How would you describe our relationship with our brother, David, growing up?

JANE: When we were kids, David was just your little brother, just like I had a little brother; they were annoying, but we liked them. Then in high school, when David started having some trouble, I just remember thinking it must be so hard for him with the two of you as sisters. How could it not be? And your mother on top of it. I mean, three strong women in that family, how could he not have struggled the way he did? And now I think you're both incredibly supportive of him and it's lovely.

ABIGAIL: What do you mean when you say, 'it must be so hard for him with the two of you as sisters'?

JANE: Well, you and Robin were sort of famous. You were smart, you had each other. *You had each other.* I mean, being the younger brother of twin sisters who were as close as you two had to be so hard and lonely. The pressure. I feel like there must have been extra pressure for him in that house.

❧ ❧

I interviewed my brother, David Pogrebin, months later in my living room.

ABIGAIL: Do you remember Robin and me leaving you out?

DAVID POGREBIN: There were times, particularly in adolescence, when it was hard because Mom and Dad were such a tight unit and you and Robin were such a tight unit that I felt literally like a fifth wheel, and I had no one to be a unit with. But that wasn't till adolescence.

ABIGAIL: Then things got bad?

DAVID: I don't think things were terrible, I think it's a function of odd numbers; I was the odd man out. You and Robin had such a strong relationship. I've always felt that you two were so much each other's soul mates, and I think there was a part of me that would enjoy when you would fight; in fact, I think there still is a part of me that gets a secret pleasure when the two of you are not on the same page.

ABIGAIL: Do you feel like we're insular even now?

DAVID: There are times where I've felt like, Why bother? Not that being close to somebody is ever competitive, but there are times where I think, She gets everything she needs from her sister. . . . And the fact that I was the one who broke from the family mold, so to speak . . . I felt you and Robin took the path Mom and Dad wanted; I took my own path. If one of you had gone to Yale and the other went to a non-Ivy school, for instance, it would have been easier to wedge myself in, or feel like, 'I can get closer to her or to her.' But once you both went to Yale, that sealed the deal for me. There was a way in which it felt inevitable. . . . So I made choices to compensate. I did things to bolster my own feelings of specialness to counter yours. . . .

ABIGAIL: So would you say, looking back, it was hard to be the nontwin sibling?

DAVID: Not so consciously, because it's all I knew. All I've ever known is having twin sisters. I will tell you the one thing Alina [his ex-wife] said is that the reason I'm overweight, and have been since I was ten, was that I wasn't part of a twin. That I ate to be big enough to get noticed. I would try to make myself two people or a bigger one person. But I don't put a lot of stock in that theory.

ABIGAIL: Did you think we had it better being two?

DAVID: Not always. I didn't think until I was older about how hard it must have been for you to be twins. To constantly split the attention.

ABIGAIL: Do you see Robin and me as competitive?

DAVID: I would guess there's some subconscious competition. There are things you both do around the same time—have children, get second homes. You can't look at that and say there's no looking into your sister's yard. There must be something subconscious about the timing of your children, because that was just a little bit strange.

ABIGAIL: If someone asked if you are close to your sisters?

DAVID: I would say yes. I feel I can talk to you about almost anything. But I think there's a judgmentalness that has kept me from being a closer brother.

ABIGAIL: Both Robin and I are judgmental?

DAVID: Yes. In a way I'm not. I think being the least financially successful in the family has given me a unique perspective that makes me less judgmental.

ABIGAIL: Do you feel you have to treat Robin and me equally?

DAVID: Yes. I feel like if I call you, I should call her within the week.

ABIGAIL: Why?

DAVID: Out of fairness. Fairness between twins is a big thing for the nontwin, not wanting to ever blow the equilibrium. I'm painfully aware of that, in terms of everything. I don't want either of you to think that I'm closer to one of you, that I like your children more than her children, your husband more than her husband. I don't want Robin to feel that I'm closer to you than her. Which is a little odd, when you think about it, because I've felt that way my whole life—that you were closer to each other.

ABIGAIL: You wouldn't say that you're closer to one of us?

DAVID: There have been times in my life where I've been closer to each of you. And I stand by and stick to that story.

ABIGAIL: Can you describe our differences now?

DAVID: That's a difficult question to answer.

ABIGAIL: Really? What if you had to speak at our funerals tomorrow?

DAVID: I'd have to think about it. [Laughs.] It would not be something that would just zip out there.

ABIGAIL: I just want to say for the record that if Robin and I die at the same time, we should have separate funerals. I just realized that. Will you make sure?

DAVID: Don't even say that.

ABIGAIL: Seriously, if we died together, God forbid, and we had one funeral, that would really suck. I have different friends, different worlds.

DAVID: If you and Robin died together, God forbid, why would you have separate funerals? What a waste! I can't believe it. [We're laughing.] You want me to have to go through that twice? Why should Jane Harnick and I have to go to two terrible occasions and endure? That would be terrible. It's already going to be double the grief.

ABIGAIL: I've lived my own life. I want my friends to be able to talk about me without being cut short so Robin's friends can get equal time. This really never occurred to me until this moment. I don't want any efficiency at my funeral— two for one. I can just hear Mom saying, "Let's use the leftover lox for Abby's reception. . . ."

DAVID: You're insane.

✳ ✳

5 RISKY BUSINESS: THE SHOALS OF BIRTHING TWINS

Not being able to have a baby can be heartbreaking. But having too many at once can be even worse.
—Health reporter Christine Gorman, *Time*, 2002

Ricki and Steve were like so many couples trying to get pregnant: anxious and ill-informed. Though this couple, in their early thirties, went to one of the most reputable fertility clinics in New York City, they heard few specifics about what they might be in for. "No one informed me of the risks of multiples," says Ricki, a genial woman with shoulder-length black hair, who works part-time in her suburban library. "I just thought that with twins, you got more uncomfortable at the end of the pregnancy and were more likely to have a cesarean birth. I didn't realize how common premature birth was with twins."

Ricki's husband, a furniture maker who is dressed in his company work shirt when I meet him, recalls trying to obtain some hard data. "I really felt that I had to fight tooth and nail for every number, every statistical fact, every probability," says Steve, whose baby face contradicts his graying hair. "I'm well versed in calculus and statistics and things, but whenever I wanted to see real solid IVF numbers and probabilities, I felt that, at best, the doctors were extremely evasive and not forthcoming. They would say something like 'I don't have those figures, and even if I did, they wouldn't be meaningful to you.' I don't think it's a nefarious conspiracy on their part. But I do think that perhaps on some unconscious level, their impetus is numbers: They want to be able to point to statistics and say, 'We have a certain percentage higher success rate than the next clinic.' To a large extent they were more motivated to push you through the process than to make you aware of what can go wrong. If you were going to go out and buy a car and the dealer said, 'You have a two percent chance of this car killing you as soon as you leave the parking lot,' you would never buy the car. It would be considered statistically absurd to take that kind of risk. If they told you the real numbers for prematurity and birth problems, a lot of people might be dissuaded."

"But what if it meant no car at all?" Ricki calls from the kitchen, where she's making tea.

There's the hitch: no risk, no baby—or that's what Ricki and Steve were led to believe. They don't regret their sweet twins for a moment; they just wish they'd had a more realistic sense of what might lie ahead.

They ended up having premature fraternal twins, born at twenty-four weeks (full term is from thirty-seven to forty-one weeks), each weighing a precarious one pound, twelve ounces. Both babies were immediately intubated, hooked to respirators, and rushed to the Neonatal Intensive Care Unit (NICU). Sammy fought for his life in his early weeks; part of his intestine became infected and failed, so doctors inserted a drain in his side. When his condition worsened, they performed surgery for seven hours to remove a third of his small intestine, and later confessed they were surprised he pulled through. "One doctor told me, 'I'm not supposed to say this, but it must have been the hand of God,' " Steve recalls, " 'because we didn't think it would make it. Not one in ten children would have even survived that surgery at his size.' "

Today, at three years old, Sammy has mild cerebral palsy—he has worn leg braces, and until recently, his speech was unclear. But he holds his own in a regular nursery school class with his brother, Stevie. When I meet the boys at their noon pickup on a sunny fall day, they appear chipper and healthy. During the short drive home, they sing along in their car seats to "Here Come the ABCs" by They Might Be Giants, and ask Mom what's for lunch. Sammy takes my hand to walk up the steps to his house, and when he passes his father in the doorway, he blurts out matter-of-factly, "I missed you today, Daddy."

Both parents say they feel lucky, but it's evident they were traumatized by the roller-coaster events of the boys' earliest months. "There's a lot of shock," Ricki admits over mugs of tea at her blondwood kitchen table, "a feeling of free fall and dread. I remember thinking I would have given everything I owned just to give them another week of gestation. Because it makes such a difference." She adjusts her titanium glasses. "I remember feeling so much guilt that we did infertility treatments and caused them to be born; that maybe I hadn't taken it easy enough during the pregnancy and I caused them to be born early; that they'll have to deal with this prematurity and low birth weight the rest of their lives. During the first six months when they came home, there were times when I felt like I shouldn't have done this."

Most people are aware of our national twin boom: According to the Centers for Disease Control and Prevention, twin births in the United States have increased 70 percent since 1980. Between 1980 and 1995, the number of triplets (or "high-order multiples") born to white mothers ballooned by an astounding 500 percent. Today, one in thirty-one births is a twin. (In 1970, it was one in sixty births.)

Credit goes chiefly to reproductive technologies like IVF (in vitro fertilization), and to delayed maternity—women conceiving between the ages of thirty-five and forty—when there's a greater chance of releasing two eggs in one cycle. From 25 to 35 percent of IVF pregnancies produce multiple fetuses, and there are an estimated three million–plus IVF children in the world today. (Natural twins will happen only one or two times in a hundred births.) Which means the vast majority of these twins are fraternal (dyzygotic), the result of two separate sperm fertilizing two separate eggs, and, as with any other two siblings, roughly half their DNA is shared. Identical twins (monozygotic)—which occur when one fertilized egg splits—share 100 percent of their genes. Identicals are always a gestational fluke, although studies show the accident is more likely with reproductive technology. Fraternal twins can run in families when the mother has a genetic predisposition to hyperovulate, meaning she releases more than one egg during her monthly cycle; identical twins are not hereditary. And there's no proof that twins skip a generation: "An old wives' tale," says Dr. Louis Keith.

Obviously, reproductive technology has answered the prayers of countless couples, and the high success rate of IVF is a potent justification for the craze. However, I was struck during my research by the intensity of some doctors' concerns that the hazards are not always highlighted, and even when they are, couples pay no heed.

The fact is that multiple births are high-risk. Neonatal death is five times higher for twins than for singletons. For triplets, the chance of infant death is eleven times higher than for single babies. Twins and triplets are often born too early and underweight (50 percent of all twins are premature, 90 percent of triplets), which can cause developmental problems in utero, at birth, or later on. Twins who are small for their gestational age suffer motor deficiencies, mental retardation, visual abnormalities, behavioral disturbances, and speech problems. A twin is four times more likely to be born with cerebral palsy.

"It is true that modern reproductive technologies and medications started an epidemic of multiple birth," says Dr. Avner Hershlag, the venerable head of the fertility clinic at Long Island's North Shore Hospital, who happens to be Natalie Portman's father. "The reason why multiple pregnancy became such a problem is because the principle of fertility drugs is to make *multiple* eggs, which can result in multiple babies. . . . I know that your perspective is twins, but the main concern is actually over supertwins—triplets and higher—because that really increases the risk to the babies and the mother."

Hershlag, who speaks with the Israeli accent of his birthplace, rattles off the risks to the newborns: "severe respiratory problems, liver problems, blindness, and mental problems, with delayed developmental milestones. There's the need for long-term admissions to the NICU, huge costs incurred to the system and to the parents, and it goes on. There is also significant mortality. I'll give you a number I just read today: that in the UK each year, one hundred and twenty-six babies born after IVF die as a consequence of multiple birth."

He turns immediately to the mother's risks: "Everything that can happen adversely in pregnancy happens more with high-multiple birth, including diabetes in pregnancy, premature separation of the placenta with abruption and bleeding, hypertension, increased discomfort in the pregnancy, increased bed rest—including loss of working days—and that's all before delivery. The most major impact is probably *after* delivery, and that is the social change in people's lives as a result of multiples. There are studies that specifically address the parenting anxiety index. An article from 2004 in *Fertility and Sterility* says the anxiety increases severalfold as you conceive with multiples and deliver them, and any additional baby increases your stress by that much more. We in our practice would not have to do any surveys; we know that reality; we live it."

"The majority of twins do pretty well," says Dr. James Grifo, of NYU's fertility center in Manhattan. "A singleton pregnancy is complicated; a twin pregnancy is *more* complicated; a triplet pregnancy is even *more* complicated. But the reality is that a twin pregnancy generally has a very good outcome." In May 2009, six months after my interviews with Hershlag and Grifo, new research upped the ante on the risks of multiples: Europe's leading journal on reproductive medicine, *Human Reproduction*, published an international study that found that twins born *as a result of fertility treatment*—not just twins in general—have a higher risk of "adverse outcome, including preterm birth, low birthweight and death, compared with spontaneously conceived twins." In other words, it's not just that fertility treatments lead to a higher chance of a multiple birth—which is, in itself, always more high-risk—but twins born of fertility treatments were more likely than spontaneously conceived twins to end up in the NICU or to be admitted to a hospital during their first three years of life.

I tell Grifo that some doctors I've spoken to say that even though adverse outcomes are in the minority, they're a life sentence for parents.

"It definitely changes their life; there's no doubt about it," Grifo replies.

I ask whether that possibility is communicated by fertility specialists to their patients.

"We do our best," Grifo replies, "but it's shoot the messenger. No one wants to hear it; they just want to be pregnant."

When infertile parents focus all their efforts and savings on producing a child, they may not factor in the perils of producing two, three, or more. On the contrary, a couple that hasn't been able to conceive and is about to spend tens of thousands—sometimes hundreds of thousands—on IVF usually wants to maximize the chances of getting a baby out of it; and understandably, many of them are thrilled at the notion of an instant family of four. The conventional wisdom is unquestionably that getting pregnant with twins through IVF is serendipitous. Two for the price of one looks pretty good when the price tag for each stab at pregnancy is exorbitant and the biological clock is ticking.

The crude summary of how IVF works is this: A woman is given drugs to stimulate her ovaries; she produces multiple eggs, which are extracted and joined in a dish with her mate's sperm; hopefully, embryos result and are transferred back into the woman, with fingers crossed that at least one will take and develop into a baby.

Maximizing the chances of success used to mean "putting back" more embryos. "Because the procedure was inefficient to begin with," Hershlag explains, "and we could not tell which embryo was going to make it, it was very common to place multiple embryos in a woman's uterus with the hope and prayer that one of them will take and become a baby. And in those years, people were putting tons of embryos—could be five, six, seven—in a woman who was in her mid-thirties. Since then, as IVF has become a more efficient, reliable, and reproducible method of treating infertile patients with almost pre-dictable pregnancy rates, we doctors have started to relax. Patients have also started to relax; they're not demanding that as many embryos be transferred, and we are being much more cautious."

Grifo has, like Hershlag, cut down on the number of embryos transferred regularly in his clinic, but he says parents are not always as "relaxed" about it as Hershlag describes. "I spend more time talking people *out of* transferring too many embryos, rather than the opposite. Patients say to me, 'Look, I want four embryos,' and I'm sitting there saying, 'No, no, no, this isn't what we should do.' The idea that *we're* actually driving this is totally false."

He explains that they've been able to cut back on embryos because of new methods that discern the most promising ones in the lab: quality over quantity. "Now we can take our data and say to the patient, 'Look, I'm happy to put two embryos back, but my recom-mendation is that we put *one* back, because if we put back a second embryo, we're not making more pregnancies; we're just making more twins, and that's not our goal. Are you willing to let us put one back, knowing that by putting one, I'm not hurting your pregnancy rate; I'm just giving you a lower chance of twins?' And the response from many patients is, 'I want twins. Do it.' " He sighs. "The fact is, patients have a say in their care; that's the way we practice, and it's the right way to practice, even if the patient is asking for the wrong thing. It's our job to educate them, but at the end of the day, it's their cycle."

Hershlag says, "I sit down with my patients and talk about triplets, the complication rates, prematurity, the lifestyle of having triplets. I say to my patients, 'It consumes your life, and it's wonderful on the one hand, but on the other hand, it's probably not how God meant for us to have babies.' And in many cases, after they hear my whole speech, they say, 'Okay, Doctor, we really appreciate your concern. Now can you put in three?' They say, 'It's my last IVF cycle. . . . My husband just lost his job, and this is the last time that his insurance will pay for it.' "

"The average couple doesn't know what they're getting into," says John Wood, who lives in a small Minnesota town with his wife and two-year-old twin boys, one of whom has cerebral palsy. Since Wood happens to be a family physician himself, he's embarrassed that even he knew so little about the risks. "As a doctor, I've had to tell many people bad news, but it was quite another thing to hear it." Wood can only watch as his son Ben enjoys the normal childhood that his twin, Peter, never will. "Peter is just beginning to crawl," Wood says. "Meanwhile, Benjamin is running."

Dr. Wood pointed me to a sobering 2005 University of Florida study, which found that multiples are at higher risk than single babies for developing twenty-three of forty birth defects affecting the brain, heart, bladder, and liver. Though the frequency of handicapped multiples is still relatively small—about 3.5 percent, compared to 2.5 percent of singletons—the Florida researchers say the impact is colossal. "It can be life-altering," said one coauthor, Jeffrey Roth, in his university's newsletter. "For the affected family, it doesn't matter that what has happened to them is a rare event." Dr. Yiwei Tang, one of the study's lead researchers, said prospective mothers should be warned: "In offering these options to women, full disclosure of an increased risk of birth defects should be made."

Ricki and Steve remember being nudged by their fertility physicians to transfer as many embryos as possible. "They were pushing ICSI," Ricki recalls, referring to intracytoplasmic sperm injection, when doctors actually inject a sperm into the egg by hand before inserting it. "We didn't want to do that because we felt that was too technological," Ricki said. When she opted for IVF (where the egg and sperm are merely combined in a dish and left to fertilize or not), the doctors made her feel like she'd wimped out. "On the day of the transfer," she recalls, "the doctor said, 'There are three embryos left alive. Two look okay; one doesn't look that good. We would have had more to choose from if you had done the ICSI.' He said, 'So we're going to put all three in,' and he left the room. There was never any talk ahead of time about what we'd want to do if there were several embryos to transfer, about the odds and risks of twins or triplets; there was no conversation like that."

Steve adds, "At the point of transfer, the tilt in the conversation was very much that 'If you're not really serious about trying this, why are you even wasting everyone's time and resources?' It was almost implied that if they didn't implant the maximum number of embryos, then there was basically no chance we were going to have any children at all."

"I do think there are some doctors who are out of control," Grifo allows, "but often it's because their pregnancy rates aren't so good, so they're trying to make up for their suboptimal pregnancy rates. And sometimes they're trying to make up for their patient who has a really poor chance, so they take the damn-the-torpedoes approach and put three embryos back three times, and if that fails, they put four embryos back, and they end up with triplets. It's all well-meaning, but it's sometimes a mistake. There are things you can do to remedy that, like reduction (aborting one fetus) to reduce the risk of the high-order multiples, but that's not risk-free, either: You could lose the whole pregnancy."

Dr. Isaac Blickstein of Hebrew University, the rumpled, affable but blunt OB-GYN I met at the International Twins Conference in Belgium, is widely considered to be one of the leading experts on multiple births. He is unabashedly exasperated that the hazards of aggressive fertility procedures are still underplayed. He strikes me as a testy Paul

Revere, riding to alert infertile patients: *Be careful what you wish for.* "Usually you just see the happy stories," he told me. "You don't hear stories about handicapped twins, twins who had difficulties in life."

I ask Dr. Keith about the tantalizing promise of *People* magazine covers with celebrity moms holding rosy, healthy pairs. "What you don't see on those magazine covers," Keith replies, "is those multiples who are still in strollers at the age of ten."

The International Twins Conference happens every three years and draws every major researcher, scientist, and physician in the field. Inexplicably, it gets scant American press, but the collective expertise in one place is striking. I attended the June 2007 assembly in Ghent, Belgium. A charming medieval city one hour from Brussels, it is built around a picturesque canal. One presenter after another drove home gloomy statistics about multiple births. More than any other message at the three-day conference, what came through like a drumbeat was one consensus: *We need to stop this locomotive.*

One of my Ghent evenings was spent dining with Drs. Keith, Blickstein, and Blickstein's Israeli colleague, Liora Baor, who has a warm aspect and a thick Israeli accent. A social worker and professor at Bar-Ilan University, Boar specializes in counseling parents of twins and twins themselves. She was drawn to her specialty after having a set of her own—fraternal boys (nineteen years old at the time we meet), who, she says, are each other's "best friends, though they can fight until there's blood."

Restaurant Keizershof is a formal café overlooking the Korenlei Canal, which carries sight-seeing boats under arched stone bridges. Blickstein orders a local beer and excuses himself to go have a smoke. As he grabs his Marlboros, I notice he has scrawled four capital letters on the pack: "T.I.M.E." He says it stands for one of two things: "This is my end" or "This is my energy," depending how you look at it.

Baor takes a long time to order because she's allergic to gluten. She proffers a laminated card to the waiter—it explains her allergy in every language—and asks him to show it to the chef. After much discussion about ingredients, she settles on lobster bisque and carpaccio.

I return to the issue: "Why do I keep hearing about the dangers of twins at this conference?"

Keith is concerned about my reporter's spin: "Do not write about this as 'doctors talking negatively,' " he warns me. "We are talking about *facts*. . . . The American public is absolutely brainwashed. They don't want to hear about the obstetric realities of having multiples. But the deafness has nothing to do with the doctor's *obligation* to tell them the truth."

I confess to Dr. Keith that I took Clomid, a fertility drug, in 1996, when I had been trying to get pregnant for five months and was beginning to worry about whether I could. (Okay, I admit I'm neurotic and five months was too soon to start taking fertility drugs.) My doctor never discussed with me the fact that Clomid could beget multiples or what the risks were. "That discussion should have been had with you even then," Keith insists.

My doctor just gave me the prescription; he didn't explain much at all.

"Yeah, he gave it to you like he was giving you aspirin for a headache," Keith says dryly. "And I bet if you went back to him today and said, 'Doctor, do you remember me? You gave me Clomid. Do you know that Clomid causes multiple pregnancies in x, y, or z number of patients?' Fifty cents to your dollar says he doesn't know. He's not thinking that way. He wants you to get pregnant." (In fact, I did—and there were two dots on the sonogram at first, suggesting the possibility of twins; later, the second dot was gone, and I had one healthy baby.)

Blickstein has written about the fact that in the United States, contrary to Europe, nothing requires a doctor to enumerate—let alone emphasize—the risks. "There's no obligation right now for fertility specialists to lay out the facts," he says.

There's also no law which mandates that doctors transfer one embryo at a time.

"Our field is aiming at self-censorship, which would achieve the same results," says Hershlag. "And we are currently doing it and will do more."

Grifo is outraged at the idea of legislation. "We are already the most highly regulated area of medicine in the world. Period. FDA, CDC, New York State Department of Health, you name it. Now, are these regulators telling me how many embryos to put back? Not yet. But you know what? That's next. And guess what? When they do, they're hurting my chances of making my patients pregnant. . . . I don't mind having limits set, but I think doctors still have to be able to give individualized care. Because when the patient has done four IVF cycles where she's had two embryos put back, and she is doing her fifth IVF attempt, I don't think putting two embryos is necessarily the right thing for that patient. Sometimes those patients need more embryos because they've already demonstrated that a larger percentage of their embryos aren't good. So that's where you can't regulate and legislate medicine."

But the UK and several European countries have. The British Parliament decided to set a limit on embryo transfers—no more than two would be covered by national health insurance—in part, because of the 1998 dissertation findings of Keith's advisee, Chris Jones, who chose to analyze Britain's IVF data on the costs of raising preemies. "You keep on adding a zero to the end of the figure when you add an extra baby," Jones tells me. "So if it's five thousand dollars with a singleton, it's fifty thousand dollars with twins. And with triplets, it's five hundred thousand dollars. It becomes so expensive because of the number of days these premature babies are spending in the NICU. Because we're now able to care for such low-birth-weight babies, babies who weigh five hundred grams are kept alive. They won't do very well—they might be blind and have cerebral palsy and all kinds of awful things. But they'll be kept alive. And each day in the intensive care unit costs as much as a single IVF cycle." (This means between ten thousand and fifteen thousand dollars.)

Jones tells me his 1998 numbers are still "very current" because treatments have remained the same, as have the costs: "My research was the first to put a pound-sterling value on this epidemic, showing that IVF costs the UK National Health Service up to GBP sixty million per year due to multiple births and related neonatal services."

I tell Keith and the Israeli doctors at dinner that I thought parents themselves were paying these bills.

"NO!" Keith and Baor bellow simultaneously.

"Do you really think that preterm baby care in the United States is paid for by the parents?" Keith asks. "Once the insurance—if there is any—runs out, the bill goes to the state. The hospital doesn't lose money. It gets reimbursed one way or another."

Jones feels strongly that insurance companies could turn this ship around. "If the insurance companies were to take responsibility for the conception side of things, they could prescribe the conditions for implantation. They could say, 'We're not going to pay for you to be loaded up with embryos because we'll end up paying for it in the NICU. . . . If you got the conditions right for a cycle *in the first place*, you could avoid the costs of the NICU. Because the babies are going to be healthy if you don't put back so many embryos, if you don't do what's called 'embryo overdose.' "

Jones says his message hasn't been exactly popular. "I've angered the fertility clinics," Jones admits. "They define success by getting women pregnant on the fewest possible tries. By and large, fertility clinics want to line their pockets."

Hershlag counters firmly: "I don't think that greed is the major motivation for our being in this field. I hope it's not. We are all very privileged to be a part of people's lives, allowing us the honor of helping them make a family. I resent the fact that people who may be seeing sick multiples on the other end say that it is a result of doctors' immorality. We are all constantly talking about ways of combating this epidemic, but let's not forget why we did it: We did it to put babies in people's homes. . . . Fertility treatment is now the key to a lot of people's happiness; we see it every day, and you are welcome to look at our walls"—his entrance hall is lined with holiday cards of beaming babies and kids—"and understand what this has meant to people who were childless."

Grifo bristles at the suggestion that he's profit-driven: "I got news for you. I work my ass off. And I get paid a lot of money, but you know what? When I was thirty-three years old, working a hundred and fifty hours a week, making about ninety cents an hour, I didn't have any-body complaining about my salary; no one cared. And now, all of a sudden, I finally get to age forty-something and I start making money—after decades of killing myself—and all of a sudden I'm a criminal? And all I'm doing is helping people have babies? These peo-ple who criticize, they don't know my stress. They don't know how hard it is to come to work every day, what it's like to tell somebody they just had a miscarriage, to have a patient want to kill you because their IVF cycle didn't work, though you did your damndest to give them their best shot, and they're writing blogs about all the things you should have done because they don't know where to put their anger."

Grifo does acknowledge that an insidious competitive climate has been fostered among clinics, but he faults Senator Ron Wyden's 1992 law, the Fertility Clinic Success Rate and Certification Act, which requires clinics to publish their pregnancy rates. "What do you think happened as a result?" Grifo asks. "Patients could now look at this government-sponsored Web site and see what the highest pregnancy rates were, and if your clinic didn't have the highest pregnancy rate, you weren't busy. That was an incentive for everybody to have the highest pregnancy rate; it wasn't an incentive for somebody to have the highest *singleton* pregnancy rate. Because of that law, American doctors were transferring too many embryos, no question."

Blickstein illustrates how clinics' so-called success rates—which even the CDC warns don't tell the whole story—foster a bad pattern: "Let's say I am an American woman," he posits. "I don't have much money, I'm infertile, and I need IVF. You, Abigail, have a clinic on

Fifth Avenue; Louis has a clinic on Seventh Avenue. You do IVF, and he also does IVF. By American law, you must publish your results. . . . You have published the fact that you have a twenty-two percent take-home baby rate. Louis has twenty-one percent. And IVF costs ten thousand dollars a cycle. So: I'm working very hard to have enough money, and I have finally saved ten thousand dollars. To which clinic should I go? To the twenty-two percent or to the twenty-one percent?"

"Twenty-two," I reply.

"Of course. So this is the first motivation of patients: to go to the clinic that has the higher chance of getting them pregnant. Now, I go one step further: I am now an American citizen with ten thousand dollars. I want a cycle of IVF. I am pretty sure that I won't have time to go through this procedure again in the next five years and that I won't have another ten thousand dollars so soon. It's now or never. Now, if I had a *twin* pregnancy, I get two babies for the same price, and I have an instant family. You want a new family within one cycle: It's good! . . . ninety-five percent of the couples will have a very good outcome. So why should you care about those who don't have a very good outcome? Parents say, 'Who cares? I am a lucky person. Nothing will touch me. I smoke, I drink; nothing happens to me. So why should I think that something will happen to me during a medical procedure? As long as the doctors are not against it,' and they're not: They're IVF doctors who want their numbers to be higher. And once those IVF doctors produce a pregnancy in the United States, 'Ciao, madam.' They don't see you anymore. The women are transferred to the obstetricians, who will deal with the complications of a twins pregnancy.

"This is not the end of the story," he continues, "because the obstetricians sometimes give up at twenty-eight weeks; they cannot stave off early labor anymore. And so at that point, they can transfer the problem further: to the neonatologists, who are light-years away from the infertility people."

Keith adds, "The guy who gets them pregnant is '*successful.*' The guy who gets them delivered is '*successful.*' The neonatologist who gets them out of the ICU is '*successful.*' After that, the parents have to deal with it."

Blickstein: "The infertility people do not *know* what is happening in the NICU."

Keith: "They don't want to know."

Hershlag rebuts this when I recount it. "None of us want to see sick preemies resulting from what we have done."

I ask Grifo to respond to the same charge—that fertility specialists don't end up seeing the unhappy endings.

"That's not true, because patients call to tell you," he replies. "And believe me, you don't feel so good about it; but no one knows that part of the story. Plus, we're getting sued for it; no one knows that, either. Look, we're trying to do good. . . . The reality is that every time you take a breath, you take a risk. And we have to deal with that. People want to legislate perfection. It's not possible."

In 2008, the American Society of Reproductive Medicine recommended limiting the number of embryos transferred to cut down on higher-order multiples. Both Hershlag and Grifo show me data that indicates great strides in reducing triplets in the last few years. But they haven't managed to cut down on twin rates. "That's because we're still putting two embryos in," Hershlag says. "So in about a third of the cases, both embryos take."

Which is why *single*-embryo transfer may be the wave of the future. Dr. Thomas Toth, director of Massachusetts General's IVF program, has garnered attention for relying on the single zygote for 25 percent of his patients—an unusually high rate, considering the rate for the nation is 2 percent. Forty percent of his patients over thirty-five do get pregnant. In women under that age, the rate jumps higher, to between 50 and 55 percent.

Toth, like Grifo, has honed a method that keeps zygotes in the lab longer before they're transferred. He uses the analogy of a horserace to explain the benefits of more time: "It's easier to predict who might be the winner coming up the back stretch than predicting only half or a quarter around. Watching cells develop gives us the idea of which embryos or cells might have the most potential. 'Leaving them in the dish,' as we say, helps us to determine which might have a fighting chance."

With his patients, Toth clearly walks the line between urging restraint and understanding why they hate that concept. "Until you've walked in someone's shoes, it's hard to say, 'I would never put in two or three embryos.' Patients are emotionally and financially invested; and clinicians are helping them achieve a goal that's heartfelt."

When I'm getting ready to leave Ricki and Steve's house, Ricki seems disappointed that I can't stay to watch the speech tutor work with Sammy, so proud is she that her son, whose life was once tenuous, continues to defy the odds. "He has a very special personality. His therapists have always said that when he falters, he just gets up and tries it again. It's funny: Sammy's the one who had all the medical problems, but he's got such a strong spirit—he's braver than his brother."

She puts the tea mugs in the sink and starts to prepare the boys' sandwiches. "I went from being someone who never dreamed premature birth would happen to me to someone who is profoundly grateful for normal, everyday things like watching my kids in a regular pre-school class, doing all the things the other kids do. And I'm also well aware that the effects of prematurity can show up years from now, in learning, psychological, or physical problems that simply can't be seen yet. If I could go back in time and have the boys born separately—as singleton babies—I would, so that Sammy would not have to deal with all this. But overall, I am very grateful to the doctors who helped conceive them and who kept them alive. I love my kids madly, and I count my blessings every day."

6 TWIN SHOCK 101

If you're a well-to-do parent expecting twins in the New York metropolitan area, you've probably heard of Sheri Bayles. She's the trainer to the stars, or at least to any couple who can afford four hundred dollars for a six-hour (two-session) primer on multiples.

"Despite what the doctors told you," Bayles says, addressing the dazed fathers-to-be in the room, "after six to eight weeks, your wife will *not* be interested in having sex again! Why? Because she's got two babies hanging off her boobs all day!"

Bayles has allowed me to sit in on one of her parent classes on a snowy Valentine's night. Six couples have gathered awkwardly (husbands wedged next to engorged bellies) in a pediatrician's waiting room on the Upper East Side. Bayles, a slim fifty-year-old with a helmet of red hair, is dressed in a blue sweater, white turtleneck, and white socks. (She left her wet boots outside the door.)

"I brought cookies this time," she announces. "Because last week nobody touched the vegetables."

When she begins, I'm glad I'm running a tape recorder, because it's impossible to take notes fast enough. Bayles delivers her years of wisdom like a drill sergeant: what a baby nurse costs (from $280 to $600 per week, "depending how important they think they are"), the downside of hiring one (she'll make you feel inadequate), what a doula means literally ("Greek slave"—she takes care of the mother, not the baby), why a twins club is indispensable ("It's like an AA meeting—you'll need it").

Don't overrely on nannies: "Why is it that all of us feel we can't take care of our own children?"

Subscribe to *Twins* magazine: "Every article is all about you, and they're short."

Don't accept hand-me-down toys without checking the PSC (Product Safety Commission) Web site.

Be wary of relatives visiting: "You should never invite anyone in your family who is more high-maintenance than your babies."

Be prepared for laundry: "Each baby generates a load every day."

Keep premature infants in the same bassinet: Cornell did a study that found it's beneficial.

Keep twins in the same room: "Most single kids try to climb out of the crib at eighteen months; twins don't. Because they have each other. There's no reason to leave."

Buy infant swings: "In the World of Twins, we call it 'the Neglectomatic.' Because you can put them in there and walk away for a half hour."

Bayles used to be a nurse at Cornell, specializing in lactation/baby-care classes, when she herself got pregnant with IVF twins in 1994, after three years of trying. Her calling became clear: She would teach expecting parents of twins what to expect. Thirteen years later, she now coaches approximately twenty-two couples every six weeks. The doyenne of twins advice, she's aware of her popularity. "I've been told I'm a fantastic teacher," she tells me. "It sounds so egotistical, but everybody tells me that. And it's not like I hear it once—I hear it all the time."

Bayles rattles off equipment—cribs, double strollers, car seats, bouncy seats, swings, changing tables. You don't need positioners and you don't need dividers: "The twins were next to each other inside the womb; why would you divide them out now?" Bayles asks.

She returns to that Cornell study: "They started putting all these preemie babies together in the same bassinet so they could cohort them, and the twins started regulating their heat and breathing better; they started growing; neurologically they did better. So researchers realized, You know what? They really need to be together to thrive."

Bayles's directives continue: Feed both twins at once, every three hours. If you feed them one at a time, give each only thirty minutes on the breast. "If they're not finished by thirty minutes, *cut 'em off*," Bayles insists. "Let me explain this: We have 'gourmets' and we have 'barracudas.' Barracudas are the babies who get to that breast and go"—Bayles makes a kind of sucking, growling sound. "Within five minutes, they've emptied a five-ounce bottle. And then there are the gourmets: They're like the people in your family who sit around the dinner table and are still eating their salads while you're on to dessert."

Sleeping: "From twelve midnight to six A.M., let them sleep. You never wake a sleeping baby between twelve A.M. and six A.M. *However*, one exception to that rule is: If a sibling wakes up, YOU MUST WAKE UP THE OTHER SIBLING. If you have a boy and a girl and one wakes up at three-thirty A.M. and the other is sound asleep, it will kill you to do this—it will *kill* you—but YOU MUST WAKE UP THE SIBLING." (I remember those blurry, sleepless nights with my first child, and I can't fathom having awakened my baby just to keep him on schedule; but Bayles is adamant.) "If you don't keep them on the same schedule at nighttime, they're going to start messing up the day-time schedule. Because then, an hour later, the other twin wakes up. And then the next hour, the other twin wakes up. And you're going to say, 'I'm going crazy here.' It will *kill* you to wake that sibling up, but YOU MUST DO IT. In the morning, they'll be back on schedule again."

One parent asks how to breast-feed both babies at the same time. Bayles smiles, as if she's been waiting all night to be asked. "It's doable!" she declares. She snatches up her demonstration dolls—one dressed in blue, one in pink—and launches into the Nursing Show, with Bayles gamely shoving dolls under each of her breasts in varying positions to illustrate all options. There's "the football"—one twin under each armpit; there's the "back-to-back," where each twin can face a mother's arm while it sucks, or one can come up over the right shoulder while the other is cradled under the chest; or "There's a really weird one that no one ever does, where you crisscross your babies."

She tosses the babies on the floor. End of nursing lesson.

Bayles pulls out the next prop, a poster that says DAILY GOALS.

"If you can achieve these on a daily basis," Bayles proclaims, "you will have won the lottery."

They are:

1. Babies are fed!

   "That is your biggest job."

2. Shower every day.

   "You'd think I wouldn't have to write this down. But you will be amazed that your spouse may leave you at seven A.M. in your robe and slippers—you haven't brushed your teeth, combed your hair, or taken a shower. He comes home at seven P.M. and finds you in the exact same robe and slippers. And your husband says, 'What have you been doing all day?' And you hand him the two babies and say, 'I'm leaving now and going to have a drink at the corner bar.' TAKE A SHOWER AND GET DRESSED."

3. Feed yourself.

   "I ate four thousand calories a day to nurse twins. You burn one thousand a day breast-feeding one baby. Two babies is two thousand. So you're burning two; you're eating four—that's a Weight Watchers diet! If you don't eat, you don't make milk."

4. Take a lot of naps.

   "Turn the phone off and sleep or you won't catch up."

5. Delegate and accept help!

   "This is a really tough concept for some women. If you don't feel comfortable asking your friends to take the laundry basket downstairs, they're not your friends."

The parents in the room look like they've been listening to a ghost story. One tentatively raises her hand. "How long does all this realistically last?"

Bayles smiles. "Do you want the real answer or the fantasy answer?"

"The real answer," the mom replies.

"Your first year will be an absolute blur."

Later, in our private interview, I ask Bayles why she paints such a bleak picture. "Because it is bad. Because you're sleep-deprived. You have a very short fuse. You don't have any patience whatsoever. Someone says boo to you and you start crying."

I tell her I noticed almost a resistance in the room—a disbelief that it could be that hard. "People are not prepared to listen to the bad stuff." Bayles nods. "Everybody thinks they run their lives so well—especially in this city. You have to be type A to survive here. And then all of a sudden, there's no control. Years ago, I remember this CEO—she had her life organized to the nth degree and then she had twins and called me, sobbing, 'I am not in control!' " Bayles recreates the hysterical blubbering. "I told her, 'Yes, the babies are running things now.' "

She acknowledges that complaining is taboo because twins are considered such a blessing. "Guess what?" Bayles says. "There are moments when you really wonder why you did it. You're supposed to be happy."

Back in class, Bayles segues to the upside: "Once the good stuff starts happening, you are so thrilled that you had two or three babies. Now let me give you the good stuff."

Someone in the room exhales, "Please."

The "good stuff": Twins will have built-in play dates, Bayles promises. They'll be socially advanced because they've learned how to share and interact early, and the family becomes a gang unto itself. "You will think it's the most wonderful thing in the world. As much as it's work, you will find yourself standing over their cribs and crying with joy. I can't tell you how many times we found ourselves just weeping because we're so happy to have them."

Bayles's last subject of the night takes me by surprise.

"Those of you who had siblings," she says, addressing the room: "Was there a favorite in the house that you knew about? Because we knew, in my house, who the favorites were. Was it obvious to you who was the favorite in the house? Come on! Don't look at me that way. There's a point I'm making here, so please answer me."

No one does.

"The reason I'm bringing this up is because when you have two babies at the same time, there's one baby that complements your personality, and one that doesn't."

What?

"You may find something in that baby's personality that you find more attractive than the other baby's personality. . . . If both my sons were crying on the floor, there was no question in my mind who I would have gone to first. Because one of my sons has a very complementary personality to me, and the other: We have different thoughts and ideas about how things should be done. And so luckily enough, he complements my husband. Which is how it all worked out for us. . . . It became almost obvious to everyone that Aaron was my husband's favorite and Zach was my favorite. To the point where we made a big boo-boo—and I learned from my mistakes. On weekends when we split up to do errands, my husband and I always took the same kid. And then you don't really get to know the other kid as well."

She encourages the parents to keep a journal that includes who took which baby each weekend in order to make sure to keep things even and to find ways to connect with your less favorite child. "The son that is my husband's favorite actually loves the theater and I love the theater, so we have found a way to connect. Whereas I'll take my other son to sporting events."

I'm stunned that Bayles would normalize the idea of preferring one child. Apparently, I'm not the only startled one. "I remember once that I was teaching this to my very first year of twins parents," Bayles recounts, "and some mother took great issue with this conversation. She came up to me and said, 'I can't believe you spent any time on this at all. It was just disgusting.' I said, 'Okay, that's your opinion.' Three months later she called me and said, 'You were right. I have a favorite.' I said, 'I know you do.' It's really hard not to, when they both come at the same time. They always tell you never to compare your children, but guess what? When you get babies at the same time, you compare them all the time."

It's the only time I speak up in the class: "Isn't it hard for Aaron to know that you prefer his brother?"

Bayles considers. "I'm sure it bugs him a little bit, but he knows his daddy is on his side at all times. He'll run to daddy first. He does know there are things that we have that are very special that Zach and I don't have. So you try to bring those points out."

In our subsequent interview alone, I bring up her homily on favoritism. Why raise the prospect at all?

"I raise it because I think everybody feels very guilty about feeling favoritism toward one versus the other; both kids are crying and they always run to that one baby. I just think it's important. I certainly knew in my family who was the favorite. We all knew it. I don't think that it hurt. I don't think any of us suffer from it. My mother and I have an amazing relationship now, but I wasn't the favorite. Do you have a favorite in your house?"

"No," I reply, feeling like it's the wrong answer. "I really can't say we do."

"Congratulations. That's unusual. There's usually one child who sticks out in every mother's mind as being the better child or the best child or the one that's most amenable. I would have to say that the toughest one in my house is the one that I have the closest relationship with, while the other one is so easy. It's frightening how easy he is. And he's not my favorite. He's just not."

"How can you say that?" I ask her. "Imagine him hearing that."

"Well, he knows that Daddy is crazy about him. And he feels it, too, from his end: I don't think he feels a connection to me like Zach does. I don't understand it, either, to be honest with you. I don't know what it is."

"You are admitting a preference as a mother," I say.

"Absolutely," she admits.

"That's the most taboo thing you can do."

"I know," Bayles replies. "But if I had a choice—if I had to make a choice—say I was getting divorced and they told me, 'You can only take one boy—*Sophie's Choice*—I know who I'd take. I actually know who I would take."

It makes me squirm: The *Sophie's Choice* reference is an upsetting analogy, and I also can't help but take her candor personally. I'm not going to be the Twin Avenger, but I can't imagine how it would have felt knowing I wasn't my mother's first choice.

"It is a very difficult thing," Bayles acknowledges. "I'm crazy about both my sons."

I couldn't get Bayles's lecture out of my head. It irked me that parents were paying four hundred dollars to learn they'd inevitably prefer one child. I sought a second opinion when I went to visit clinical psychologist and twins specialist Dr. Eileen Pearlman in Santa Monica. An identical twin herself, who married a fraternal twin, Pearlman founded TwInsight, which offers counseling, workshops, and psychotherapy for parents of twins and twins themselves.

Pearlman confirmed Bayles's perspective: "I don't think parents love twins the same," Pearlman told me. In fact, in her coauthored book, *Raising Twins: What Parents Want to Know (And What Twins Want to Tell Them)*, she lists twenty modern myths about twins, and number six is: "When parents have twins, they love them both equally." "Sometimes a parent identifies with the twin who is more like them," Pearlman explains. "Often parents relate to the twin who relates to them more or *likes* them more." So she doesn't counsel parents to resist this partiality? "I tell them just to acknowledge it," Pearlman says calmly. "It's normal. When you take away the judgment, 'I'm being bad,' then it takes away the tension from it."

She says the first few months of infancy can lead to a preference. "Maybe one baby is the better eater, so it's an easier child. Maybe one is always complaining."

Indeed, there is evidence that because so many twins are born premature and have a low birth weight, parents sometimes prefer the more robust twin. The *Multiple Pregnancy* textbook cites researcher Jane A. Spillman's 1991 study on "The role of birth weight in maternal twin relationships": "Spillman observed that 72% of mothers had a favorite twin, and for 84% of them it was the heavier of the pair. A mother looking after one baby attends to his or her needs without consideration. In contrast, a mother of twins must constantly choose which one is more upset, which one should be picked up first, which one is hungrier, etc. and this forces her to make distinctions."

"That's why I talk so much about labeling," Dr. Pearlman continues. "I tell parents, Stop the labeling: 'This one is the fussy one.' 'She's so easy.' Don't label." She sees parents lean on labels because they don't get to know twins as quickly as they would singletons. "They bond with them, but it takes a little longer with twins because they have to get to know two children at once."

It's something I never focused upon: the idea that parents of twins might have a harder time connecting individually with each baby because two are so much more demanding in terms of basic needs and constant care.

The renowned late pediatrician Elizabeth Bryan writes in *Multiple Pregnancy*, "It is known that mothers of preterm twins . . . tend to have less physical contact and talk with their twins less. . . . The traditional transcultural image of motherhood portrays dedication to one baby at a time. Mothers of multiples may understandably feel deprived of this experience, and frustrated by the sheer impossibility of giving undivided attention to either child."

My cousin Alisa tells me the early months with her premature twins were crushing.

"It was miserable," she says unambiguously, sitting on an armchair in her graceful modern apartment overlooking Central Park. "Nobody slept. Eli cried; he had gas. He would only be walked around; he wanted to sit in the thing with the vibrating seat. And I was just pumping milk."

At the time Alisa and I talk, Eli and Grace have become adorable, hyperarticulate, spark-plug four-year-olds, who show no discernible trace of how delicate they were at birth. But the memories of those early, draining months are still fresh in Alisa's mind. "People said, 'Oh you'll get on a schedule with your twins.' *What* schedule? The whole thing was just such an endless cycle! It never ended. Every day was so much like the last. It was like the worst Groundhog Day. We spent so many days in the house. It was hard to ever get the babies outside, even in the nice weather. Every time you'd get them ready to go out, someone would poop or you'd have to pump again. There was really not much joy for the first months. Everyone tells you the infancy is going to go so fast. We'd say, 'Really? You come to my house tomorrow. And come the next day. And then come on day three. And you'll see it's NOT going fast at all.' "

The experts call it "twin shock": the slap in the face that many mothers of twins feel after they get their twins home, no matter how wanted or loved the twins are. Alisa had wanted a baby desperately at thirty years old, and after five IVF attempts, two miscarriages, and $150,000, Grace and Eli were a gift from God. But that didn't stave off the melancholy.

"I was so depressed," Alisa admits. "I didn't even realize it at the time. But in retrospect, I was. It was just so daunting. And then, physically, I was not myself. The hormones I'd just stopped taking after the pregnancy made me have night sweats for six weeks; I was changing my clothes all through the night." Her weight—normally, waif-thin—had ballooned. "I filled up with tons of water. So after I gave birth, I actually felt huge. When I was pregnant, it didn't bother me, being so gigantic. I thought it was funny. I did not think it was funny after I gave birth. I was pretty upset. So I was depressed about the way I looked and I had all these hormones. I started feeling better at the fourth month or so, but the first three, I was like, 'What did we do to our life? What were we thinking?' "

Needless to say, she wasn't experiencing that new motherhood euphoria you hear so much about. "I didn't have that initial falling-in-love feeling the minute I had them," Alisa admits. "I just didn't. It was like a terrified feeling of 'Are they going to be okay?' For a while they were so little, I was scared to bathe them. They were just *fragile.*" [Eli was three pounds, five ounces; Grace was three pounds, fourteen ounces.]

That feeling of being in control didn't happen till they were eighteen or twenty months old, Alisa says. And then it was just barely. "For us, age two was so different. They talked and made sense. Before that, when we went to the beach, all these other kids would be sitting playing calmly with buckets; our kids would just be running crazily in opposite directions. And this idea we'd heard that 'Oh, your twins will play with each other'? All they did those first years was fight over toys. So if you were sitting in any room, it was just a constant 'No, you can't take this from her.' We were constantly giving one thing to the other."

No one prepared her for this. "Only other mothers of twins know what it's really like," she says. "There are a lot of mothers with that eighteen-month gap between children, or a fifteen-month gap, and their life sucks, too. But it's not the same thing. They'd already been a parent by the time they had the second. They didn't have those two infants at exactly the same time. It's a different ball of wax. Every parent goes through new-parent shock, but with one baby, you can deal. We never realized how much support two little babies needed."

I ask her if, during the worst of it, she thought about those mothers who didn't have the luxury of baby-sitters or housekeepers. "Oh, I couldn't imagine." Alisa shakes her head. "I do have a friend who didn't have that support. She had a nervous breakdown—for real. She went on Paxil. She lost about thirty pounds. She's a mess. Chainsmoker. It really killed her."

Alisa says she encountered few mothers of twins who fit the profile of blissful new mom. "There have to be a few out there who *are* feeling blissful," Alisa replies. "If you have twins who go full term and they come out at big weights, I think you have a very different beginning than if you have premature twins. Our first two and a half months were with babies who shouldn't have been here yet. That's a different experience."

Did she feel a sense of inadequacy? "I felt bad that I didn't enjoy it more," Alisa admits. "I was envious of the people who had single babies. And then I'd immediately scold myself: Don't think that way, because God forbid something should happen to one of my children. . . . But I was envious of that mom pushing that *one* baby in the stroller, relaxed, listening to her iPod while the baby slept. We just never had that kind of calm moment when the baby takes a nap next to you in bed. Never happened. Not once."

I ask if she felt a pressure to be cheerful because others expected it of her. "It wasn't like I had the kind of mother who came in and said, 'Why are you so down in the dumps? This isn't hard at all!' My parents were like, 'Oh my GOD, here we go again today.' They were in it with us every step of the way and they needed their own breaks. We were all so beaten up from the whole thing. . . . I didn't feel bad for the *children*; I think the children were very well taken care of."

I ask Alisa what advice she'd give to other mothers of twins, especially those who resorted to IVF to have them. "I'd tell them, 'It's going to get better at six months, but it really only gets better closer to two years. It's going to be a hard first two years. And make sure your husband is on board to be an equal parent.' I also got a lot of on-line support from other twin mothers, and I did meet these other miserable twin mothers in the park. Nowadays, when I'm out with my kids and see people with little twins, I say, 'Don't worry, it's going to get better!' And they shout, 'WHEN?' I'll ask how old their twins are and they'll tell me, 'Five months.' I'll say, 'Not for a while!'

"You have to be prepared that your life is going to be harder than you imagined, and don't feel bad about yourself if it is, and it's going to get so much better. And then, because it will have been so bad, when it gets better, it will be like the biggest weight has been lifted off of you. So when people are complaining about the terrible twos or difficult three-year-olds, you're just going to be laughing. Because your hardest days will have been over."

I ask Alisa if she had it to do over again, would she want twins?

"Now that it's all over, it's great. We had this unique experience."

And would she wish it for Grace and Eli—the experience of having their own twins someday?

"I can't even conceive of this idea that they're going to have sex." She laughs. "Much less have children. Much less grow up and make their own sandwich."

The answer to whether twins would wish to parent their own twins seems obvious to me: I would be unhesitatingly thrilled if my son or daughter could have that adventure. But apparently, that's not so obvious to everyone. When I met Liora Baor—the Israeli social worker who counsels parents of twins and has twin boys herself, she told me, "Most twins say no. Most twins, when you ask them, 'Would you wish your own children to raise twins?' they say no."

For what reason?

"They've heard about what it takes to raise them," Baor replies.

It's a recurring theme in the presentations at the 2007 International Twins Conference in Belgium, where I met Baor: the quiet truth that raising twins can be so overwhelming to some mothers that they struggle more than they let on; society doesn't give them permission to be as despairing, or shell-shocked, as they sometimes are.

"Going through IVF is not a picnic," Baor tells me. "It's depleting all your resources. Mainly the psychological ones. The successes are not high with IVF, so it can take many cycles. Up to fourteen. Twenty. It depends how much you can endure. By that time, you are building an expectation. And then you come to the moment and you deliver the twins. And because it's a pressured pregnancy, doctors tend to deliver them early, so as not to have any risks. And most of the time they are born premature. Premature babies are small, not social, not nice. They do not smile so soon as the others and it's hard to interact with them. They don't know how to give cues to the environment like a full-term baby when they are hungry or they are wet. And the whole day they are crying. The couple have now become parents very early—earlier than they prepared themselves. Not only that; they are saying to themselves, 'Even this—the birth itself—we couldn't do normally.' "

In other words, they couldn't get pregnancy right and now they can't do infancy right? Baor nods. "It's a roller-coaster."

Fathers are less discussed but are also impacted. Parent coach Sheri Bayles warns her dads-to-be that they're going to be much more hands-on than they might have been with one child, because moms can't do it alone. Dr. Bryan says fathers often feel the added financial burden of supporting two kids—and all their needs—at once. They also get frazzled from interrupted sleep before a workday, and exhaustion can strain the marriage.

My mother, Letty, had zero twin shock; just twin rapture. I can just imagine how annoying her testimony would be to those mothers who struggled, but I know she can't invent angst she didn't have. "I remember so many times putting you down for your naps when you were in bassinets, and sitting and reading a magazine and saying,

What is hard about this?" Mom recalls, curled up on her couch in my childhood living room. "You both just slept. You were only troublesome between maybe four and six o'clock in the afternoon; but if one cried, the other didn't. So it only meant dealing with one at a time. And whoever cried first kind of co-opted the crying for that day. But I remember sitting down in the living room and saying, I really should go back to work; this is not hard."

Paris Stulbach, a former television producer, started Twins & the City in 2003, a Manhattan support network whose members swap advice in cyberspace and during dinners on the Upper West Side. (The Web site quotes Walt Whitman: "I am large, I contain multitudes.") "I felt very alone at the beginning," Stulbach says about why she created the group. "I was a mess. The babies were a mess. The house was a mess. I was a hormonal train wreck. I couldn't possibly eat and drink and sleep enough to take care of two infants. A few weeks of living like that, and my confidence was shattered. You feel like you're failing all the time."

There's nothing like veteran parents of twins to tell the uninitiated how to deal with feeling isolated, which car seat to buy, how to keep two children from running into the street, or whether to separate twins in preschool. "The advice covers everything from the worst situations—people whose babies die—to which neighborhood restaurants are twins-friendly," Stulbach explains.

I ask her what she personally wonders about when she looks ahead to her twins growing up. "Whether there is a price to pay for having a mother who was not at her best for the first few years," she says.

In *Multiple Pregnancy*, Elizabeth Noble, author of *Having Twins and More* (2003), writes, " 'Twin shock' can overwhelm the best-prepared mother. . . . At all costs, the 'supermom' image should be tossed aside."

Liora Baor offers perhaps the most realistic counsel: "I don't know if you know of Donald Winnicott, a British pediatrician," she tells me, "but he said that *There is not a good mother; there is a good*-enough *mother.* You just have to expect less."

I ask Alisa if there was anything about watching Robin and me grow up that informs the way she's raising Eli and Grace. "The only thing your parents have said that really made an impact on me is that the one thing they really regret is not spending separate time with you. So in the smallest ways, we've done that. On weekends, we switch off. We do different things. I can see one day going on a trip with one of them and then the other."

Pediatrician Dr. Elizabeth Bryan observes that often "parents are reluctant to separate their twins even for short periods, so that they might spend quality time with each one. Others find that even short separations are hard to organize for practical reasons. Still others believe that by letting someone else, even a relative, look after one of the babies, their 'special' status as a parent of twins may be diminished or their competence questioned."

Robin and I give one piece of advice to parents of twins: *Spend separate time with each twin.* It seems so simple, but our parents never did it, and Robin especially feels that this oversight cemented a feeling of our having been blurred together.

When I ask my mother why she and Dad never took us separately, she looks pained. "Because we didn't think that way. We just thought in terms of the family. I feel I should have been aware of it because I should have been smart enough to figure out that something is gained when you're alone with a person. I should have realized that. I didn't. . . . I don't know. It never occurred to us. It always was a matter of "Let's." Not: 'You come with me and you go with him.' "

She said they realized their mistake in one powerful instant when I was eighteen and they invited me to go with them for a weekend at a bed-and-breakfast. "You said you were uncomfortable coming along because you'd never been alone with us. It was like somebody shot us between the eyes; we couldn't believe it. 'How could this have happened?' We never noticed that we had never been with one child."

"It was clear that you felt you had a performance level," my father recalls, "and you felt that, without Robin, you wouldn't be able to hold up your end in terms of pleasing us, as if that was anything you had to do. So that was a real realization that we'd missed something. I think we were always so careful to have equality of treatment that it turned out to be undifferentiated. We'd never done anything individually with you, all this time."

Dad adds, however, that we also "bought into the constant togetherness. Anytime there was the slightest deviation between you, you girls would accuse us of being unfair. So it was mutually reinforcing. Like if you would have an experience that was better, the other would resent it."

Dr. Joan Friedman, author of *Emotionally Healthy Twins*, who has a bohemian style with long blond hair, says parents must insist on separate time with each twin, even when the twins balk. "If you haven't introduced alone time really early, you're going to get resistance," she says. "The parent has to believe that having that separate relationship is crucial."

She is adamant about this because she says individual time gives rise to distinct relationships, which gives rise to concrete identities. "If you don't, as a parent, make a solid attachment with each twin, then you're left with the twin parenting the twin," she explains, which means one twin's overreliance on the other for a sense of self, one's confidence, one's place in the world. "Because of the parents' failure to work hard toward developing a separate relationship with each child, the children, by virtue of their proximity and their developmental age when they're growing up together, end up attaching more importantly to each other, and they shut the parent out. 'I want to go with my sister; I don't want you to take her and leave me home.' The twinship ends up becoming so powerful, and parents are afraid of it. They're afraid if they do anything to disrupt it, they'll ruin the twin attachment. . . . So by virtue of the parents not understanding what each child needs, the twinship becomes powerful, and the parents get left out. . . . My discovery is that, while it may seem counterintuitive, when both twins are securely attached to the parents, the twinship becomes a more cherished, healthy, balanced relationship. The counterintuitive piece is that if you separate twins as much as you may have to—in order to encourage that parent bond—then people think you're hurting the twinship."

She says her patients report the same regret my parents have. "I can't tell you the number of times a mother says to me, 'Why didn't I ever take them separately? Why didn't I think about it? I could have left one home.' These women had nannies; they could have done it. But they didn't want to. In their minds, they'd be breaking up something so wonderful that they couldn't justify doing that. Or their twins resisted the idea and they listened to them. Even though everybody knows—it's not my research—every attachment theorist tells you every infant needs alone time with its mother."

Jean Kunhardt, cofounder of the Soho Parenting Center in Manhattan, echoes Friedman. "The intimacy dance is such a one-on-one thing, it's a *monogamous* thing. My biggest urging to new mothers is to really take the time to have an individual moment with each twin. Twins demand it less because they don't need it as much. So it's the quiet moments of engagement with your baby that are sometimes missing with twins."

Skipping one-on-one time seems to backfire both ways: Twins miss out on forging a clear identity, while parents miss out on a specific intimacy.

Even back in 1954, psychologist Dorothy Burlingham wrote in her study of identical twins that mothers can't connect to their twins until they get to know them apart from each other. "Several mothers have plainly said that it was impossible to love their twins until they had found a difference in them," Burlingham wrote.

According to psychologist Michael Rothman, one way mothers of twins compensate for the disquieting feeling that they don't really know their twins apart is to categorize them. If they can tag them, they must know them. "Labels or personality styles are assigned to each twin and scripted by the mother and family quite early," Rothman writes, "likely as a means to soothe their own anxieties."

Joan Friedman agrees. "The labels are created in order to convince yourself you have a separate attachment. And if you don't do the work and *really* have the separate attachment, then you've just created sort of a myth that helps you define one child in relationship to the other. . . . That's the difference between being *known* and being *noticed*. If you're not *known* through your attachment to your parents, then you're *noticed* because you're *like* your twin or you're *different* from your twin. It's not about who you are, but how you compare to this other person."

Being known versus being noticed. I realize that this is what Robin had been trying to tell me—that twinship had made her feel noticed but not known. She was never sure if friends really knew us, or even if our parents did, and so the fact that we always got noticed by people, and still do today, is no consolation. Friedman tells me that not feeling "differentiated" can make a person feel lost. She speaks from experience. "My sense of self was organized around my sister, so once she and I were apart in college, I had no idea who I was. . . . I think that's an extreme case, but it gives you some sense of what can happen if your identity is only organized around the twinship."

I interviewed our childhood friend Pamela Koffler, a film producer, who first met Robin and me at age twelve at a summer camp in New Milford, Connecticut. Though she lived in Tenafly, New Jersey, and we lived in Manhattan, we stayed in touch after camp, and then we all ended up in college together.

PAMELA: I was thinking, as a mother who's had an infant recently, what a profoundly different experience it is to have two infants—for the *infants*. Usually you have this baby and you are just gushing love—and you're just this dyad: mother and baby. But with twins, there are two babies. You just don't get an undivided mom ever. You never got that. And how does that feel? How does that change things? How is it better or worse? It never occurred to me to think about that until I had a child. It's such an intense bonding experience, being alone with a baby. It actually made me want to find out: How does the attachment process happen with two babies? How is it different? Does the physical contact of those babies create that attachment with each other when it can't happen with the mother?

ABIGAIL: What is it like to be friends with identical twins?

PAMELA: I was friends with you and then I was friends with Robin. And I don't remember the in between. But I remember that your mom did kind of call a meeting about it, to talk about "Why are you now better friends with Robin?"

ABIGAIL: Who was there?

PAMELA: The two of you, your mom, and me—in your living room. I think her intention was to kind of negotiate what had occurred among the three of us. It was a separate discussion from the question of who was going to light a candle at my bat mitzvah. I think Robin did.

ABIGAIL: What do you remember about the meeting?

PAMELA: Just somehow Letty wanted to manage the expectations, to head off hurt feelings. And I remember feeling uncomfortable, a little on the spot, not at all mature enough to cope with it, but also wanting to be good and to say the right thing.

ABIGAIL: Do you remember thinking, This is too much to ask of me—to navigate their twinship?

PAMELA: No. I felt so privileged to be a part of such an intimate dynamic. I remember thinking, This is ground zero of a family's stuff, and *I* matter. It was a little bit heady, I guess. I can't speak to why I was friends with you and then I was better friends with Robin. I feel like some triangulation happened and that's it. I can't honestly say at twelve or thirteen, there was more of a kindred spirit in Robin. But I do remember noticing you were different from other twins I had known. There was one set of twins at my public school, and the identicalness of them was irrelevant; nobody thought of it. They were shy; they were quiet; they just were. There wasn't a *thing* about them being identical twins. But when I met you guys, you already had, at twelve years old, a sophisticated sense of "We are individuals; but we're also twins." And it was this culmination of the power of the twinness, but the distinctiveness, too. The effort to be distinctive.

ABIGAIL: And you remember that?

PAMELA: Yes. Plus, you were dynamic and theatrical and performative. And the combination was big and alluring. . . . It was almost like the identical twinness wasn't even a good-enough gimmick for you two. You were going to be interesting, fascinating, exciting friends, and oh, there's this other cool thing too, which is that you're identical twins.

ABIGAIL: Do you remember that we played on our twinship?

PAMELA: No. It was the opposite. You had almost settled into the identity of "We're sisters, we're twins, but we're going to be so much more." I had to catch up to that, because identical twins by themselves are so incredible. It's such a huge, crazy thing to see two people who look exactly alike who aren't the same person.

ABIGAIL: Do you remember meeting us for the first time?

PAMELA: Yes. I remember you had really long hair and Robin had short hair, and I thought that was already so ballsy, like "We're young twins, but we're going to have different hair."

ABIGAIL: And then college—do you have memories of us there?

PAMELA: I feel like I was finding my social footing freshman year and you guys weren't a part of it. For some reason, my identity there needed to be separate from what came before. I think it had to do with the ease with which you guys socially found yourselves—or I perceived it that way. . . . Then I really noticed how you and Robin found different social strata, and I often thought about it because yours seemed more interesting to me—the theater people who were sexually ambiguous and all of that. And Robin's was "square," "jock." That seemed not true to her some-how; but back then, we were in college, and I made an allowance for it—like, We're not all ourselves quite yet. But it seemed a little unfair that you got that crowd and she got the other crowd. And then Robin and I reconnected junior or senior year.

ABIGAIL: Did you feel the twinship complicated your friend-ship with Robin?

PAMELA: I don't feel like it was complicated, because I feel like somehow the environment of friendship with one of you instantly creates an ease with the fact that you can't be best friends with both. So it was really uncomplicated. It was just an absolute given: At a certain point I was Robin's friend and that's the friend I had. It felt like a force field. A magnet goes here—you just don't go to the other pole, because of maybe some rules that you guys wrote between each other that got communicated nonverbally. But a nice artifact of that is, I always felt de facto friendly toward you

and that there was a loyalty because of my friendship
with Robin. Like, Okay, there's some refracted friendship
here. . . . Maybe it has to do with a nice aspect of being a
twin, that you double your circle of friends because of the
closeness.

ABIGAIL: Tell me as honestly as you can, even though I'm
sitting in front of you, since I know some people in college
felt "the Pogrebin twins," as we were sometimes called,
were just too *much*, too visible and self-satisfied, did you
see us that way?

PAMELA: I think it's unavoidable; I think it has to do with your
personalities. You guys were a force. It had to do with your
interests; even at twelve years old, you liked to perform.
You were creative; you made up clubs. . . . While I sat
and read Archie comics. It didn't occur to me to be in a
dramatic, interesting fantasy world. I think it was that,
combined with the twinness; I don't think they can be
separated. Because there were other twins who didn't have
that effect. You guys were dynamos. . . . And there are two
and you're identical.

ABIGAIL: Do you think our twinship made us cocky?

PAMELA: Not cocky at all. You were generous, inclusive people.
There was also a kind of naïveté mixed in with your self-
possession. You guys weren't edgy. There was a sweet
innocence to how worldly you were. It was an interesting
combination. There was a guilelessness to how you guys
were just "Ta-da!" about yourselves. And I think what
people responded to is the jealousy of being that young,
mixed with the lack of guile, because I think a lot of people
don't have that.

ABIGAIL: How do you see Robin and me now when we're
together?

PAMELA: I would have said it's an ideal relationship, except that I know from discussion with Robin that nothing is perfect. I would have said there's a fluidity of intimacy that is special: how well you know each other, a lack of the discomfort that I sometimes feel with my siblings, that I imagined you didn't have. Very normal, very close, very at ease, supportive. And when we were younger, I imagined a secret intimacy.

ABIGAIL: Is there anything you have wondered about in terms of Robin and me?

PAMELA: I guess, not having had a sister myself, I wonder: Whatever isn't perfect about your relationship, you still have to admit that it's an extraordinary closeness, right? It has to be.

ABIGAIL: It is.

PAMELA: That, to me, is the precious thing.

* *

7 MAKING THE BREAK: SEPARATION

The "pushing away" and "holding on" . . .
—Ricardo Ainslie, *The Psychology of Twinship*

On April 22, 2008, Carl Zimmer wrote a *New York Times* science article about how genetically identical *E. coli* bacteria differentiate themselves. In the article, entitled "Expressing Our Individuality, the Way
E. Coli Do," Zimmer explained that despite the bacteria's exact likeness at the moment they split in half, they ultimately go on to display
their own personalities and behavior. He addressed society's assumption that when two beings are genetic copies, that must mean they're
the same. "We put a far bigger premium on nature than nurture when
it comes to our individuality," Zimmer wrote. "That's one reason why
reproductive cloning inspires so much horror. If genes equal identity,
then a person carrying someone else's DNA has no distinct self."

In my nonscientific, lay-twin opinion, this hits upon the core
twin anxiety—especially for identical twins: *If I'm the same, how can I
be distinct?*

Zimmer answered this, albeit unwittingly, in his analysis of the
microbes: "A colony of genetically identical E. coli is, in fact, a mob of
individuals. . . ." (Italics added.) "At the very least, E. coli's individu-

ality should be a warning to those who would put human nature down to any sort of simple genetic determinism. Living things are more than just programs run by genetic software."

Ah, so science affirms that individuation *is* possible. Yet, for so many twins I've talked to, identical or fraternal, establishing separateness seemed to be *the* primary stumbling block.

Steve and David Colman, handsome, assured thirty-seven-year-olds, say they needed to live closer together to be able to pull apart.

Gretchen Langner, forty-three, balked at one attempt by her twin, Belinda, to put some distance between them; she told Belinda that a decision like that couldn't be made unilaterally.

In the case of the identical Farley boys, twenty-five, one of them went so far as to become a woman in order to differentiate himself from his twin.

I meet Steve and David Colman for lunch during an August heat wave. Both have blue eyes, smallish ears, and pink complexions, although Steve's lips are thinner, his nose wider, and he has longer, downtown sideburns. (He's a performing artist.) Both have freckles on their arms. Both order panini sandwiches.

The Colmans grew up in New Jersey; their dad was a Presbyterian minister and their mom was a feminist activist in their church. They have an older brother, John, with whom they tried to downplay their twinship so he wouldn't feel left out. They say it wasn't until they were adults living in the same metropolitan area after ten years in different states for school and work that they were able to make an emotional break. "I think the physical separation prevented us from getting to a point where we could separate in our relationship," says Steven, younger by eight minutes and a performing poet who cowrote and costarred in *Russell Simmons Def Poetry Jam on Broadway* and won the National Poetry Slam championship as a member of the Nuyorican Poets Café slam team.

"We couldn't separate until we started talking," says David, who, at the time we talk, teaches labor history and African-American history at Ramapo College in New Jersey.

"And with the distance we weren't talking as much," Steve continues.

"When you get closer, then you can separate," says David.

"I think there was an *assumption* of closeness before, which inhibited real communication," Steven says. "Because we made these assumptions that we didn't need to communicate verbally. Where maybe we did."

David nods. "Honestly, it's really been in the last couple of years that we're actually talking about all this. . . . There aren't a lot of models and frameworks for helping twins navigate this territory. Society glamorizes or fantasizes twinship and assumes all sorts of things about the relationship."

Despite their newfound division, one commonality unites them: The two white brothers married black women. David's wife, Crystal, is finishing her Ph.D. in history at the time we talk. Steven's wife, Sarah Jones, is a poet/performer, with whom Steven often collaborates, as he did on her highly acclaimed one-woman-show, *Bridge and Tunnel*, which was coproduced in 2004 by Meryl Streep.

I ask the Colmans what they make of the fact that they both ended up in interracial marriages.

"We grew up in a predominantly black community in New Jersey," David replies, "and there was a lot of cross-cultural dating because that was just what happened in that context."

"It just became what we were familiar with," Steven adds.

They do admit that it is "striking for people," as David puts it, to see both Colmans and their wives together.

Steven smiles. "When people see us sitting at a restaurant, they totally react. They'll look first at Dave and me, and think, They look alike. Because identical twins are already weird to see. But then, seeing people who look like us, they're obviously thinking, White twins with two black women: What's going on? Do they have some . . ." He doesn't finish the sentence.

"Fetish?" I ask.

"Exactly," Steve says. "You notice that people are trying to figure it out; I would be, too. If I saw twin guys walk in with two black women, we'd be like, 'What's the story there?'"

"I'm aware of it," David agrees, "but Crystal and I have lived in mostly white places through most of our time together. So we really don't pay attention."

David and Crystal's relaxed approach affects Steven's. "They're better for Sarah and me," Steve says. "Because they don't pay attention."

Though as twins they felt they needed to let each other go, their parallel marriages reunited them in some way, since as couples, they face many of the same issues and situations—like walking into stores or boutiques. "I'll be the one to return any gift in our family," David says. "Because Crystal's sister was almost arrested for returning something. And she had a receipt! I never used to take the receipt out of the store when I bought something, but I quickly learned that you always keep the receipt *until you get home.*"

"That's why Sarah just sits in the car sometimes while I go inside." Steven nods. "I'm like, 'Let me just do this.' For instance, if we're in the Catskills and there's a Yankee-looking country store—"

"Oh, totally." David nods.

Both brothers have given thought to having mixed-race children.

"I just hope they're dark," Steven says, smiling. "That's the joke with all the mixed couple friends we see: Pray to God the kid doesn't come out too white. Because the black women don't want to look like they're the nannies."

"It's also a black-pride thing—having a black baby," David interjects.

Steven nods.

The summer I meet the Colmans, they've been spending a lot of relaxed time as couples—a noticeable contrast to the time when they were too busy to attend each other's weddings. (They don't have great explanations for that: "2001 was a crazy time for us," Steven says. "It was probably another one of those moments when we weren't talking," says David.) Now Steven and Sarah have rented a house in the Hamptons, which David and Crystal often visit. They all went to South Africa together when Sarah and Steven were booked to perform there; David and Crystal did academic work in the region. "It's really a foursome now," Steven says.

He says it's taken work to get back to the closeness everyone always assumed was there all along. "Biology determines a lot of your relationship," says Steven, "but it's what you do with it that makes it real. Or makes it work. And if you don't do anything with it, then it just becomes a fantasy."

Psychologist and identical twin Joan Friedman insists the idealized fantasy of twinship—which both the twins and their parents buy into—ends up forcing, or reinforcing, a togetherness that ill serves twins in the long run.

"Twins are completely crippled by the fact that they had this other person *with them* all the time," she says. "So they were always fine socially, comfortable in school; they always got a lot of attention. But they didn't have to *work* for anything. Without doing much, they were always 'so cute, so special.' "

My father bears this out. "You always were special, kind of a gimmick. That had its good side and its bad. . . . Think back on all the things you got together; I don't know if you would have gotten any of them apart."

Friedman continues: "Resilience for children comes out of mastery of a challenge, or facing a fear. And twins, with their ridiculous star power, lose out on mastering some of life's challenges. That's why parents simply have to spend separate time with each of them, have to separate them from each other regularly, let them fall on their faces and deal with it. Twins should have separate friends, separate teachers, separate teams. Parents should say essentially, 'Deal with the fact that you're in different preschool classes, or your twin brother gets invited to a birthday party and you don't. Yeah, it hurts your feelings and it's hard. But you're two different people and he's going to the party alone.' And that's life."

Her example strikes a chord, because that exact scenario happened to Robin and me: In seventh grade, she was invited to a big Halloween party that I wasn't. It was a crisis in my house. My parents' reaction was outrage; why would Becky, who was friendly with us both (though clearly closer to Robin), do us such an injustice? Dad encouraged me to confront Becky, and it's hard to believe I did, but to no avail. Robin skipped the party in solidarity.

"In my estimation, that was wrong," Friedman says when I recount the story. "Twins aren't equal just because they look alike. . . . Twins need to get the message early that 'You aren't the same. And that the two of you will end up in very different circumstances, just like you would if you were plain siblings.' It's never fair with siblings: Someone ends up with more kids, smarter kids, more money, a better marriage, more sex. It's never equal. And yet I think twins expect that when things aren't equal, their sister or brother is the winner, and then they're caught up in that old vortex and they're resentful and confused and they push the other one away."

Ainslie underscores this point: "On the one hand, some of these twins articulate an ideal fantasy of twinship. . . . On the other, they suggest a sense of dislocation. They seem to feel that they themselves have become disconnected from that utopia."

Once you start talking to the experts, it's clear that achieving individuation is an obstacle course. There's so much in the way: the incessant message to twins that they're equal and therefore one shouldn't exceed the other; the fact that twins spend so little time apart and therefore lean on their closeness and miss out on separate attachments; the romanticization of the twin ideal, which parents and twins swallow and even fake if necessary.

Eileen Pearlman, who runs TwInsight, a counseling resource for twins and parents of twins in Santa Monica, says the separation muddle starts even before cognition. "With twin babies, they have to learn what's me and what's not me," she explains in her serene office. "So when they're very young, you'll sometimes see that one twin infant has their hand inside the other one's mouth, or their foot. . . . There is this kind of confusion. Eventually they touch up against one another and they learn there's a separate person. . . . This separation/individuation process continues through life. From birth to three years old, there's one stage. Another one is around the adolescent stage, when the child is trying to figure out more of an identity, and then when graduating from high school or in early adult life. There may be a little more bumping up against each other then. Some twins do it earlier; some twins do it later. And the bumping up—or the individuation—may be gentle, but some could be quite volatile. . . . Maybe one is ready to separate before the other one. Maybe one feels good about separating but feels bad about leaving their twin. So there is that feeling: I don't want to hurt or abandon my twin, but I need to find out who I am. And the twin who is left behind may feel abandoned."

Thinking back, I realize I did my severing from Robin when I switched schools in the ninth grade. Finally I had an alternative universe, a new crew that was all mine. It was the first year of my life when people met me as a singular person, not as a set or as part of a spectacle.

At my new high school, I found a social cocoon surprisingly fast—maybe because, as psychologists have told me, I was built for companionship: Twins know how to do intimacy. When my school friends eventually met Robin, it was like meeting a stranger; she was Abby's similar-looking sister; not Abby all over again. She was just an additional interesting fact about me—a sister I was undeniably proud of—but she was not people's initial introduction to me.

My new friendships were intense: Rachel's apartment became my second home, Daisy knew as many show tunes as I did, Julia lived exotically on Avenue A and wrote tortured poetry, and hazel-eyed Julie made me feel oh-so-much cooler than I was, though I still dressed in denim pantsuits and Danskin turtlenecks. I didn't feel lost without my sister; I felt new.

The shift in me was a challenge for Robin. After watching the excitement of my fresh experience, she decided to apply to different schools the following year. But her new home didn't turn out to be the same cushion or haven. She had friends, but she didn't feel they really knew her. She performed in theatrical productions, while most of her new friends were athletes. She worked hard but got fewer pats on the back. Where my high school hoisted me up while I tested singleness for the first time, Robin was on her own.

I don't want to oversimplify. It's not that I was always on a cloud while Robin was under one; I spent plenty of nights in teen angst, putting on my Janis Ian record and writing overheated journal entries about the "raw truths" I confronted while rehearsing *No Exit* and about how Jason would never love me. But for me, high school was emboldening; Robin wouldn't say the same.

Until now, I don't think I've ever appreciated how hard it must have been for her when I left "our" school and suddenly seemed recharged. It didn't matter that until then she'd had the easier, happier social life; the point is that once I left, I was in many ways *gone*, distracted by my intense schoolwork, rushing off to weekly sleepovers or to rehearsals for shows she wasn't in.

I don't recall our relationship changing at that time. But it must have.

One diary entry from December 1979 affirms that there was tension: "*Argument with Robin . . . Accuses me of not caring for her anymore . . .*"

Only now do I appreciate how generous she was to let me go, without making me feel guilty. Only now do I wonder if her retreat from me in these last few years was a mirror of my earlier break.

Despite all the evidence that a split is inevitable and essential between twins, I have been stubbornly unsympathetic to what Robin needs, in part because it feels like an odd time to need it. No matter how many "experts"—Pearlman, Friedman, Ainslie, Rothman—tell me that disentanglement is crucial, and often occurs later than one would think (not during adolescence, when typical fissures happen, but deep into adulthood), I keep feeling impatient for this "stage" of our twin development to be over.

Is this distance really necessary? Robin and I are fully functioning, self-reliant adults. Isn't that "good enough"? Who determines how separate separation has to be? In our interview, Robin said, "I'm not rejecting you; I'm claiming something." But that "claim" has been a genuine deficit for me. It's the "hole" Robin assumed I feel sometimes. Aren't we apart enough? We have separate families, neighborhoods, schedules, work, friends, vacations, yoga classes. I don't need more space. Her boundaries feel artificial and confining; they fight the pulse of our earlier relationship—which wasn't to be joined at the hip, but to be unfettered in our nearness, our prioritizing of each other. When did the twinship get in the way of the friendship?

Joan Friedman almost scolds me when I ask her to decode this dynamic. "Your sister simply wants to have her own sense of self. She doesn't mean to hurt your feelings, but of course it does, because it's not something you identify with, or are feeling right now, so it demands that you be this bigger person, to recognize that she's needing space, not because she's upset or resentful, but so she can grow apart from you, which will ultimately enable her to be close to you."

Friedman says Robin's choice has nothing to do with me, but I balk at that. Of course it's personal; I'm the one who complicates her identity.

"It's not you," Friedman insists. "It's in *relationship* to you, by accident of birth. She's dealing with issues of the twinship and, yes, you happen to be her twin."

Ricardo Ainslie noted this dichotomy in his book: "One striking feature in many twinships was that the twins seemed to be differentially invested in the relationship. In these instances, one twin appeared more committed and involved, whereas the other was more disengaged, more willing to de-emphasize their twinness. . . ."

"One twin feels more needy; one doesn't," echoes Eileen Pearlman, who grew up calling her identical twin "Sister" and admits that she only made her break years after she was married. "It's hard to resolve the fact that, even though this is going on, it may not be permanent . . . Some twins get scared, thinking, If I'm separated from her, does that mean that we're never going to be close again? Realizing that it's a process takes away the fear and the sting of losing someone. It's seeing that the other person is individual and you are, and then how do we find our togetherness, our *we*-ness again?"

Robin maintains that our "we-ness" is still there, and considering it dispassionately, I see she's right. It shimmers in our daily phone calls and in each rendezvous: the spa getaway my husband gave us one year, where we lounged in robes side by side in "the Quiet Room," and braved a "Challenge Course" which required climbing—harnessed—to the top of a twenty-five-foot pole and then leaping off into nothing. It's been there in the four days we've spent the past two Augusts at her summer rental without kids or spouses, making tomato salads, leading each other in yoga, working on our laptops under quilts. It's in the vivacity of our children's play dates and the fact that they've grown up so close. Of course there's we-ness.

When I look at us from Robin's perspective, I see that it's not just a matter of individuation; it's a matter of breathing, getting enough air. Decades of being grouped, lumped, and mistaken for someone else could be oppressive—not ever being sure of what is wholly, exclusively yours. "With identical twins," Burlingham wrote in 1954, "the similarity in looks and the confusion this creates may eventually make them feel that nothing is personal or unique about them. They have therefore every reason to feel misunderstood . . . and angry."

When I reunite with Belinda and Gretchen Langner, thirty-two years after we were classmates in fifth grade, they are living together again—after years spent on their own. My childhood memory of the

Langner sisters is of two exotically beautiful, willowy sisters, urbane beyond their years; they are still luminous today, with broad smiles, dark eyes, and dancer's frames, but they seem somewhat weathered by their mother's death three years ago, by Belinda's severe bouts with environmental illness (she eats only two types of food at every single meal), by Gretchen's six-year rocky romance, and by their own twin tensions, now that they're under the same roof again.

Gretchen is a Columbia-trained psychotherapist; Belinda has a degree in fine arts from the School of Visual Arts and currently makes handbags. Close as the Langners are—they freely call each other "honey," something I can't imagine Robin and I doing—Belinda has recently felt burdened by Gretchen's incessant discussions of her turbulent love affair. "I think I'm trying to make it clear to Gretch we need to be our separate selves," she says in front of her twin. "Sometimes I set limits now—on the time that she wants to talk about it and have me try to help her figure out what to do about him."

When we all sit down to talk, Belinda is buoyant about her own current romance with an old friend ("He's very respectful and sweet with our twinship," Belinda says), while Gretchen has recently reunited with the on-again, off-again boyfriend Belinda dislikes.

"It's been a struggle to say to myself, I can be happy even if Gretch is unhappy right now," Belinda admits. "If I'm around her a lot and she's really unhappy, I have to leave to be around other people, who are happy." She and Gretchen have had couples therapy together. "Because we had begun to feel like a cranky married couple rather than a happily married couple."

Gretchen similarly describes their twinship as a lifelong marriage: "A therapist once told us, 'This is a relationship you can't get divorced from.'"

"There has always been this unwritten law that we have to be there for each other," Belinda continues. "But now what I'm seeing is that we need to be there for each other and also be independent. That is probably our life's work."

Gretchen's training in social work has given her the vocabulary, if not always the capacity, to address their hurdles. "When you have such a close relationship—and I don't think there's a relationship closer than ours—if you read the top couples therapies books, this is exactly what couples are dealing with: separation, individuation, boundaries."

Gretchen says their recent prickliness is in large part because they're unused to bunking together; up until recently, they lived two hours apart. "This has been really challenging," she admits.

"I think it's been a strain on our relationship," Belinda says bluntly. "I'm walking this tightrope between being the one whom she turns to, the one she really wants unconditional love and understanding from, but also feeling the need to tell her the truth. . . . I'm finally in a good relationship now, and I'm about to be engaged."

"She's my role model." Gretchen smiles.

"Even with my white hair," Belinda says, touching her locks, which she won't dye because of her illness. "I'm going to be a bride finally. So now I just want to shake her. I want us both to be happy now."

Belinda called me four months later to tell me her engagement was off. She didn't want to reveal the cause publicly, but she did talk about the difficulty of once again having to move back in with her twin. "Neither one of us wants to be still living together in our forties, not married and not mothers," she says quietly. "We've always encouraged each other to find someone, and wanted so desperately to be married."

In the same Langner spirit that I remember from childhood—always finding the deeper meaning of things—Belinda said she and Gretchen have chosen to see mystical signs of optimism around them. "One of the roads that intersects ours is called 'Twin Ridges,'" Belinda tells me when we speak again, months after our first interview. "There's a beautiful pond there where Gretchen and I go to sit. And on the same sign that intersects Twin Ridges is a road called

'Crossways.' " The symbolism of those street names obviously resonates with her. "We almost have this spiritual idea that we're meant to be here in this house together," Belinda says. "To have each of our lives begin again."

Psychotherapist Dale Ortmeyer believes twins have distinct but harmonizing traits that combine to create one shared self, so it follows that twins would need to be physically together in order to feel complete. As Ortmeyer puts it, "The need to be with each other is heightened." He elucidates further by citing a myth in which one twin is absent. Though Narcissus is generally believed to have fallen in love with his own reflection, second-century Greek geographer, Pausanias, hypothesized a different explanation: that, in fact, Narcissus had a twin sister, whom he loved totally and who died, which is why Narcissus gazed endlessly at his own reflection—to remind himself of her.

"What was Narcissus mourning?" Ortmeyer asks in his 1970 paper. "Could it be that the youth was not searching for his own reflection, but for the complementary attributes of his twin? . . . His loss, then, would not be the loss of an identical person, but of a different person, his twin, the two of them making a unity."

One result of a "unity" identity—or a unified one—is that it makes each twin lazy about developing the attributes they're missing. This may be because twins aren't aware of their "identity fusion," as Ortmeyer calls it. I can't say I was, but now that I've been forced to think about the idea, it's intriguing. Maybe it's too pat, but it's possible that Robin brought to the twinship self-possession, while I brought mirth; that she made me more intrepid, while I made her more buoyant. Robin told me in our interview that when we're in social situations, she'll defer to my talkativeness. (No wonder I lost my voice.) "You say what you think a little more," she said; "you're more comfortable jumping in with your thoughts about what's going on and can hold the table in a dinner situation. I have felt that in family gatherings especially, I end up receding a little bit."

Similarly, when I'm with Robin, I find myself becoming more inept, absentminded, dependent. I'm the one who loses an earring, forgets the lunch date, leaves my purse unzipped in the subway. I let her be the grown-up.

Ortmeyer suggests that only later in life do twins even realize they have a deficit; it usually happens when the twin isn't by their side anymore. "In adolescence, when twins can no longer have the same degree of intimate contact," Ortmeyer tells me, "the we-self becomes a handicap. Twins unconsciously may mourn the absence of the personality traits of the other, yet not see the need to develop those traits." Diane Setterfield, in her novel *The Thirteenth Tale*, captures this perfectly: "You could view the twins as having divided a set of characteristics between them. Where an ordinary, healthy person will feel a whole range of different emotions, display a great variety of behaviors, the twins, you might say, have divided the range of emotions and behaviors into two and taken one set each."

Joe, who prefers a pseudonym, says he misses his twin brother, Peter, but their separation has calcified to the point of estrangement. "What does one do?" Joe asks over coffee at a tiny bakery in lower Manhattan. "I guess one starts picking up the phone or writing. Stuff like that. But the habit of avoiding has been a lot easier than breaking it."

Their individuation can be traced to high school, when Joe got immersed in the math team and Peter fell in love during sophomore year. "This is not a great psychological insight," Joe says, "but I feel like he replaced me with his girlfriend. . . . He spent all his time with her and they were weirdly bonded."

Joe went to an Ivy League college and never returned home to California.

Peter attended a local university with his high school girlfriend, and they're together to this day—married, with one child.

"I remember making a point of going over to their house for dinner and telling my brother, 'You're really important to me; I want you in my life,' " Joe recalls. "Peter seemed really moved by that, but the evening ended with his girlfriend getting really upset. Maybe she felt defensive or threatened. . . . I know that she always looks irritated when people would remark upon our twinness at family parties. I don't think the fact of our being twins was a delight to her."

When Peter and his wife had a child, Peter changed his last name to a new surname that his wife and baby would all share. Maybe it was another attempt at separation, but Joe took it personally. "I thought it was a strange, hostile gesture," he says now. He never told Peter how he felt. "I should have. But part of me feels very guilty—like I abandoned him; I went off to college and didn't come back. It wasn't a priority for me to live near my twin."

Ultimately, Joe married, too, then divorced after seven years. At thirty, he came out as a gay man. "My mother said she could see it in our baby pictures." He smiles. "She was very into it—'Rah, rah!' She immediately started marching in PFLAG parades." (Parents, Families and Friends of Lesbians and Gays.) "My brother was intelligent about it, sensitive to me."

I ask Joe what he makes of the fact that he and Peter have the same DNA but different sexual orientations. He tells me that losing his closeness with Peter made him seek closeness with other men. In other words, his twinship and homosexuality are linked not because of some genetic blueprint, but because of Peter's disaffection.

"I don't have the sense of my sexuality being this thing that I was born with," Joe says. "It felt much more circumstantial. Because, who knows? If Peter and I had been really close friends and been twinlike, I just wonder—would that have somehow freed me to explore different kinds of relationships, to be in the world differently? There was always a profound sense of insecurity in my friendships in my teens and twenties, which was wrapped up with him. . . . When I would typically enter into relationships, they had the dynamic of my expecting too much and being disappointed; the person I loved, who wasn't a twin, would see me as obsessive or needy. So I'm wondering if having a twin who's actually *there*, who's always checking in with you, that must be pretty nice. That must make you pretty secure and confident. Right?" He really seems to want an answer: "Don't *you* have that?"

The cashier in the three-table café is giving us dirty looks because we're nursing our coffees, which barely meet the minimum charge. Before we leave, I ask Joe if I can contact Peter. "I'll have to find his number," he says, appearing surprised himself that he doesn't know it by heart or even where he keeps it. "I'll have to get back to you on that."

I relate to Joe's story in this way: I think I, too, may have sought out—or gravitated toward—more intense female intimacy in my adult friendships because of what's absent from my twinship. I have longer, weightier discussions with Rachel, Marcia, and Dani than I do with Robin, partly because my friends probe deeper and draw out the minutiae of whatever I confide. Our exchanges are in many ways more tender, more comprehensive than mine with my sister.

My husband falls into a category of his own: He is the person who undoubtedly knows me best, whom I trust the most. But Dave is not a gooey girlfriend. He doesn't fill that place I may be wired to need filled. I have what feels like a congenital clarity of what it is to be wholly close to another human being—what poet Karl Jay Shapiro, in his 1942 poem "The Twins," called "the instinctive partnership of birth." Twin after twin described the same primal sureness. Once you've had it, it's hard to let it go, or to settle for anything less. Dave is unfailingly patient with this need, partly due to his equanimity, partly because he grew up with identical twin sisters himself.

Robin, on the other hand, hasn't so much collected new intimacies as found it tricky to tend them. She said in our interview that our closeness made her "sort of a lazy," then added, "When you have a twin, you don't really need friends or a best friend. All through my youth, I wasn't that open to close friendships. You were enough. Now I feel like my eggs are in one basket a little bit and I resist that."

Eggs in one basket—that's just the phrase Joan Friedman used when we spoke in Los Angeles: "Twins understandably, genetically, put all their love in one basket. For some reason, you were more capable of spreading it around. She's had to shut off the love that she has for you in order to feel as if she has enough love for others."

Separating from one's twin can require more conscious effort than we expect, and multiple attempts before the individuation sticks. Some move to different cities, some go to couples therapy, and some extricate themselves gradually. Others mark a line in the sand by the striking clarity of their self-definition.

Perhaps the most extreme example of this is offered by Clair Farley, who, thanks to a sex-change operation, is no longer Alex Farley. Her identical brother, Mark, is still male, still Mark, and a homosexual. They both live in San Francisco because lately they want to be near to each other. Clair is, when we meet, the transgender economic development coordinator for the Lesbian Gay Bisexual Transgender Community Center; Mark is still mulling career paths after coproducing a highly praised documentary, *Red Without Blue*, about his and Clair's story. (The title refers to the colors their mother dressed them in as babies—Mark in red, Alex/Clair in blue.)

When I meet them for dinner at the Mandarin Oriental Hotel, Mark is somewhat underdressed for the stuffy restaurant, wearing a white long-sleeved T-shirt under a short-sleeved one; Clair, on the other hand, is turned out in a black-and-white herringbone jacket, black top, skirt, and heels. She's pretty—softer-looking now than when I watched her on film a year earlier. Their voices are the only feature that is still identical about them, which, Clair admits, sometimes gives her away as a former man.

Both twins answer my questions in measured tones; neither reveals any feeling, despite the intensity of their story. Clair is more overtly at ease than Mark, more talkative. Mark seems chary, despite the fact that their story has already played nationally on the Sundance Channel—or perhaps because of it.

"I wouldn't say that surgery fixed everything or solved all my problems," says Clair, "but definitely I feel like I was reborn in many ways and can start fresh. That's the most powerful part of it: I've been given the opportunity to start over in a new body."

They spent their childhood as inseparable playmates in Missoula, Montana. The film includes home movies of the boys dancing merrily together. At one point, Mark says on-camera, "We were just in love with each other from the day we were born," and their mother adds, "They know each other in ways you and I will never know."

In seventh grade, Alex came out as a homosexual. Mark was still in the closet, but their classmates assumed he was gay, as did their mother. The twins were going through an angry phase, fighting with each other constantly; Clair admits she was physically abusive to Mark. In the film, Mark says their sameness magnified their adolescent awkwardness: "We were definitely really self-conscious at that point in our life, and having each other as a mirror of what we didn't like about ourselves."

At fifteen, they decided to commit double suicide. It was Mark's idea. "I asked Alex to make a promise," he recounts on film. "I told him he had to say yes before I told him what it was. I started telling him that I didn't feel anyone really loved us and that we had a place in this life. Things had to be better somewhere else."

Alex agreed to Mark's plan. "We both had been depressed and suicidal," Clair recalls. "Why wouldn't you end your life with the person you began it with? Why would you want to live on without him?"

They drove to a bluff overlooking Missoula. Both did a large amount of cocaine; then they directed the exhaust pipe into their car and turned on the ignition. "We closed all the windows and started breathing in the fumes. He kept kind of shaking me and we were both in the backseat. He wanted me to get up—'Get up, get up.' You know, 'You can't die yet. No, we have to die together; wake up, wake up, wake up.' "

"We stayed in there for hours," Mark recalls, "and I remember at one point saying, 'This isn't working; we're not dying.' And so we talked about driving the car off the cliff."

" 'I don't want to drive off the side of the cliff,' " Clair recalls saying. " 'Please let's not do this. I just want to go home.' "

"So I got out of the car," Mark continues, "and took the hose out of the exhaust and drove us home."

When they got home, drugged and sickened, they confessed everything to their dad, who rushed to the hospital; they were sent from there to a mental facility, then for four years to separate drug rehabilitation centers, Alex in Oregon, Mark in Idaho. They saw each other twice during that entire time.

"This came after a fifteen-year relationship of spending every single day together," Clair says now over her salad. "Suddenly we had to survive without each other. For the first time, we created an identity that was separate."

Though their phone conversations were monitored, Alex did tell Mark at one point that he had decided to become a woman. Alex also told his mother, who, in the film, offers her own take on Alex's choice to change genders. "[It was] his attempt to not be a twin. To be totally isolated from us. And it worked. Do I think it's real? Yeah. For the time being."

I ask Mark if there was a point where he asked his twin not to go through with it.

"Never," he replies firmly.

Today, Mark minimizes the question of whether Clair's decision was a reaction to their twinship, but in the documentary, he tells Clair he was somewhat offended at the time. "It's still hard for me sometimes," he tells her on-camera, "because we were born as twins; we were born as boys. That's part of our identity; it's part of my identity. You said you don't like what you're like—your physical body—and you don't like me because we look so much alike. I explained to him that I don't look at you [now that you're a woman] and see myself. Part of who we were was lost in that transformation."

Their relationship, which had been so intertwined as children, suddenly felt annulled.

Mark: "It was almost like you were cutting this cord that we had: this twinship. This identical identity. I just couldn't imagine you desiring to be someone else because it was who I was and who you are. You didn't want to be like me and that's why you hated yourself and hated me at times."

Clair: "But I'm still the same person."

Mark: "You're the same person, but it's not Mark and Alex anymore."

I tell Clair it's difficult not to see her sex change as a repudiation of Mark—at least to some degree. "I would say that growing up, I did have some resentments about him because I saw those qualities in him that I didn't like in myself," she explains. "But to say that it was because of him is not the case. It was more a rejection of the person I had been."

"I do remember feeling just a kind of abandonment in a sense," Mark tells me, barely touching his entrée, "because Clair had told me that she didn't want to be my brother any longer and she wanted to transform her body into something else. And to me, not understanding what that process is all about, it felt like a rejection and it felt hurtful."

Clair concedes: "I think there was probably some unconscious desire to have individuality or space. When I was separate in boarding school, I was able to explore these things for the first time and say, 'I have to have a personality that's not connected as a twin.' I think that's when I started to realize that I really did want to transition."

I ask Clair if today she feels like a woman.

"For me, gender is not as simple as 'I'm a woman.' Yes, biologically now my genitals are female, but I wouldn't necessarily say that my expression and behavior and spirituality are female. I feel like it's evolved past those qualifications or those labels. My spirituality is nongender. . . . We're all much more than a woman or a man. None of us is based on these inherent stereotypes; we're all much more than that."

Does Mark consider Clair his sister or his brother?

"She's my sister," Mark replies. "There's no hesitation at all. . . . I could say I've stopped using 'Alex,' but at the same time I don't feel bad about using 'Alex' when I'm speaking about Alex and a memory of my brother. Because that's still real and it existed. But I never make the mistake of calling Clair 'Alex' today."

Does he feel like he lost his brother?

Mark shakes his head. "I feel there are things about Clair that are gone. Some things I'm glad are gone: some of the anger and the tendencies to be aggressive—those qualities that I saw in Alex that I feared a little bit or didn't like. I see those are gone and I don't miss them at all. And the qualities that I always enjoyed about Alex, I still see in Clair today. . . . It's amazing just to see how far she has come."

And he'd still say she's his identical twin, though they're not a match anymore?

"Of course," Mark replies.

I wonder, chiefly because they share the same DNA blueprint, whether Mark has had similar urges to have a different body.

"I'm happy with my penis," he replies. "But I wouldn't say the whole of me is male. I agree with Clair that there are aspects of me that are female."

"You have worried about people wondering if you're trans," Clair reminds him, meaning transsexual.

"Now people think Clair's voice is too low"—Mark smiles—"but for years, my voice has been too high. People have inbred in them that 'this is what a man sounds like; this is what a woman sounds like.' "

Though Clair made perhaps the most dramatic symbolic separation of any twin I've met or known, I find it remarkable the extent to which her breaking away has brought them closer than ever. "If a week goes by, I totally need to see him," Clair says. "I think I'll always have that feeling of wanting to connect with someone I've loved for my entire life." Though they spent years apart during and after boarding school, they now choose to live in the same city, talk daily, and honor a weekly date every Friday. Mark's longtime boyfriend, David, is understanding that Mark's twin takes precedence.

"There's just a huge responsibility I feel to be there for her," Mark admits. "It can take me away from my own life."

Clair's decision to "transition" from male to female has been the dominant event of their lives for a while now—because it was such a radical, public metamorphosis; because their mother was embarrassed and vehemently resistant for so long; because it required drastic, expensive medical procedures; and because they chose to put their story on film.

"There will be times Mark feels more caught up in my own experience," Clair says almost apologetically. "The worst part of being a twin is feeling responsible for the other person's situation, and feeling like you have some control over it. When you don't have control, it can feel like heartache. I really don't want to see him in pain or for him to see me in pain."

Mark seems to want to make clear that he doesn't resent for a moment being his twin's chief supporter, and, in some sense, her supporting player. "She's still the wisest, strongest person I've ever met," he tells me. "I feel honored to be part of her life."

ROBIN: I have really felt like what's interesting to me about
your doing this book project is I feel like there's a huge
amount we take for granted. It's almost an ignorance of
what really is there between us. It's this major, defining
thing that I haven't really paid attention to, given credence
to, as a shaping element. That's true for every permutation
of it. There's a sense with which I carry you with me all the
time. I think back to those childhood days as halcyon days.
I kind of preferred a blissful ignorance. All the stuff now
that weighs on me is more of a burden. I kind of liked the
uncritical time, when it was all just great. But I realize that
that's why it's maybe rearing its head now. I'm sure there
are things that the research would turn up about twins'
attachment that would tell me something about myself,
that has to do with not appreciating what the space would
be without you. The degree to which I can go forth in the
world because of you, all of that. It hasn't been a point of
inquiry for me.

ABIGAIL: But when you think about how your life would be
different if I were gone?

ROBIN: It would be broken.

※ ※

8 AND THEN THERE WAS ONE

So when I looked into a mirror, even the small things that made my face my own made my face into his, and if I waited long enough he would begin to speak to me. He would tell me about heaven, about all sorts of little details. . . . He said he was watching me all the time. . . . And always the last thing he said to me was, "When are you going to come and be with me again?"
—Chris Adrian, "Stab," *A Better Angel: Stories*

"A twin doesn't know what alone means until you lose your twin."

Gregory Hoffman is a broad-shouldered, ruddy-faced Long Island native, dressed in a U.S. Open windbreaker when we meet over a burger, medium rare, in a pub-like restaurant called Churchill's in Rockville Centre. He lost his identical twin, Stephen, in the Twin Towers on 9/11, when they were both thirty-six years old.

There is no way to overstate the emotional wreckage; Gregory was undone by it. "Those times I've thought about killing myself, I'd say, What would Stephen want me to do now? When I asked myself that question, the right answer was always, Stay alive. Sometimes I have to divorce myself from the pain I'm in, and put myself in a position of being able to ask that question. That's been helpful through this."

He still hasn't gotten "through" it, and he seems to bristle at the idea that he's supposed to. "I hate the words *move on*," Hoffman says briskly. "You move forward. There's no moving on."

Stephen Hoffman, three minutes Gregory's junior and a bond broker at Cantor Fitzgerald, was—even according to his twin—the more gregarious of the two, which is hard to imagine, because Gregory's personality is outsized: energetic, high-volume, and bursting with twinship. More than any one thing he says about it, what comes through is rapture at their alliance—an unbreachable, almost hallowed union.

"One day you talk to somebody," Gregory says, "and the next day, they're just *gone*. I remember the first night I went home by myself and I was hyperventilating. I was looking at pictures; they weren't enough. I *had* to watch Stephen talk; I had to see him *move*. I started watching football tapes from when we were coaching together. I needed to see him alive. I had never had such a strong urge, like I couldn't breathe. I was going through major twin withdrawal."

Gregory remembers the sickening escalation of that awful Tuesday morning. "I'm looking at the North Tower on television and I'm counting down from the top of the building, trying to see his floor. And I say to myself, If that plane flew into their floor, they're all dead. People were calling in: 'Have you heard from Stephen?' I was initially calm. I said, 'Stephen was in the Towers in '93 and he got out; he's going to get out again.' But I remember looking at the screen and saying, 'How the hell are they going to put out that damn fire?' So I'm calling him on the phone, and suddenly he picks up. And I say, 'Steve! It's Greg!' To hear his voice . . ."

Greg looks so relieved for a split second that I actually have the fleeting hope maybe the story can turn out differently. "I'm sure it was so reassuring to hear my voice, too," he continues. "He says, 'Greg, I'm okay,' and the next thing you know it's 9:02, and the second plane smashes in. I'm watching CNBC on my computer screen at work, and it was just disbelief. I hear Stephen say, 'Oh my God. Look at that.' He was talking to somebody, and then the cell phones went dead."

The night before 9/11, Greg left Stephen a phone message, suggesting they go surfing at dawn near their homes on Long Island; they often started the workday that way. "If we had gone surfing, he wouldn't have been at his desk at eight o'clock," Greg says. "How often I've said to myself, If I'd only have made him go surfing."

Hoffman seems eager to recount this nightmare to a fellow twin. (He has signed all his e-mails to me "In twinship.") "I have trouble explaining this to people," he says. "I tell them, 'Remember when the North Tower was burnt out like a shell but still standing; to me, that's what a twinless twin is.' You're still there, but you're not. And you never will be. There's not a day or a moment that goes by that I don't think about him. But he's alive in my conversations, like this one. If you want someone to truly be dead, stop talking about him. If you ask me why it's so great to tell you all this, it's because it keeps him alive. I could talk about Stephen all night."

He takes a bite of his burger.

"You know how twinship is such a tactile thing," he continues. "You reach out and touch your sister. Imagine suddenly you don't have that anymore. I have two beautiful daughters, a beautiful wife, ten other brothers and sisters, my mom and dad, great friends, but I still felt like I was in an enormous, inescapable black hole. I remember Saint Patrick's Day, 2003, I was walking across the Brooklyn Bridge; I stopped and I looked out over the edge and I said to myself, Three steps and my pain is gone. That's how bad it got sometimes. You just wanted the pain to stop." He calls to mind this description in Diane Setterfield's novel *The Thirteenth Tale:* "The separation of twins is no ordinary separation. Imagine surviving an earthquake. When you come to, you find the world unrecognizable. The horizon is in a different place. The sun has changed color. Nothing remains of the terrain you know. As for you, you are alive. But it's not the same as living. It's no wonder the survivors of such disasters so often wish they had perished with the others."

Gregory's wife, Aileen, a social worker, is a petite, attractive woman dressed in a blazer and slacks when I meet her separately in my apartment. "He really spiraled down," she says in a calming voice that suits her profession. "It has changed him profoundly. There are some days that I feel like we're starting all over again. I'm grateful I have Gregory alive. But it comes with a huge change."

Aileen decided to track down other twin survivors of 9/11 so that Gregory could connect with people going through the same unique torment. She found seventeen twins at first, but when the *New York Times* ran an article about her search, other twins came forward. "I ultimately found forty-five twins," Aileen recalls. "We had two social events when we brought all the twinless twins—I hate that phrase— together. It was very moving."

She and Greg also attended an annual gathering of twin survivors, organized by a group called Twinless Twins, which has ten chapters in the United States and four in Canada, Australia, and the United Kingdom. "Twins spend four days telling each other sad stories about how they lost their twins," Aileen explains. "In some ways, it really saved Greg." In July 2008, some eighty people attended the Twinless Twins gathering in Toronto, according to the *National Post*. One twin explained why the loss is acute, whenever it happens: "You meet your twin before you meet your mother." Another twin, Davona Patterson, forty-four, who lost her twin to cancer, told the paper, "It's not an occasional breakdown, it's an everyday breakdown. There's only one of me now."

Gregory tells me that Aileen could fathom his bottomless anguish, but it was more complicated dealing with Stephen's wife. "Gabrielle and I had The Fight—about which is more important, a spouse or a twin," Greg says soberly. "And I said, 'Gabrielle, don't ask me to answer that question. Because you're not going to like the answer.' She was going through her shit and I was going through mine, but I *wasn't* going to minimize my twinship. I told her, 'Stephen and I were together since we were conceived.' I wasn't going to stand there and say I loved him more, but one thing I did say was, 'You can go find another husband; I can't go find another twin.' She stormed out, yelled at me. It was hurtful to her. And I've never brought it up again."

Aileen, who remains extremely close to her sister-in-law (they have daughters fourteen months apart), saw the friction building between Greg and Gabrielle. "People were trying to measure who had more grief," Aileen says. "I think when you're in pain, especially in a tragedy like this, you want to stand on the rooftops and say, '*I'm in so much pain.*' And if you have a way to measure it, to say that one is more than the other, you try."

Aileen describes the Hoffman twins' friendship as "magnificent." She met them her first day at Buffalo State College (she was a freshman; they were seniors) and remembers being dazzled. "They were electric." She smiles. "Literally the friendliest guys you've ever met in your life." Both loud, both economics majors, both Republicans, both working at the student union flipping eggs, they talked very fast, and were the hub of the social scene. "Everybody knew Gregory and Stephen," she says decisively. "The two most popular guys on campus."

Even on her wedding day, Aileen says, Greg and Steve were still riffing on their twinship. "Gregory wore a button that said 'I'm the groom' "—Aileen laughs—"and Stephen wore one that said 'I'm the best man.' And people still got them mixed up. When the wedding was all said and done and we went back to my house, Greg and Stephen were saying good-bye to each other outside; they were hugging, and they kept touching each other. It was as if they were saying good-bye to that chapter of their life."

Gregory admits he is still grappling with how to be an uncle to his twin's daughter, Madeline, eleven, when we meet, without appearing to insinuate himself as a replacement father. "When Madeline hugs me, I don't mind if she pretends it's her dad she's hugging. Because I know how much I look like him. I remember right after he died, she said, 'Uncle Greg, can I call you "Daddy" now?' What an emotional bomb that was. I said, 'Madeline, your dad is your dad. Not that I mind being called that, but it's not fair to him. I'm never going to replace your dad.' That's what I said to her when she was six years old."

It's clearly a sensitive subject—that he doesn't see Madeline more often; he's not sure how much Gabrielle wants him around, and he admits he doesn't always know how to be with his niece. "I feel terrible about that," he says. "I ask myself, Would Steve be happy with the time I'm spending with Mad? No, he wouldn't be. But he probably understands."

I ask if Gregory has ever wished he could trade places with his brother.

"The answer is, I wouldn't want Stephen to go through this kind of pain. He had a horrible death—I can't imagine what a horrible two hours he had, but then it was over and he was at peace. For me, it's five years and counting, and I wouldn't wish this on him. It's the one downside of being a twin: if you're the one who survives losing the other one. It's knowing what you had and knowing you'll never, ever, ever have anything quite like it again."

I tell him that I doubt Robin and I think about the fact that one of us could be gone at any moment. "You shouldn't," Gregory insists. "But recognize what you have. Stephen and I always understood how great we had it. My sense from you is that you and Robin don't take each other for granted. That's not going to change the fact, Abby, that one day it's going to happen to one of you. And you know what? It sucks."

Hoffman gave me not only a glimpse of destabilizing sorrow but also what felt like an urgent message: Live consciously. Know that you can't fathom what you would be—or would no longer be—alone.

I've never thought of myself as being held together by Robin but neither have I considered whether I'd fall apart or be diminished without her. Hoffman's description that "you're still there, but you're not" tells me that I might ultimately be not just one without Robin, but *less than* one. He suggested she's more integral to my daily strength and character than I realize. Who am I without my twin? Do any of us twins discover that without being forced to?

Nancy Segal's studies on twin bereavement found not only that identical twins have higher initial "grief intensity ratings" than fraternal twins but that the grief ratings for twins are equal to those for bereaved spouses. My guess is that most twins would expect those results.

In his book *Wish I Could Be There*, Allen Shawn talks about his lost twin, Mary, and maintains that the age-old maxim "We are born alone and we die alone" is inadequate in his case: "For twins, this statement needs to be amended. We are born with company, but we die alone."

Former *Baywatch* actress Alexandra Paul said five words in the middle of our interview that make her weep abruptly: "If something happened to her . . ." She couldn't continue for a moment. And then she echoed Gregory Hoffman exactly: "It would be worse than if my husband died. You can fall in love again, but you can never get another twin."

Liza and Jamie Persky, near forty when I interviewed them at a Manhattan café, admitted that they constantly think the worst when they can't reach each other. "If either one of us is not where we say we're going to be, we think we're dead," Liza stated.

"We think we're dead all the time," Jamie affirmed. "And people will hear about it. Like I'll get home and there will be like eighteen phone messages: 'Your sister thinks you're dead.' "

Liza: "I panic."

Jamie: "We also have a code—"

Liza: "We made a code thirty years ago that if anything was ever wrong with one of us, like if you have a gunman holding a gun to your head and you can't let on, you'll pick up the phone, and the code is—"

In unison: "How's Dale?"

Jamie: "That was our Irish setter when we were like nine."

Liza: "We know if you ever hear that, then you're really in trouble."

The world of twin loss—and it feels like a whole universe once you enter it—extends powerfully to parents who have lost a twin. One pioneering organization, CLIMB—the Center for Loss in Multiple Birth—was started in Alaska in 1986 by Jean Kollantai, who lost one of her fraternal-twin sons just days before his birth; his brother emerged healthy.

I meet Kollantai, forty-seven, at the Ghent International Twins Conference. She's dressed in a patterned blue skirt and black sandals, and we sit in a grassy courtyard with our egg-salad sandwiches on our laps. "My introduction to parenthood," she says in a gentle voice, "was literally holding these two full-term babies, where one was alive and one was dead."

She says she did not get hysterical right away, and having spoken to hundreds of grieving parents over these last twenty-plus years, she attests that most do appear calm at first. "You have to experience it yourself before you know how you would react. It takes a long time. And I guess a lot of the calm was my thinking, Well, if I'm really good for Christmas, he'll come back."

Kollantai felt lucky to be able to take her deceased son, Andrew, and his surviving twin, Berney, back to their house in Palmer, Alaska. Though it may sound counterintuitive to want to take a dead baby home, that's exactly what she suggests outsiders don't grasp: how important it is to spend time with both twins together. "After the autopsy was done, we took both of them in the car," she says almost proudly. "So we were able to be home with both sons."

The story gets more agonizing: They had to keep Andrew's body outdoors overnight so it would not decompose. "It was zero degrees that spring, and we had to leave him outside," Kollantai recounts. "It was really strange to come home from the hospital and leave one baby in the car all night in zero degrees. But that was the only way we could have him with us."

Kollantai's written guide to counselors of grieving parents stresses the importance of holding the lifeless baby, even if he or she was deceased before birth. Apparently, parents are more likely to get the chance to hold their dead infant if it was alive at birth and *then* died— hours or days after. But when a twin is *born* dead, it's often whisked away, and the surviving twin is treated, Kollantai writes, "as if he was a single baby, all there had ever been."

During Andrew's makeshift funeral service at home, his mother remembers, his twin, Berney, became unusually agitated. "He'd been very mellow until then," she recalls. "Then he started screaming and never stopped."

They buried Andrew with family photographs, on which she'd written messages, plus a few of the toys they'd bought for the twins they'd been expecting. (Kollantai's guide for counselors also suggests other keepsakes, such as footprints or locks of hair.)

She says so many people said the wrong things to her at the time that she resolved to create a more compassionate resource for parents experiencing the same kind of heartbreak. CLIMB's first newsletter was published in 1987, and the response was overwhelming. "You have no idea how many people have had multiple-birth loss."

Kollantai tells me few realize how complete a human can seem without ever having made a sound. "This was a baby whom I already loved," she says of her son Andrew. "He was a baby I'd wanted and had been very aware of in utero. I was dealing with the shocking loss of a child, the concept that he was really not coming back. Ever."

She says she had to let go of the image of her twins growing up together. "If I was buying something for Berney in a store, I'd think, I should be buying two. If it was quiet in the house, I'd think, It shouldn't be quiet like this; both of them should be crying. I felt I could nurse on only one side because the other side was Andrew's."

There was also the question of whether she should tell people that she was the mother of twin boys, or one son. "I'd go into stores and people would say, 'Oh, he's the most beautiful baby I ever saw.' And I'd say, 'Yes, well, he was really twins.' I'd just blurt that out."

I ask Kollantai if she still marks Andrew's birthday, or whether she thinks that's morbid. As soon as I utter the word *morbid*, I notice her stiffen. "You have to get rid of abstract terms like *morbid*," she cautions me. She says it gently, but I know it's a rebuke. "It's easy to put judgments on things."

I see why *morbid* could seem judgmental, but I want to hear Kollantai's reasons, because I *do* think society expects people to get over it—especially when one child is alive. Indeed, Kollantai has written about the fact that "all parents are under tremendous internal and external pressure to 'focus on the living baby,' consider themselves lucky, consider the one who died at best a nice extra that didn't work out. Many are told that their grieving would 'hurt' the living baby."

In her guide, she challenges the attitude that mournful parents should focus on the twin they have, not the twin they lost: "We have had to find, the hard way, that truly no one replaces anyone—not even a genetically identical person or people born also to you at exactly the same time."

While Kollantai and I meet, Berney is busy applying to college; Kollantai says she believes he was never burdened by the twin he never knew. Still, when he was growing up, Andrew was very much a presence. "On Berney's tenth birthday," Kollantai recalls, "I said, 'If you could spend an evening with anyone in the world, who would it be?' Berney is a history buff, and I thought he was going to say 'Winston Churchill.' But he said, 'The baby.' "

Elizabeth Pector, a family physician who works with Kollantai and who also lost one of her twin boys, enumerated the issues that surface after the loss of an infant twin:

- The surviving twin can grow up feeling guilty that he/she survived, or feel unprotected by parents who weren't able to save the other twin.

- The living twin can feel the burden of being a constant reminder to his/her parents and relatives of the twin who didn't make it—especially if they're identical.
- Parents can feel overprotective of their surviving twin, even convinced that they'll lose that one, too. Or they can neglect the living twin because they are still mourning the dead one.
- Some parents feel robbed not only of their second child but of the specialness of being a parent of twins—all the attention, status, and adventure that would have conferred.
- Parents can feel strain in the marriage—especially if one parent feels the other is grieving too long or not enough.
- Finally: If a mother is depressed, says Pector, she's more likely to project some kind of depression onto her surviving twin, thinking, "Oh, my poor baby is so lonely—every time he stares into space, he's thinking about his twin." Pector herself couldn't help but read into her son's "uncanny awareness of his shadow," and his obsession with mirrors as a baby: "If he saw himself in a mirror at Kmart or Target, we couldn't get him away from it."

◦ ◦

Simon Mills, who lives in London, lost his identical twin, Nicholas, in 2004 to suicide. The Mills brothers were both serious heroin users and dealers, and the night of Nicholas's death, they had argued about the fact that Nick was still shooting heroin instead of smoking it (apparently, the former is more lethal), when suddenly Simon stormed out. He returned later, to find his brother asphyxiated by a shoelace he'd tied to a window ledge.

The Mills twins were cheerful, athletic boys who morphed into heroin junkies by age sixteen. After Nicholas's death at age twenty-six, their schoolteacher mom, Elizabeth Burton-Phillips, wrote a book about how she'd been an unwitting enabler: *Mum Can You Lend Me Twenty Quid?: What Drugs Did to My Family.* Simon helped write the book, he says, to make sure it was accurate; he felt it wouldn't help another family if it wasn't unsparingly true.

"We were doing a thousand dollars' worth of drugs a day and selling thirty thousand," he tells me on a long-distance call. He describes how they actually exploited their twinship to support their habit. "We used the whole identical thing to steal from shops: we'd have one of us going around to the alcohol counter, picking up a couple of bottles, making it look obvious, and then the other doing it less obviously, so the more obvious one *looked* like he was stealing, and then put the bottles on the counter right before he walked out. Just to confuse them."

When Simon buried his brother, he enclosed a poem he'd written, the last two lines of which read: "Please forgive me as I forgave you/As I know as a single I will always be two."

Simon is a member of the Lone Twin Network, based in Great Britain, which was founded by attachment therapist Joan Woodward, whose own twin died at three years old. In Woodward's book *The Lone Twin: A Study in Bereavement and Loss,* one of her central findings was not surprising: that losing a twin is "profound"—more so if the death was "traumatic" or when the twins were of the same sex.

But Woodward's more startling discovery was that those twins who described their loss as "severe" tended to have lost the other twin before the age of six months. Woodward attributed the heightened distress in those who lost their twin in infancy to the fact that the surviving twin had no speech to express and process grief. She also posited that the surviving infant twin would absorb a parent's devastation more enduringly.

Simon Mills has listened to these "twin survivors" in support groups, and he finds it hard to believe that the loss of a newborn twin could compare to his. "At the annual meeting, you'll have twins there who never even *met* their twins: Their twins died at birth, but they feel they're missing something. . . . They're not whole. I found it very difficult to deal with at first. I said, 'You never even knew them; I spent twenty-seven years, day in and day out, with Nick. How could you possibly know what I'm going through?" But the more you go to these meetings and the more you realize how disturbed these people are, whether it's a twin who died before birth or after, they're still there and they're still mourning."

In Kim Edwards's best-selling novel, *The Memory Keeper's Daughter*, a mother, Norah, talking to her husband, David, insists that their fraternal-twin boy surely misses the sister he lost at birth:

> "He can't possibly remember," David replied sharply.
> "Nine months," Norah said. "Growing heart to heart. How could he not, at some level?"

The trauma of early twin loss—as early as in utero—has garnered a certain legitimacy in recent years. No concrete science exists to support the psychological impact, but there is compelling anecdotal evidence that people who started out as one of a set of twins and ended up being born alone report similar feelings of loneliness, incompleteness, and fear of abandonment.

I heard Althea Hayton speak on the subject at the triannual International Twins Congress in Ghent, Belgium, in June 2007. Hayton, fifty-five when I meet her, is an Oxford graduate working as a social worker in Britain, and the editor of *Untwinned: Perspectives on the Death of a Twin Before Birth*. "I am, I think, a survivor of a twin pregnancy," she announces at the podium. "But I have absolutely no proof." She doesn't deny the lack of substantiation, but she puts more credence than most in the hundreds of personal testimonies she's collected.

"Until about twenty years ago and the development of pre-natal psychology," Hayton writes in her book's introduction, "it was generally assumed—if one thought about it at all—that there is no way a surviving twin would remember being with their twin in the first months of born life, let alone being in the womb with a co-twin who died early in pregnancy. . . . It stretches the imagination somewhat to learn that a dead twin, who was presumably never known to the survivor, can be the subject of a sense of grief and loss, but clearly this is the case, at least for some."

Hayton is imposing in person; tall and sturdy, with a gray helmet of hair, she speaks with a plummy English accent and great fervor. I felt like I was being instructed by a stern but compassionate governess as she explained her mission. "I'm using my own intuition and my own sense of my surviving-twin experience to try to establish a pattern or a characteristic response that sums up what I'm seeing, that I can then convey to people who've *not* lost a twin and haven't a *clue* what I'm talking about," she tells me. "I get no resistance from people who have lost a twin; they take it as completely normal. And then other people think I'm totally off the wall, that I must be completely mad."

Though Hayton's work is controversial, the founding premise is not: It's well established that one out of ten or eleven pregnancies begin as *twins*, but somewhere during the first trimester, one twin dies and is frequently absorbed in the uterus, essentially disappearing. (At the same conference, Dr. Jan Gerris, head of gynecology at the University of Ghent, puts the number of so-called vanishing twins at between 10 and 20 percent of pregnancies. Salvator Levi of Brussels's University Hospital found that, out of 6,690 women he examined, "71 percent of twin gestations diagnosed before ten weeks were singletons when delivered."

Often there is no physical trace of this nascent second life, but there can be indicators, such as unusual placentas or third-trimester bleeding. Hayton says she's even been told of "residue" of the lost twin being left in the womb—an additional finger, ribs, or "bits of bowel." (Twin Kay Cassill, a journalist and the author of *Twins: Nature's Amazing Mystery*, wrote, "The potential exists that such an undiscoverable twin *might* be hidden away within *any* singleton.")

"Even as early as the Greek and Hindu physicians," says cultural historian Hillel Schwartz, "they had found these remnants of the fetuses of one twin: 'fetus papyraceus'—the dry tissue that sometimes appears along with the afterbirth of one child; the assumption then was that it had been another twin that hadn't survived in the womb. And this was the biological origin of the notion of a vanishing twin: a twin who was there at some point but, even before birth, disappeared.

"But then in the 1970s, when they began using ultrasound in pregnancy, they discovered larger and larger numbers of fetuses whose evidence was clearly there in the first three or four months but who were never born. Eventually, they began to speculate that a third to a half of all conceptions are conceptions of twins—maybe even more, depending on whom you read."

When I was listening to Althea Hayton in Ghent, I suddenly remembered the day my own gynecologist pointed to a second black dot on the sonogram screen, early on in my first pregnancy. He said it could develop into a twin but that it might not. Sure enough, the next time we looked, it was gone.

"The loss of a twin in the womb does have a psychological effect on the survivor," Hayton asserted. "It's vague and difficult to talk about." Thanks to 350 questionnaires and scores of interviews, Hayton pieced together a psychological profile of a surviving twin:

1. Deep down, I feel alone, even when I am among friends (70%).
2. I have been searching for something all my life but I don't know what it is (64%).
3. I fear abandonment or rejection (62%).
4. I know I am not realising my true potential (62%).
5. All my life I have felt in some way "incomplete" (61%).

I have the strangest thought listening to her list: *She's describing my son, Benjamin.* It doesn't fit exactly—Ben is much more buoyant and sure-footed than those five statements suggest—but it does echo aspects of his personality: a fear of being lost or left, a conviction that he's not doing as well as he should be (even when he's excelling), a sense of being incomplete (that something's wrong, though he can't put his finger on what), and an awareness that he sometimes stands apart from the group, even when he's in the thick of it.

I called my husband, David, and read him Hayton's list. He was intrigued but not convinced; he thought Ben's traits could be due to the way he's wired and have nothing to do with a vanished twin—if, indeed, there ever was one.

At a cocktail party the evening of Hayton's talk, I cornered her to tell her about my son, and, not surprisingly, she thought my description confirmed what she'd heard so many times. "It sounds to me like he has all those characteristics," she said. "I've been given this information over and over again from people who say, 'This is how I feel,' who have a real sense of their twinship, and all they have is ultrasonic information. It says something about the twin bond, about the nature of consciousness. It says something about the nature of self. It is so huge that sometimes it takes my breath away. All I'm saying now is, 'Let's listen to these people's stories and just think for a second, *Is it possible—just remotely possible—that some of what they're saying has to do with the fact that they've lost a twin?*' And explore that. That's what I'm doing."

I ask if these self-identified "womb survivors" talk about anxiety, which has dogged Ben at times. "They're often fearful." Hayton nods. "But they don't know what of." That rings true for Ben. "And so they come across as shy." Ben used to. "And they get bullied." He did as a toddler. "And they worry about nothing." True of Ben. "And they feel guilty about absolutely nothing." True. "They're always apologizing." Also true.

Hayton can see that I register a familiarity with the personality she's describing. "Bless his little heart," she says sympathetically, which I half appreciate and half resent, because I don't like the presumption that Ben fits some prototype or thesis, especially one so unproven. "Do you know," she goes on above the cocktail hour din, "that Benjamin is the name I gave my *own* womb twin? I called him 'Ben' because if he had lived, he would have been the second son in the family, and Benjamin means 'the second son.' " She's referring to the fact that Benjamin in the Bible is the second son of Rachel and Jacob, but the name actually means "son of my right hand." "Maybe you unconsciously named him for his missing twin," Hayton ventures.

I can imagine readers rolling their eyes, so I challenge her.

"How do you handle people saying there's no science to support this? No data?"

"Well, there's data," Hayton counters. "There's plenty of data." She means the stories she's gathered. "All I can say is that this is the sixth version of the questionnaire I've done, and I'm getting the same top twenty results that I've had from the beginning. Some of the questions are new questions. Like the loneliness one—it goes straight to the top ten in one leap—and then the 'feeling different,' the searching, the feeling something's missing. I didn't invent that. People have been talking about that for years."

I push Hayton a little further: "When people tell you this is hogwash—that it's just convenient for people to say, 'So *this* is why I'm depressed!' or '*This* is why I feel lonely!'—how do you answer them?"

"I would say that there are so many different reasons that psychiatrists and psychologists throw at you to explain why you're lonely or depressed. They say you were abused as a child; they'll say you didn't bond with your parents; they'll say it's because you were adopted or went to boarding school; they'll say you were beaten by your father; they'll say you were transcultural and you don't know who you are. They'll throw thousands of different reasons at you about why you have a very poor sense of self, and then you don't believe any of them. You go from one therapist to the next and they tell you all this crap. Hallo! I said 'crap,' didn't I? I call it 'crap' because it's a completely reversed alternative perception."

Reversed alternative perception?

"Everyone's got it all upside down! It's got nothing to do with what happens after birth. It's what happened *before* birth that mattered! These people were *born* like this. Nothing has *made* them that way. They were born with a predisposition because they'd lost a twin. And then, if nasty things *also* happen later, like adoption or whatever, then they *really* suffer, in ways that other adopted children won't. So it's not the actual *events* of childhood that are distressing; it's your *response* to those events because of an earlier loss that shaped you. It's like your boy, Ben; should *you*, for example, lose your husband tomorrow, he'd be wrecked. Because he won't be able to handle death at all. Another kid would just be okay and say, 'So we'll get on with it, then.' But if you have a very sensitive, empathetic, intuitive kid who's picking up on pain everywhere, whenever a really bad event happens, he's completely squashed. Totally lost. So they come across as very vulnerable."

Does Hayton believe these twins *remember* their vanished twins in some way?

"Well, it's not in their memory," she replies. "It's a kind of imprinting. I call it 'the Dream of the Womb.' Because it's like a dream. It's in the deepest, darkest place in your mind, right at the very back. But it's also right at the very front. So you see the world through it. Everything is seen as the loss of your twin."

It's interesting to see that two of the OB-GYNs who specialize in twins and who clearly respect each other—obstetricians Louis Keith and Birgit Arabin—disagree on the legitimacy of "vanished twin syndrome." Whereas Keith heartily recommends Hayton's book (and wrote the introduction), Arabin is skeptical. "I don't think that any fetus will remember what has happened between weeks four and eight," she tells me. "Though there are paramedical psychoanalysts who think that you already felt pain at the conception. I heard a lecture once and I was really laughing—about 'conceptional pain.' So there are deep psychological experts who discuss it, but scientifically I doubt."

When I send Arabin an e-mail a year later to confirm her comments, she's quick to modify them. "I become older and more cautious," she writes. "Scientifically there is not (yet?) an explanation but God knows what might happen. . . . There is more than pure science between heaven and earth. Maybe the reasons that I myself chose to work with twins is because I was a member of an early twin— you never know."

Twins researcher Nancy Segal, however, is unequivocally dismissive: "There's no such thing as intrauterine knowledge of being a twin," she tells me. "I think that's just a misguided, romantic notion."

Hillel Schwartz refers in his book to Plato's Symposium on love, the philosophical dialogue that asserts that all human beings start as two: In it, Aristophanes gives a speech about how a double human was split by Zeus and doomed to seek his other half forever. "If it was true that initially all human beings were *conceived* as twins," says Schwartz, "but only some were *born* as twins, then all these people that are called 'singletons' must go through life aching for that complete companionship of a twin. But at the same time, they go through life with a terrible guilt. Because one way or another they were responsible for devouring the other twin in the womb."

If this premise were true—that we all start as twins but that most end up being born alone—I'm curious if Schwartz believes that the average person functions in the world as if he or she is missing a partner. "I don't think that the average person would explain it to you that way," he replies, "but if you would ask him what his ideals are for a partner, it always has to do with another half. Not someone diametrically different from you, but another half. This is probably not something people would have said in the sixteenth century; I think it's a relatively new romantic notion that there is another half that will perfectly match you."

Maybe that "romantic notion" of a perfect match is why I relate somewhat to the concept of a vanished twin. Robin is obviously (thank God) still around, but there's a sense in which her uncoupling has felt like a kind of disappearance, leaving me with some of the same feelings that Hayton describes: longing, incompletion. Robin told me in our interview, "You feel a hole sometimes." Maybe that gap is her: my "vanished" half.

David Teplica, a plastic surgeon in Chicago, is convinced that he lost his twin in utero. This became the genesis for an entire second career: He has spent twenty years photographing naked identical twins.

Teplica's black-and-white pictures, some of which are in collections such as that of the Chicago Art Institute, and one of which is the cover image for Wally Lamb's best-seller *I Know This Much Is True*, are unflinchingly close-up and intimate. The portraits feel more private than the typical side-by-side, 'Gee, can you believe how much they look alike!' twins photos.

One image shows two nude twin brothers, coiled around each other like they're still in utero. Another shows two eleven-year-old girls' faces—nose-to-nose, freckle-to-freckle; the sameness of their features is startling. Another is of two male twins biting parts of each other's faces.

Teplica is an elegant, slim man—a towering six three and a half, with slicked-back silver hair and sizable sideburns. He lives with his partner, Kalev Peekna, in a fifteen-thousand-square-foot mansion with stained-glass windows, a castle incongruously situated among modest row houses in downtown Chicago. "I had been doing twin research as part of my plastic-surgery world for about four years," Teplica explains as we settle ourselves into his attic studio. "And I was gravitating toward photographing twins pretty wildly. One day, the president of the foundation that was supporting my work"—the Center for the Study of Multiple Birth, run by Louis Keith—"came up to me and said, 'So why are you so interested in this stuff?' And I said, 'I don't know.' And he said, 'Why don't you ask your mother why you're so interested in twins?' And I said, 'I'm not going to ask my mother; that's ridiculous.' And he repeated, '*Why don't you go ask your mother?*'

"So the next time Mom was in town, I asked her. And she turned *white* and said, 'I never thought you'd hear this, but when I was pregnant with you, I was told that I was carrying twins. But then, in the fourth month, I started passing some clots and tissue, and in the end, only *you* were born.' This was before ultrasound, so there was no way of confirming that I was part of a miscarried twin pair at that point, but she probably miscarried my other half."

Teplica says this revelation filled in the blanks for him. "For a while I'd felt I was a freak, just obsessively diving into the twin issue. This validated things."

Teplica says his twin identification has played out mostly in his photography. He says he asks himself, "Am I yearning for a relationship I had for the first four months of my gestation? I don't know; I think that's a little bit of a stretch. But maybe. In fact, we do know—Louis and his brother, Donald Keith, published a study about the vanished twin syndrome: Eighty-five percent of single-birth people like me, who align themselves with twins, are from pregnancies where there was heavy bleeding in the fourth month. That's statistically significant. So it's likely that there is some brain chemical or anatomy thing sensing a need for a relationship like that." No such need has been scientifically established, but Teplica believes people who have lost a twin in utero feel incomplete in their adult life.

"I live it," he replies.

A photo titled *Ovum* captures nude twin sisters who happen to be waitresses at Hooters. "They were nervous as hell at first." Teplica smiles. "I said, 'Ladies, I'm gay.' They said, 'We're not worried about *you*. We don't want to be naked in front of each other.'"

I don't blame them. The thought of Robin and me naked and entwined together makes me flinch and blush. I can't fathom a situation in which I would feel comfortable doing that. Of course, on occasion we still see each other's bodies—in a clothing shop, for instance, if we're sharing a dressing room. But I wouldn't say our closeness translates to much physical interaction. It's odd to think I'd be so shy in front of Robin.

I ask Teplica why he insists that his twin subjects be naked. "Oh my God!" Teplica exclaims, as if to say, How could it be more obvious? "All the barriers are gone. It's like returning to the uterus. And the twins just relax. It might be awkward at first, but suddenly they cuddle, and do things they haven't done in thirty years. Then I get very *rich* stuff. Giggling and biting and punching and hair pulling—I've seen it all. For instance, two straight guys, twenty-one years old, training as actors in London, ask me if they can please just suck each other's thumbs because that's what they did for the first five years of life. Society would think that they're freaks, except that the photographs are lovely."

Teplica says the twins who pose for him have a comfort level together that goes back to the womb. "You're smashed against another living beast for nine months!" he exclaims. "It's not like they're floating around separately. *There's no extra space!* They're two tiny objects smashed against each other in one closed uterus. And the reason the uterus grows is because the smash becomes too tight, and it pushes the uterus out and stretches it over time. So for the entire pregnancy, these two little fetuses are cuddling. They're kissing and stroking and touching and urinating and playing with each other's faces and limbs and toes and holding hands. It all happens in there."

The final photo we discuss, *Reunion*, is the one most viscerally moving to me: Two newborns are suckling each other's noses. Teplica took the shot just minutes after the twins emerged from their mother; they'd been separated briefly for their newborn tests, then reunited in a bassinet. "I kind of postulated that they would recognize each other and instantly start clinging and coiling around each other," Teplica says. "So I was hovering over the bassinet as they placed the two twins into it, and the very first thing that happened was that one twin stuck its fist down the mouth of the other twin. As a physician, I was so shocked and worried that he would be suffocated or something that I did not push the camera shutter, and instead lurched toward them to try to see if I could get the fist out. But instantly the twin pulled its fist out, and they recognized each other—by this act, apparently—and started suckling each other's noses. So it's clear there was this thing that used to happen in the uterus, where they would stick their fists into each other's mouths and suckle each other's noses. And they realized they were back, reconnected with each other after having that very painful and traumatic time during delivery where they were separated, and then they were very peaceful after they were rejoined."

I ask how he felt personally—watching that. "It was pretty earth-shattering," he admits. "It also helped me validate my own obsession with twins, right? If there is this bond that happens in the uterus, and I can *prove* it, then I'm not crazy for having these feelings. So on a personal level, it meant everything to me."

Teplica's *Reunion* photo brings to mind the biblical twins Jacob and Esau and their reunion in Genesis after decades apart. When Jacob sees that Esau is arriving with an army, he assumes it's to exact revenge for his childhood theft of Esau's blessing from their father, Isaac. But Esau embraces and kisses his brother instead, and maybe even nibbles him. Los Angeles rabbi David Wolpe explains the nibbling: "In the Hebrew, there are these dots over the word *kissed,* and nobody knows exactly why they are there, but the rabbis suggest that Esau bit him, that he didn't just kiss him. He was aggressive."

Not aggressive, maybe, but, rather, instinctively affectionate: the prenatal impulse of one twin to connect with the other after such a long time apart.

⋄ ⋄

When I interviewed Kollantai and Pector in Ghent, each emphasized how little emotional vocabulary exists in American society for handling twin loss. It struck me that the antithesis is the Yoruba tribe in southwestern Nigeria, which every twins expert knows well because the tribe has the highest rate of fraternal twin births in the world: forty in every thousand births, compared to twelve in a thousand in the United States. (There is no clear cause of the high twinning rate, though many believe that the species of yam they eat has properties that enhance fertility.) Because there are so many twin births, and often twins are premature and underweight, there are inevitably frequent twin deaths; the Yoruba honor the dead twin with a statue called ibeji ("twins"), a carved wooden figure that the parents commission from a local artisan and which they honor and cherish, even going so far as to bathe, dress, and feed the statuette. The ibejis are not meant to be likenesses of the deceased newborns, but to represent their souls; the soul in the figurine is supposed to balance the soul of the living twin, which is considered in jeopardy.

"If one twin dies," explains Nike S. Lawal, professor in Harvard's Department of African and African American Studies, "parents have to do something for the remaining twin, some ritual so the one who died won't try to take the other twin along."

Every year, Yoruba mothers dance with their wooden twin effigies, singing songs they often write themselves. In an art book of ibeji photographs by George Chemeche, one of these songs is excerpted: "Twins-child, please do not leave me/Twins, please don't go away and leave me."

Dr. Louis Keith says that he and Donald do think ahead to the time when one may lose the other. "Of course it won't be easy," Louis says matter-of-factly. "I went to a funeral of a twin who was killed in a terrible accident. It was a Jewish funeral, and as they were getting ready to lower the body into the ground, the surviving twin started talking to his brother *through the wall of the coffin*. I was watching this very closely, because I knew I was able to see into it in a way that other people couldn't. I was thinking to myself, If my brother dies before me, I will only lose his physical body, because I will continue to talk to him. In the coffin, in the shower, wherever."

Donald agrees: "Our conversation started a long time ago," he says. "And it won't end when one of us is gone."

ABIGAIL: Who is more brave?

ROBIN: I guess me.

ABIGAIL: More private?

ROBIN: Me.

ABIGAIL: More hardworking?

ROBIN: Totally equal.

ABIGAIL: Body-conscious?

ROBIN: You.

ABIGAIL: Athletic?

ROBIN: Equal.

ABIGAIL: More sensitive?

ROBIN: You.

ABIGAIL: Emotional?

ROBIN: You.

ABIGAIL: Sentimental?

ROBIN: You.

ABIGAIL: Social?

ROBIN: You.

ABIGAIL: Argumentative?

ROBIN: You.

ABIGAIL: Political?

ROBIN: Equal.

ABIGAIL: Creative?

ROBIN: Equal.

ABIGAIL: Eager to please?

ROBIN: You.

ABIGAIL: Superstitious?

ROBIN: You.

ABIGAIL: Religious?

ROBIN: You.

ABIGAIL: Spiritual?

ROBIN: Me.

ABIGAIL: Generous?

ROBIN: I guess, you.

ABIGAIL: Ambitious?

ROBIN: Equal.

ABIGAIL: Impatient?

ROBIN: You. I've been working on it.

ABIGAIL: Shy?

ROBIN: Me.

ABIGAIL: Maternal?

ROBIN: Equal.

ABIGAIL: Who needs the other one more?

ROBIN: I guess you. But you don't know what's going on inside me.

ABIGAIL: Why don't you tell me?

ROBIN: Because if I needed you, I would tell you.

＊ ＊

9 SPLITTING THE DIFFERENCE:
WHEN IDENTICAL TWINS DIFFER

The study of twins is about the best natural experiment that we have in any aspect of human physiology or behaviour. If one is interested in the question of how important genes and environment are, you look at identical twins.

—Dr. Nick Martin, lab head of genetic epidemiology, Queensland Institute of Medical Research

In June 2008, a cheeky, athletic twenty-year-old twin from Gloucester, England, named Emily Blunt learned she had a rare bone cancer. Her identical sister, Kath, did not. One month later, Emily was dead. When the press first published her grim diagnosis, her twin, Kath, was quoted as saying, "I just feel so guilty. . . . We have always fought each other's battles—but this is one fight I cannot win for her. It leaves me thinking, 'Why did it happen to her and not me instead?' "

Why indeed?

One identical twin gets cancer and the other doesn't.

One gets Alzheimer's; the other doesn't.

One has schizophrenia; the other doesn't.

Same DNA. Different fates.

Twins provide the perfect storm to study disease because their identicalness highlights any difference. What "goes awry" in one case and not another?

Kathy Giusti, fifty when we speak, is an attractive Harvard Business School graduate with two school-age children. She used to be an executive at a pharmaceutical company, but now she is living with multiple myeloma, a rare blood cancer that afflicts fifty thousand Americans and which few survive. Her identical twin, Karen, a former attorney for *Time* magazine, doesn't have it. Since Kathy's diagnosis in 1996, she's become nationally renowned for creating a nonprofit organization that funds groundbreaking research. The Multiple Myeloma Foundation has raised $105 million and launched four FDA-approved drugs on the market in the last four years.

When I talk to Kathy on the phone, in July 2008, she has survived eleven years, despite being initially told she would die in three. "Telling my sister the diagnosis was devastating," Kathy recalls. "I think when you grow up as a twin, you believe the twin will always be there for you. I had to explain that I wouldn't be. I had already researched the disease; everything about it was 'incurable,' 'fatal,' 'only going to live two to three years.' By the time I made that phone call to Karen, I knew I was going to die. I said to her, 'You know I'm usually a fighter, but there's no hope with this disease.' She refused to accept that. She was like a pit bull, calling everyone she knew, doctors, sending articles, helping me figure out what my next step should be."

Karen not only used her contacts at Time Inc. to mount the first of many successful fund-raisers but she didn't hesitate to give Kathy her bone marrow for a transplant. They had to confirm they were identical—"We'd never known for sure," Kathy says—in order to make sure they were a match. "That moment was a turning point for me," Kathy tells me. "I thought, Okay, this is the most horrible thing that could have happened, but maybe there's hope."

Hope was an understatement. The transplant put her into "complete response," which means doctors can't find the cancer cells anymore. That doesn't mean the cancer is gone. "I can relapse anytime," Kathy explains. But for the time being, she's alive, feeling stronger, and thrilled to be able to watch her daughter's cheerleading squad and her son's all-star games. "With an incurable cancer, you always live your life on the edge," she explains. "I know that whatever I'm seeing could be the last time I ever see it. So I'm just happy watching any moment that's important to my family. Do I think my son will get into another all-star league? Yes. Do I think it will happen again in my life-time? No."

Kathy Giusti has no resentment that she was the twin who got sick, but she is curious about the biological or genetic reasons for it. "There are times when I say to myself, Something else must have happened to me," she says. "I do believe there are viruses—like mononucleosis—that happen to you along the way. Or I could have a weaker immune system. I tended to get sick more than Karen when we were kids."

When Kathy was first trying to entice researchers to study her cancer, she leveraged her twinship, knowing that scientists hunger for cases where identical twins are discordant for a chronic disease. But some doctors, according to Kathy, were initially reluctant about exploiting the information Karen carries inside her. "The last thing anyone wants is to take a healthy twin and make her sick," Kathy explains. She said that she and Karen had to convince researchers that they were not only willing to accept the risks but eager to do so. "It's one thing to create a foundation to fund the research," Kathy says. "But we wanted to *be* the research. I think twins care so much about each other, they're willing to do anything."

In 1997, Kathy moved to southern Connecticut to live near her sister, in large part because she wanted Karen close enough to help raise her two children, Nicole, then four, and David, then a year old. "If anything were to happen to me," she says, "I knew she would be there to help my husband, Paul. Karen and Paul are the two rocks in my life. I've needed to be strong for my children and for the foundation, but the people I can fall apart with are my sister and my husband. My sister is a great mom, and she has three phenomenal children, all incredibly close to my children." She adds a thought that chokes me up: In thinking about her inevitable absence, she was comforted by the assurance that her kids, Nicole and David, would continue to know her through Karen. "Because she's so similar to me," Kathy explains. "My kids see that Karen and I are different. But I always felt that if they wanted to know what their mom was like, they would know me by knowing her."

Dr. Thomas Mack's life's work has been centered around these kinds of cases—where one twin is chronically sick and the other isn't. He says identical twins tell a story others can't because they start the same genetically and when one diverges, the cause can often be traced. A towering, burly lumberjack of a seventy-two-year-old, Mack is dressed in suspenders when I meet him in Los Angeles. He graduated from Columbia Medical School, worked in Pakistan for the Centers for Disease Control, became a professor of epidemiology at Harvard's School of Public Health, and now teaches preventive medicine at the Keck School and USC/Norris Comprehensive Cancer Center.

Mack gives the example of Hodgkin's disease, which he and his wife, Dr. Wendy Cozen, have studied for years. "Someone years ago suggested the hygiene hypothesis," he tells me over a soda water in a loud Los Angeles restaurant, "which means the cleaner you are, the more you are at risk for certain diseases, including asthma and Hodgkin's." So Cozen suggested they ask twins which of them put more dirt in their mouths. "And we also asked about every other difference like that, which we could pick up between them. And it turns out that those are, in fact, pretty substantial determinants."

How can twins know who put more dirt in their mouths over a lifetime?

"Well, the nice thing about twins—are you a twin?"

I say yes.

"So if I asked you, 'Who put her thumb in their mouth more often when you were kids, you or your sister?' you'd know."

Robin did.

"See? We find that both identical twins agree as to which one did. So we tested that, decided it was a reliable determinant, and then looked at the one who did it more often."

The one exposed to fewer germs was more likely to get Hodgkin's.

So the dirtier you've been, the better off you are?

"Right. Now we haven't published that yet, but the evidence was fairly strong."

He found the same counterintuitive result with sun exposure and multiple sclerosis (MS): the more sun, the less chance of disease.

"If we're right that sunlight does, in fact, protect," Mack says, "and I don't know if we are right, because we don't know the mechanism by which it would happen, but if we're right, then because we know that MS is, in fact, a strongly familial disease—in other words if you have it, your kid has a four or five times increased risk of having it—then I'm going to tell you, 'Get your kid out in the sun.' Now I don't want to tell you to do that *too* much because I don't want you getting melanoma. But we know that the sun has both negative and positive aspects and you should get a little of the positive as well as the negative. Keeping that kid in the dark all the time is not a good idea."

I would have assumed that the identical twins in his MS study would have had similar sun exposure in childhood and thus would not have been helpful to test the hypothesis that more ultraviolet light means less chance of having MS. "Obviously, we wouldn't have learned what we did if there hadn't been some twins who were in the sun differently," Mack explains. "We only can use the twins when we're very sure there is a difference; one of them wanted to be on the beach all the time and the other one didn't want to. One of the other questions about MS when we started that study was, 'Could it be caused by a virus coming from dogs?' So we asked twins who slept with the dog the most. And we got very clear answers about that."

Mack has also studied lupus, childhood diabetes, breast cancer, and melanoma. He said the hardest part of his research is recruiting enough twins. He built his twin roster one twin pair at a time. "Years ago, I put an ad in the *Los Angeles Times*, asking for twins with chronic disease, and eighty pairs responded. I put an ad in the *Seattle Post-Intelligencer* and the *Des Moines Register* and I got exactly the same response. I received several grants and began putting ads in papers all over America. Over the long term—over the course of ten years, I got seventeen thousand pairs with chronic disease. If we could just get enough twins with a given disease, we could characterize their genome, and then look within pairs to see what the environmental exposures are by controlling the genome." In other words, look at two people who have the same genetic code and do detective work to track where their environments or exposures varied. That variance may tell you what caused the disease in one but not the other.

"But that's hard," Mack admits, "because it takes a lot of twins."

So is Mack saying that environment, not DNA, is ultimately the determinant of whether one gets sick?

"It's both," Mack states. "It's always both. And twins are the best single example of why that is necessarily true. There are going to be diseases—like some of the metabolic diseases—that are due to one single gene abnormality. For example, Tay-Sachs—the Ashkenazi gene: You will find twins who are concordant when that gene is present. But for almost all important diseases, twins are *not* concordant. For example, in Hodgkin's disease, twins are fifteen times as likely to be concordant—both affected—if they're identical. But that meant that most twins *weren't*—just ten pairs out of 350 twins were affected. So something else has to be responsible for all that other difference. And that's always the case."

The new frontier for understanding the mechanism behind discordance in twins is called epigenetics. The field is considered groundbreaking because its premise defies the conventional wisdom that genes dictate our destiny. Epigenetics tells us genes can actually be changed by environmental factors over the course of a lifetime. They can be turned on or off—expressed or repressed—based on our behaviors or exposures. *Epigenetics* literally means "on top of genetics": It's now widely believed that there is some force "above the genes"—chemical modifiers or "methyl groups" of hydrogen and carbon—that attaches to a chromosome and renders it dormant. Methylation can be instigated by environmental exposures, some of which include tobacco smoke, diesel exhaust, radioactivity, pesticides, bacteria, basic nutrients, and certain viruses.

"What it means," Mack explains, "is that the methyl group gets in the way of the function of the gene; it's like putting a cap on the gene. Tissues develop in different ways because some genes are turned off."

And environment is one force that can turn them off?

"It must be," Mack replies. "Because we know that differences between identical twins become greater as they get older." In other words, the longer Robin and I live, and the more our habits, vices, behaviors, or environments diverge, the greater the differential impact on our genes. Mack makes sure I understand how the term *environment* is used by scientists: "When we say, 'environment,' we mean 'everything *but* genetics.'"

Identical mice have been the involuntary pioneers for this science. In one 2006 experiment led by Eric J. Nestler at the University of Texas Southwestern Medical Center in Dallas, researchers put small, genetically identical mice in a confined space alongside larger, aggressive, mean mice—bullies—and watched how the smaller mice reacted. (The model is actually—hilariously, I think—called "social defeat.") While some of the identical small mice became cowering, anxious, and depressed, interestingly, some of the small mice stood their ground. To oversimplify: For those mice who became depressed, the intimidation had a chemical effect, deactivating the genes that normally make a mouse resilient. So theoretically, if one could prevent that chemical change, or counter it once it has occurred, those "defeated" mice would not have been so flustered by the bullies. That is what conventional antidepressants are supposed to do: counter dejection. Though drugs may not prevent it—"social defeat" still takes root—scientists can counteract it, emboldening the mouse.

Even more intriguing is that the effects of the intimidation on the relevant genes—even if the behavior is mitigated successfully by a drug—may still be passed on to the next generation. The genes may have been altered in such a way that the behavioral traits get inherited. A monthly journal on how the environment affects human health, *Environmental Health Perspectives*, called a similar 2005 report "startling" because it suggested "that epigenetic changes may endure in at least four subsequent generations of organisms."

Psychiatrist Peter Kramer, who wrote *Listening to Prozac* and writes a regular blog on *Psychology Today*'s Web site, said the bully mouse study shows "how adversity might reach inside the brain and scar the gene within the nerve cell. The research also points toward a medically exciting, if ethically complex, future in which traumatized people might be restored to the neurobiological state of their resilient twins."

One rat study in 2004 demonstrated that it's not just chemicals or foods that influence a gene's expression; affection, or the lack of it, may also have an impact. The experiment, conducted at McGill University, in Montreal, found that rats who were not licked and groomed by their mother as often as their siblings went on to exhibit more stress. Dr. Moshe Szyf and his colleagues discovered that the mom's neglect had the effect of *turning off* the rats' stress-mitigation response, thus spiking their anxiety levels. Rats that weren't licked as babies ended up with methylation on a particular gene that normally produces a coping brain receptor. "The offspring of the high-licking moms exhibited better response to fear," explains Dr. Szyf, who headed the research.

The trauma from maternal disregard was not irreversible: Drugs could bump off the methyl group, change the gene's activity, and reduce a rat's stress. In an e-mail to me, Szyf explained that derailing the methylation—which had muzzled the gene in the first place—allowed the rat to get a grip and cope.

In the summer of 2005, a research group led by Manel Esteller at the Spanish National Cancer Center in Madrid, found that out of eighty sets of identical twins, 35 percent of the pairs differed from each other epigenetically, and the older the twins were, the less identical. Those who had spent the most years living in different places with different lifestyles showed the greatest DNA differences, more proof that epigenetic differences can account for why one identical twin gets a disease and the other doesn't. For example, both twins may start with the same genes that normally battle tumors, but one twin's tumor-fighting DNA is rendered impotent by an epigenetic change, and that twin ultimately gets cancer.

I asked Dr. Mack how he would counsel my sister, for instance, if I were diagnosed with breast cancer. "I can actually reassure her," Mack replies. "I would tell you that it would be more likely than not that she would never get breast cancer, but she would have a substantially higher risk than an ordinary person. It still would be less than fifty percent. Fifty percent refers to lifetime risk. But if most women have a twelve percent chance, she might have as high as a forty percent chance. So it's substantially higher than the average person but still less than fifty percent."

Mack urges me to put in perspective the studies that say identical twins prove certain diseases are inheritable just because they're found to be more alike for disease than fraternal twins. "Almost always conveniently, these studies omit the fact that identical twins tend to consciously adopt similar behavior," Mack cautions, "and therefore have the same exposures not because of specific parts of the genome but because commonality of the entire genome makes them identify with and therefore copy each other."

I tell Mack that the following day I'm scheduled to meet his compatriot, biologist Dr. Eric Vilain, a professor of human genetics based at UCLA's David Geffen School of Medicine, who is applying epigenetics to the question of homosexuality—what makes one identical twin gay and the other straight? He and Mack are on similar quests, except where Mack is deconstructing predictions of disease, Vilain is trying to crack sexual orientation. "To me, he's trying too many possibilities," Mack says bluntly. "I think it's a long shot. If it really works, in the sense that I mean it, it's going to be a revolution—because we will know the biologic basis for homosexuality, or one of them. And if it's epigenetic, well, we know we can influence epigenetics, so in theory, we could influence homosexuality. For example, if you eat a lot of broccoli when you're little, and you get a lot of folic acid, you may have different epigenetic patterns than if you don't. Well, so in theory, if you think a kid is susceptible to homosexuality, you might change eating habits to impact the genes. Now that's pie in the sky. It's predicated on Eric being right—substantially right—and everything falling into order, so I don't think that will really happen. But let's give it a shot. Because I think a lot of gay people really want to know why."

Dr. Vilain is a youthful forty-one-year-old Parisian with wide-set eyes and the pale skin of a scientist who doesn't leave the laboratory much. We talk in his sunny, cramped office, sitting side by side next to his blondwood desk and built-in bookshelf; glancing at the wall behind him, I notice indecipherable equations scrawled on a dry-erase board. He has a thick French accent and speaks in a hurry. "I only became interested in sexual orientation a few years ago. I'm not a twins researcher. We've just started using twins recently because we think it's a great hypothesis to test the idea that epigenetic/environmental influences are important in behavior. . . . We're asking the question, 'Do we see a difference in genes being turned on or off between co-twins who have opposite sexual orientation?' " In other words, is something activating or deactivating certain genes that results in homosexuality?

"People will say, 'Are you studying the gay gene?' " Vilain asks the question for me. "No. We're studying the gene that makes people attracted to either males or females. So in many respects, we're study-ing the *straight* gene; we're just using gay individuals as a model."

Does he think it's ultimately going to turn out to be one gene or a confluence of genes that is responsible for sexual preference?

"We don't know," Vilain replies frankly. "It's probably a conflu-ence, and it becomes more complicated because of the environment influences. Right now, it's still a very poorly studied area. There are several levels of evidence that homosexuality has some genetic influ-ence. The first evidence was actual twins studies—not *genetic* twins studies, just *traditional* twins studies." He means the studies in the early 1990s by Dr. J. Michael Bailey and Dr. Richard Pillard, who looked at identical and fraternal twins and tested whether homosexu-ality is genetically determined. If it is, then both identical twins should be gay if one twin is, while fraternal twins should differ more often because they share only half their genes. They found that if one identical twin is gay, the other has a 50 percent chance of also being gay; if one twin is fraternal, the other twin has a 20 percent chance of also being gay.

Vilain explains how these results argue both for and against the notion that homosexuality is genetic: "You could say, 'Well it's *only* fifty percent; if one twin is gay, the other twin is going to be gay in only fifty percent of the cases. That means it's *not* genetic.' But of course you have to hold this thought a moment, because you also have to think, Wait a second; if it was all *environmental*, then it wouldn't make any difference if it was a fraternal twin, and the frater-nal twins would *also* be at fifty percent concordance. But they're not. They're systematically *less*."

Months earlier I'd interviewed psychologist Dr. J. Michael Bai-ley—the researcher whom Vilain cites as pioneering the first gay stud-ies—in his Chicago apartment, a small walk-up with cloudy windows, an olive green rug, and the bachelor's requisite leather couch. Bailey, in his mid-fifties, was wearing jeans, loafers without socks, and wire-rimmed glasses. When I inquired as to whether he is a twin or gay himself, he said he is neither. Divorced and the father of two children, he was formerly chairman of the psychology department at Northwestern University, and obviously bruised from an onslaught of criticism of his 2003 book on transgender people, *The Man Who Would Be Queen: The Science of Gender-Bending and Transsexualism*, which was unrelated to twins.

In the two landmark twin studies Bailey shepherded—one that recruited gay twins through newspaper advertisements, one that made use of the Australian database of twins—the concordance rate (meaning both identical twins were gay) was, as mentioned, 50 percent in the first study, between 20 and 25 percent in the second. Bailey puts more stock in the lower concordance rate: "Most of the time a gay identical twin is going to have a straight twin," he asserted. "At least seventy-five percent of the time, maybe more. It's even higher in fraternal twins. So basically, if you meet an identical twin who is gay, the chances are his twin is straight. And that is surprising to a lot of people."

Of those pairs where one twin was gay, one not, Bailey said, "The twins both recalled the differences emerging in childhood. The gay twin was more gender nonconforming than the straight twin. So if it's a male pair, then the gay twin is more feminine; the gay twin is closer to the mom, the straight twin is a little closer to the dad—that kind of thing."

The credence he gives to gender stereotypes may make some people bristle. I was raised by a feminist who would strongly object to the premise that one kind of behavior is "normal" for boys or girls, but Bailey unapologetically contends that stereotypes have emerged because they're based in truth. "I've only met a few discordant twin pairs in the flesh—that is, meeting both the gay twin and the straight twin—and the ones whom I met are somewhat consistent with that picture even in adulthood: You can tell them apart. The gay one seems gayer than the straight one. There's a lot of skeptics who say, 'Well, is the straight one really straight?' and I don't doubt there are cases where he's not. But usually I suspect he is."

Bailey believes "gender nonconforming" behavior is a clue to the fact that homosexuality is ingrained early on—not "learned" or "acquired" later. "I've had several mothers who've seen articles about my research, contacted me, and said they have identical twin pairs in which one twin from early on is totally feminine, wants to be a girl, where his identical twin brother is a typical boy. I feel confident that when these children become adults, the very feminine one is going to be a gay man and the other twin is going to be a straight man. So what kind of things can make twins like that? The mothers deny that they're treating each child differently. . . . So I've always suspected that the cause of this difference is some sort of innate environmental influence. It means that it's not caused by social treatment, but it is *within* the individuals, that this difference was probably present at birth. Now what kind of things can cause differences like that before birth? I'm very curious; I think it's a huge, important question, but I don't have many good ideas. I think that this is one of the key questions in psychology and biology. We know that profound biological differences can arise in twins before birth." (These differences can be caused by a disparity in circulation and oxygenation, infectious agents, drugs, chemicals, trauma in utero. Some variations in identical twins—such as their fingerprints, which aren't the same—are explained by conditions in the womb and the position of the fetuses.)

So, whether the concordance rates between identical twins are 50 percent or 20 percent, the bottom line seems to be that, when it comes to homosexuality, it's not genetics.

Bailey corrected me: "You can't say, 'It's not genetics.' You can say, 'It's not *completely* genetics. If it was completely genetics, identical twins would always be alike."

Can you then say "It's not nurture"?

"I would say, 'It's not nurture in the case of men,' " Bailey replied. "We have been doing research on sexual orientation and sexual arousal, and I think for men, sexual orientation is precisely a directed sexual arousal pattern: Men are gay because they get more sexually aroused by men than by women. Women get sexually aroused by both men and women, no matter what their sexual orientation. It's possible that women don't have a sexual orientation, although they clearly have strong preferences for one sex or another, but it's not clear that it's caused by anything that is like what causes men to have preferences. It's a hot topic now in psychology that women are more flexible in their sexuality, that they're more changeable in their lifespan. . . . So it's very plausible to me that there is a role for nurture in sexual preference. Our results also suggest that there's a role for genes, as well."

Vilain says his biggest obstacle in continuing the research now is gathering enough twins and enough financial support. "I think there is some reluctance to fund this issue," he says.

Because people are politically invested in the findings?

"Right. Some gay activists say it's wonderful that you found something genetic, because it proves sexuality is involuntary, and so gays should have the same civil rights. Others say that sets up the stage for selective abortions. And now what we're looking at is even a little more complicated, because if it *is* environment changing biology, it's the nature/nurture debate at its worst."

But I thought the "environment" that researchers are investigating does not mean "Your mom overprotected you, which made you gay."

"It's not," Vilain replies hesitatingly, "but I don't know that for a fact. It could be a little bit."

Even something like a hovering mother could impact the genome?

"Well, the mouse study of the mother's grooming *did* impact the genome," he points out, referring to the Canadian rat study.

I'm curious as to what he thinks the implications would be if he finds "the answer" as to which genes—or which epigenetic events— "cause" homosexuality.

"First of all it would be fascinating to show for the first time that there is, in humans, an epigenetic influence in behavior. This behavior—whom we're attracted to—is fundamental behavior, essential for human survival. It's also a very dichotomous behavior: You're either attracted to males or to females. As a biologist, I think it would be a fascinating finding. Hopefully it will tell us which part of the genome is implicated. Whether I want it or not, there will be social implications. Even the way we look at evolution. People ask, 'Why does the gay gene survive?' Well, I don't know why it stays on. Maybe this will give us a clue. There are all sorts of ideas out there why it keeps popping up in each generation. . . . Other social consequences? I really think it's going to go in all directions. And people are going to take what they want to hear."

Vilain's intuition is that the environmental catalyst for homosexuality does occur before birth, not after, for the same reason Bailey cited: that gay boys seem feminine so early on. "The only reason why I think it's more likely to be prenatal than it is to be postnatal is because of children who are highly gender nonconforming," Vilain tells me. "We know that these children become gay. It's very highly predictive. And in all the cases that I know of and all the cases that have been studied, it's not like the homosexuals' environment has been different from their brothers' and sisters'; it's really not. So something is going on very early on—as early on as age three. So that's why my hunch—I can't prove it, but my hunch is it's prenatal."

In February 2008, a new study peeled back another layer to reveal why identical twins might differ in health: Their DNA isn't as alike as we thought. Scientists at the University of Alabama at Birmingham and at universities in Sweden and the Netherlands found "copy number variations" in twins—meaning that one twin might be missing a segment of DNA or might have *more* copies of that segment than his or her twin. It's possible that these disparities are to blame when one twin gets a disorder and the other doesn't. Jan Dumanski, a coauthor of the study, told the *New York Times,* "When we started this study, people were expecting that only epigenetics would differ greatly between twins. . . . But what we found are changes on the genetic level, the DNA sequence itself."

If epigenetics and womb environment explain why identical twins end up with divergent medical histories or sexualities, can it also explain the differences in personality?

Studies of twins reared apart, conducted at the University of Minnesota in the 1990s, found the most telling evidence for what does or does not differentiate identical twins from one another. Dr. Thomas Bouchard's team found, after exhaustive interviews with twins who had been separated early and then reunited in adulthood, that identical twins who'd grown up in different homes were just as alike as identical twins who had been raised together. *Just as alike:* similar habits, tastes, predilections, strengths, vices. Their different parents, homes, towns, schools, and luxuries had a negligible effect on who they became. Which means that identical twins are destined to turn out similarly (though not identically), no matter who their parents are. That tells us that genetics generally carry the day, or at least pack a significant punch when it comes to "every measured behavioral trait," as Nancy Segal puts it, "such as religious interests, social attitudes, vocational interests, job satisfaction and work values. This research has truly affected the way we think about our own abilities, shortcomings and potentialities. . . ."

"It tells you that the *specifics* of parenting are not as important as we thought," says Dr. Bouchard, who is now semiretired and lives part of the year in Colorado. "What's making twins similar is largely their genes. That seems to be what the data tells us. . . . We're not saying environment is unimportant, but, by golly, 'environment' includes a lot of things that aren't what parents are doing."

The idea that parenting is basically irrelevant in the end is so counterintuitive, it's difficult to absorb; Bouchard himself concedes that his team's findings have been "controversial," especially among developmental psychologists who believe parental influence is decisive. I'd certainly like to think my child-rearing style matters. "You are obviously important," says Bouchard, "but the fact is, I could take a different mother and put her in your place and your kids would probably turn out the same. As long as we're taking abuse out of the equation, most mothers provide an adequate nurturing environment, and these environments are practically substitutable."

Segal, who worked with Bouchard in Minnesota, underscores his point in her book: "Children's achievements might still be the same even if they were raised by different parents in different settings as long as their best abilities were encouraged and their emotional development supported." She says the evidence for this theory is in the twins reared in different homes. "In my view, the most remarkable outcome of all is that, despite the many factors creating intellectual differences between twins, the intelligence test scores of identical twins still turn out to be so alike." She adds later, "The bottom line is that living together does not make people in a family alike and that similarities are explained primarily by shared genes."

Does this mean that DNA is destiny? In his 1997 book, *Twins: And What They Tell Us About Who We Are*, journalist Lawrence Wright captured how unsettling that idea can be. "Twins threaten us because they undermine our notion of identity. We think we are who we are because of the life we have lived. We think we shape the character and values of our children by the way we raise them. We think that we are born with the potential to be many things, and to behave in an infinite variety of ways. . . . But when we read about twins who have been separated at birth and reunited in middle age only to discover that in many respects they have become the same person, it suggests that life is a charade. . . . The science of behavioral genetics, largely through twin studies, has made a persuasive case that much of our identity is stamped on us from conception; to that extent our lives seem to be pre-chosen—all we have to do is live out the script that is written in our genes."

Separated identical twins turn out the same not just because they have similar traits but also because they make similar choices. Genes don't just impact how we look and act; they prompt us to *select* certain paths or behaviors. They inform whom we marry, whether we fight with them, whether we drink too much, work hard, the names we give our dogs, which raincoat we buy. The likenesses of twins are, therefore, not just wired into us but also *constructed by us* over time as we go through life making similar decisions, responding similarly to situations, people, and events, prompting similar reactions from people, which then shape those relationships similarly.

According to some experts, identical twins reared apart turn out to be *more* similar than those raised together because twins in the same household work harder to distinguish themselves. Bouchard disagrees: "I think that's wrong. Twins reared apart were *just as* alike as twins reared together, not *more* alike. And those twins who grew up under the same roof may or may not look to differentiate themselves." He stresses that the reason identical twins reared together turn out similarly, if they do, is not necessarily because their parents treated them the same; that, in fact, twins reared in the same home will probably be treated differently depending on their personality. What's more, the term *identical* biases us in the first place. "There's a tendency for you to think you were more alike than you probably were," he tells me.

If the similarities between me and Robin can be chalked up primarily to our genes, it seems environment is responsible for our distinctions. Environment is life experience, everything nongenetic that impacts us, including a formative friendship, a powerful teacher, a thwarted romance, a scary accident, a memorable trip—everything, in other words, but our parents. And the most critical environmental influence that differentiates twins (and, in fact, all of us) may actually be our peers.

That was the surprising thesis that Judith Rich Harris put forth in her groundbreaking 1998 book, *The Nurture Assumption*. Her basic finding, after combing through every existing bit of research, was that peers are the missing link in understanding child development. *They* shape who we become. "Experiences in childhood and adolescent peer groups modify children's personalities in ways they will carry with them to adulthood," Harris writes in her book, which was a 1999 Pulitzer finalist. "Children learn about themselves by comparing themselves to their groupmates. They vie for status within the group; they win or lose. They are typecast by their peers; they choose or are chosen for different niches. Identical twins do not end up with identical personalities, even if they are members of the same peer group, because they have different experiences within the group."

Harris, a sixty-eight-year-old grandmother of four and former writer of textbooks about developmental psychology, in effect upended Freudian orthodoxy when, without an advanced degree or academic title, she immersed herself in virtually every child development study and concluded that there is zero scientific evidence that parents are our authors, role models, or puppeteers. Journalist Malcolm Gladwell deftly conveyed the shock of Harris's findings when he wrote about her in *The New Yorker* in 1998:

> If the example of parents were important in a child's development, you'd expect to see a consistent difference between the children of anxious and inexperienced parents and the children of authoritative and competent parents, even after taking into account the influence of heredity. Children who spend two hours a day with their parents should be different from children who spend eight hours a day with their parents. A home with lots of books should result in a different kind of child from a home with very few books. In other words, researchers should have been able to find some causal link between the specific social environment parents create for their children and the way those children turn out. They haven't.

"The child's parents and siblings (along with his genes) influence the way the child behaves at home," Harris tells me in an e-mail. "Other people—especially peers—influence the way the child behaves outside the home."

Reading Harris's conclusions felt like cracking the case for me personally. When I think about what marked the fork in the road for me and Robin, why she's reserved and I'm gushy, why she cares less about being liked and I care way too much, it rings uncannily true that our peer groups—friends who are, for the most part, long gone from our lives—made all the difference. Surely I can credit those merciless years of seventh and eighth grade—when my life was like an after-school special, when I was rarely at the center of the action and had one precious friend who was unapologetically uncool—for making me seek too much approval from the "in" crowd, even now.

And Robin was almost certainly imprinted by those years when she entered a new school late (tenth grade) and had to break into established cliques, warm up to students who simply weren't as warm, find a niche despite the fact that her interests didn't match the majority's.

Mom recalls the changes in both of us: "You were full of self-doubt," she tells me, "and easily deflated." And about Robin, she says, "She used to be much more of an open book, more vulnerable and expressive, but she eventually got defended and distrustful. Along the way, somehow she learned that she couldn't just be herself and thrive in that school."

I ask Ms. Harris for her take on my own situation: "I think all the things you described for you and Robin—different sorts of groups, and different experiences within these groups—played a role in widening the differences between you."

And the differences led us here, to where we both have some sense of deficit: I want more of us; she needs more of herself. The peer theory might indeed explain the outcome—why I, who handled my adolescent disquiet by connecting with others, should feel so betrayed when Robin disconnects; and why Robin, who withdrew from others in acquired distrust, now challenges herself to "claim" new relationships, while pulling away from her oldest friend.

THE RESULTS ARE IN:
TWIN STUDIES

Aggression: mostly genetic

Alcohol dependence among adolescents: largely environmental

Alcoholism: identical twins 50 percent concordant; fraternal twins 28 percent concordant

Alcohol use: mostly genetic

Allergies: mostly genetic

Alzheimer's: 80 percent genetic

Anorexia: mostly genetic

Antisocial behavior with psychopathic tendencies (lack of empathy, remorse): largely genetic

Anxiety: moderately inheritable

Attention deficit disorder: mostly inheritable

Attitudes toward sex and religion: more environmentally influenced than genetic

Autism: identical twins between 80 and 90 percent concordant

Back pain: mostly genetic

Baldness: mostly genetic

Bipolar disorder: identical twins more concordant

Cholesterol: mostly genetic

Cocaine abuse: Identical twins are more concordant than fraternal twins.

Cognitive abilities: Identical twins are more concordant than fraternal twins.

Communication: Identical twins who stay more in touch live longer than identical twins who don't.

Criminality: Identical twins are more concordant for property crimes (theft, vandalism) than fraternal (not necessarily true for violent crime, however).

Depression: strong genetic component

Extroversion: strong genetic link

Happiness: 50 percent genetic

IQ: Identical twins are more similar to each other than fraternal twins and become more alike in intelligence as they age. Dr. Nancy Segal cites the finding that "identical twins are nearly as alike in IQ as the same person tested twice."

Job choice: Identical twins choose more similar careers than fraternal twins.

Job salaries: A married twin makes more money than his or her unmarried twin (also true of nontwin siblings).

Left-handedness: more frequent among identical twins

Loneliness: 50 percent of identical twins and 25 percent of fraternal twins shared similar characteristics.

Menopause: happens earlier among twins

Moliness: mostly genetic

Multiple sclerosis: mostly genetic

Nearsightedness: mostly genetic

Obesity: Lifestyle, more than genes, impacts insulin-resistance and thus obesity.

Phobias: more likely to be concordant in identical twins than fraternal twins—therefore presumably genetic

Sleep patterns: Identical twins are more similar than fraternal.

Sleepwalking: substantial genetic effects

Smoking: between 50 and 70 percent genetic

Social life: The identical twin who has a tight-knit social circle is in better overall physical health than the one who doesn't.

Stuttering: mostly genetic

Voting behavior: Identical twins are more similar than fraternal twins.

10 CRUEL DNA: THE LORDS

Twins with the same DNA can have different fates. But sometimes DNA encodes a common heartbreak.

Identical twins Charlie and Tim Lord assumed that The Big Coincidence in their twinship would be that they had fallen in love with—and married—two college roommates who were best friends. They could never have guessed that they would also share in common a devastating event: Within six months, each lost a baby.

It's the fall of 2006 and Charlie and Tim Lord are sitting in my living room in New York, looking handsome and disconcertingly duplicate. Lanky and sandy-haired, they're sipping glasses of diet Coke. Tim lives just blocks away from me on the Upper West Side, with his wife, Alison, and their two grade school–age daughters, Annie and Mary. Charlie is visiting from Boston, where he lives with his wife, Blyth, and their two daughters, Taylor and Eliza.

As we start talking, I make my first mistake, asking Tim if he had any misgivings about attending the same college as his twin brother. "I didn't," he replies, correcting me. "I went to Brown." Oh, right. Twenty years after college, I'm still convinced that Tim was also in my Yale class, when, in fact, only Charlie was. Probably it's because Tim visited so often.

I do remember thinking the Lord boys were interchangeably winning in those days: Rangy and smart, with a kind of poetic aspect, they exuded a kind of authenticity and kindness. But the truth is, I never got to know them all that well, as my early fumble clearly shows.

The Lords grew up in various countries because their father opened pharmaceutical plants for Squibb, then switched to being a school headmaster, first in Ohio, then in Baltimore, then in Washington. Their mother, a teacher specializing in art history, taught at Washington's Sidwell Friends School.

"One of my first memories at age four is of being just walloped in the playground when we were living in Guatemala City," Tim recalls.

"I was trying to get to you and they were holding me down," Charlie adds.

"The two of us tried to protect each other," Tim continues. "There was this intense realization even then that it doesn't really matter what all else is going on, because the two of us are a team."

The Lord boys were never dressed alike, but Charlie often wore brown so friends and relatives could tell them apart by remembering the comic-strip character Charlie Brown. Tim wore blue.

The Lords say they can't distinguish themselves in childhood pictures. "I actually pretend I can," Tim admits. "Like when I'm with my daughter, I'll make something up, just because it's too weird not to know yourself in a picture."

The Lord parents didn't do cutesy, twinny things with the boys, but Tim admits, "They did some stuff that was a little icky."

Like what?

"We had to perform a song together at one of their cocktail parties." He remembers the lyrics: " 'Everybody knows I look just like my brother, but I just want to be me.' It was a rewrite of something."

They shared the same room, same birthday party. Charlie says sometimes they had to share a present.

"I don't remember that; really?" Tim is incredulous.

Charlie nods. "There was only one plastic Tarzan knife with a sheath and we had to take turns."

Tim recalls fighting over clothes. Both agree that they were not fashionable youngsters.

"We were not well dressed," says Charlie.

"We were not well groomed." Tim laughs.

I ask them about their earliest awareness of being twins.

"I do remember actually realizing that not everybody had one," Charlie says, "but then feeling sorry for the people that didn't. I had a realization when I was probably six or seven that not everybody had this person whom they were *this* close to and whom they played with all the time."

"And later, I just remember that distinct feeling of 'I'm at my most relaxed and happy when the two of us are together,'" says Tim.

"I don't have a memory that doesn't include you," Charlie interjects.

They will do this a lot—step on each other's sentences—but neither seems to mind. In fact, they seem used to relying on one another's memories to tell a complete story.

"It's very interesting, as you get older," Tim continues. "Because you absolutely love that you have this great closeness, but sometimes it's almost scary." He turns to look at Charlie. "Sometimes it's one of those weird things when you don't let people see that, because it's almost too much for people to understand."

What exactly does he hide?

"How totally close you are," Tim answers. "You do reveal it when it's just the two of you. But when you're out and about, you don't necessarily share it."

I remember that impulse: to downplay our connection in public, so that people didn't feel there was some impermeable fence around us. I know some friends still felt there was no getting close to our closeness.

"I don't remember anyone being frustrated by our friendship," Charlie says, "but I do know that my closest friends in the world recognize that my relationship with Tim is in a totally different category."

I ask how they each deal with being mistaken. Robin has a much lower tolerance than I do. "I went through a phase where I really couldn't be bothered with people who mixed us up." Tim laughs almost apologetically. "I'd just say, 'I'm not Charlie,' and walk away."

Charlie, on the other hand, was never irked by being confused; he says he knows a mile away when it's about to happen. "I know the Look," he says. "And if I see the Look—the perplexed look—I always go up and say, 'You must think I'm my twin brother.' But there's plenty of times when I don't see the person noticing, and people have later said, 'Why didn't you say hi to me?' "

"I had one incident recently," Tim chimes in, "where a woman came flying down a subway car, and I said to the two guys I was talking to, 'You're about to see a Twin Moment.' They said, 'What's that?' And I said, 'Just watch.' The woman threw her arms around me. So now, she was going to be embarrassed not only about the fact that she got the wrong twin but that she'd given me this big hug. I said, 'I'm not actually Charlie; I'm his twin brother.' People's faces just rearrange. Because there's a reality shift."

I tell them that it can be particularly awkward for me when an acquaintance at a cocktail party compliments me on my writing in the *New York Times*, where Robin is a reporter. It's not that I can't accept the praise on her behalf; it's that the person usually looks stricken when I explain that the *Times* writer is my twin, and tries to recover by quickly offering me a similar compliment. Except that they don't necessarily know what I do. And if they have to ask, it makes them feel even worse when I tell them I'm a writer, too. They clearly think they've hurt my feelings because they don't know what I've written. So then they *ask* me what I've written, and suddenly I'm in the pathetic position of having to recite my résumé so that they feel better about having made me feel bad, which they truly haven't. If they only knew how many times I've endured this particular moment; it's fleeting but strained every time. So nine times out of ten, when someone compliments the *Times* articles I haven't written, I just say, "Thank you so much," and head for the bar.

Charlie recognizes this scenario. "There will be people in my parents' life," Charlie says, "who remember us vaguely by—'There's the twin who's an actor [Tim] and then there's the one who does . . . Something else.' " (They both run nonprofits at the time we talk.)

Charlie recounts how painful it was years ago when Tim seemed to be on top of the world, studying acting at San Francisco's prestigious American Conservatory Theater, while Charlie was floundering in law school, unsure whether he wanted to be a lawyer.

"That was the hardest time," Charlie tells him. "The one time that we were each at very different places."

Did they talk about it?

"We didn't really." Charlie seems surprised to say it.

"In some ways, that was probably the least communicative we've ever been." Tim nods. "It was too weird to have a moment where I was worried about you, where I couldn't help you."

They do this a lot during their interview: address each other instead of me, really look at each other, without self-consciousness. It's noticeable because it's so relaxed, and even tender.

"That Christmas I was in this really dark time of not knowing what I wanted to do. And here's the funny part: To exacerbate the whole thing, I evaluated every Christmas present—probably, I think, rightly—through this lens of 'Tim is the California Cool Actor Guy and my parents don't really know what to do with me. And then of course Tim got cool luggage and I got a matching set of Samsonite." They both laugh.

"It's a family story we tell to this day, about the time Charlie kicked over the Samsonite, yelling, 'What do they think I am? Some little uptight fucking guy?' "

Alison Lord (née Smith) remembers meeting Charlie back at Yale in 1986. "He seemed cute, smart and 'cool,' " she says, but she wasn't interested in him. Her roommate, Blyth, was.

Blyth and Charlie started dating, which meant the girls soon met Tim, who visited from Brown. Charlie says the "Tim Introduction" was always significant for any of his relationships. "Most of my girl-friends who didn't know Tim well," Charlie says, "were always nervous to meet him. They knew it was a momentous occasion."

"The approval of Tim still really matters to me," Blyth acknowledges.

Alison says she didn't consider Tim romantically because he was Blyth's boyfriend's brother. Not to mention the fact that she wasn't Charlie's biggest fan. "I don't know that Charlie knows that I think this, but Charlie and I actually don't get along that well."

Charlie says the same thing in his own interview with me: "The funny thing is that Alison and I never really got along."

Tim agrees: "They are like oil and water."

"We're better now," Charlie says. "But at the time, it was always very complicated."

"We rub each other the wrong way," Alison says. "Which is so bizarre, when you think about it, but we do. My general inclination in the world is to be extremely organized, helpful to everyone, and I am a control freak by nature. I think Charlie views me as a meddler in other people's business."

Alison's efficient personality is glimpsed even in our short meeting. She speaks very quickly, in articulate, economical sentences—no word wasted—and betrays no self-doubt.

Blyth Lord, on the other hand, has a laid-back demeanor, and seems more ruminative. I interview her at her office at WGBH, the Boston public television station, where she's a producer. She's wearing a black V-neck T-shirt and green corduroys with a soft fabric belt. "I posed this to Charlie, actually," she says, "when he was telling me about his interview with you. I said, 'Perhaps all the ways that Alison works for Tim are where you and Tim differ.' And he thought that was very interesting, and then we got distracted and never analyzed what those things were."

Would Blyth say that one twin is closer to the parents?

"I think Charlie was always the more intense child and he had more of a temper and engaged with his parents more than Tim did. Charlie felt that was almost his role—to be more of the challenger, and Tim was more of an appeaser."

Charlie, in his interview, agrees: "I think I got more of my mother's volatility. So two volatile people will inevitably collide. . . . I was pegged as the wild man, which I never liked. I really hated it. I got pigeonholed as the temper guy, with Tim as the gentle one."

Blyth goes on: "I think because of that history, Charlie's parents have a more easygoing relationship with Tim. Charlie believes that his father is more comfortable with Tim."

Interestingly, when I ask Charlie and Tim who is closer to their mother, they each point at the other twin. They have the same response when I ask who is closer to their father.

Blyth is certain the twins' differences explain why the four spouses are not interchangeable. "Charlie could never be married to Alison," she says. "I have no idea if Tim and I could be married. I have not truthfully ever thought about that one."

Never thought about it? I certainly have at least thought in passing about whether I could be married to Robin's husband, Edward, but, yes, it feels too taboo to even contemplate.

Blyth continues: "Since I know that Charlie is really annoyed by parts of Alison, I have asked myself what parts of me must annoy Tim. And I don't know the answer to that. I will say that I have moments of insecurity around Tim; I get uncomfortable because I do feel the need for him to think I'm bright. I know he likes me, but I do have these moments of thinking, Does he think I'm interesting? Does he think I'm smart? Could he sit on a desert island with me for two days? And then I'll also say, Does he think I'm attractive? You think these things, inevitably."

Has she asked herself whether *she's* attracted to *him*?

"Well, yeah. I play that one out fairly often. I'll say, What parts of Tim are more attractive to me than Charlie? Like Tim's a better dresser now, probably because he lets Ali dress him. Charlie doesn't let me dress him. Tim's hair is looking better than Charlie's hair these days, and maybe that's because he wears hair product, but my husband won't."

"I am *not* attracted to Charlie," Alison tells me in our interview at Lowe Advertising, where she's head of human resources at the time we talk. "To me, the brothers look and sound different, and just are totally different. I think Tim is much cuter than Charlie." She has only mixed them up once—when Tim changed his T-shirt without her knowing and she mumbled hello when he walked by her, without realizing it was her husband. "I was completely freaked out," she said. "But that's the only time."

Tim and Alison finally started dating a full five years after graduation, when Tim was living in Manhattan and Alison was living with Blyth in a rental house in D.C. (To complete the incestuousness, the girls' roommates included the Lords' sister, Deirdre, and, at one point, Tim's then girlfriend, Delia.) It was only after Tim and Alison had each broken up with their mates that they started noticing each other—strangely enough, just two weeks before Charlie and Blyth's wedding day, June 27, 1992. "I saw Alison completely fresh, almost instantly," Tim says now.

"We ended up making out all night in Washington Square Park." Alison smiles. "But we basically agreed that we were not going to say or do anything about it because Blyth and Charlie were getting married in two weeks and we didn't want to make us a *thing* to distract from their wedding."

The secret didn't last long. At the wedding, Alison told Blyth the news, and Tim told Charlie. "They were delighted," Alison recalls. "But we didn't tell anyone else."

"I was incredibly excited," Blyth says now, "because I just thought that the four of us married would be really fun—assuming it worked. I did get very anxious that it might not work and that then it would be incredibly awkward if they had a terrible falling-out and all of a sudden one of my best friends and my brother-in-law weren't friends anymore. Obviously nothing like that happened."

"Alison and I were in love very quickly," Tim recounts. "But Charlie's wedding was a really emotional day for me. I remember when Charlie and Blyth left at the end of their reception, I went out into this field that was behind the tent, and my mom and dad really sweetly came out and found me. They were really conscious of things like that. They knew, I think before I did, that it was going to be an intense day. And I really couldn't even articulate it, but it was really hard. I'm sure a psychotherapist could tell you the obvious thing: Your twin has just ridden off with his wife for his honeymoon and you guys are entering a new phase in your life. But I hadn't been able to articulate that."

Tim and Alison were engaged sixteen months later, and married in September 1994.

Charlie and Blyth had a daughter, Taylor, in 1997 and another daughter, Cameron, in 1999. Tim and Alison had a son, Hayden, in 1998.

The nightmare began when Tim's son, Hayden, a towheaded, cheerful infant, started to show signs of failure. He was diagnosed first with cerebral palsy; then at eighteen months, the diagnosis was changed to Tay-Sachs disease. Tay-Sachs is a fatal breakdown of the central nervous system. The gene mutation occurs in 1 out of 250 babies around the world, predominantly in descendents of Ashkenazi Jews. Children with Tay-Sachs have, by all appearances, completely healthy infancies, but gradually they start to lose their ability to smile, grasp, or eat with their hands. Eventually they become blind and paralyzed. Few children live past the age of five. For a baby to have the disease, both parents have to be carriers, so most Jewish parents get genetic testing early to rule it out. Tim and Alison, despite having no known Jewish blood, were that rare exception: Both were carriers.

The news was devastating. Charlie's first impulse was to go be with his brother in New York.

"You were there that same night we found out," Tim recalls.

"I was," Charlie confirms.

"That was probably the most important thing—outside of Alison," Tim tells me. "That Charlie was there. And through that whole thing, I think we were more open about how we felt about each other and how much we needed each other."

"I made a decision," Charlie says, "as soon as I knew what was happening, that I was going to come down to see Tim and Hayden every three or four weeks. That I was going to come to New York. It was just unspoken that I had to be there." He looks at Tim with a kind of fierce focus. "That I had to get to know Hayden."

"The first thing that happened when he got there the Friday that Hayden was diagnosed," Tim recalls, "Hayden was upstairs in our apartment, and Charlie and I just went out in the park and threw a ball together and just talked and tried to reorder where we were. And I just knew that you and I were going to do it together. You said, 'I'm going to be down here every couple of weeks.' "

Charlie continues the story: "When I got to the apartment where I was staying in New York that night, I called Blyth to check in and to try to describe what it had been like to be with you." He's looking at Tim. "And Blyth said, 'Did you ever notice that Cameron startles easily?' And I said, 'What are you talking about?' She said to me, 'Charlie, you're obviously a carrier because you're twins. I went on the Web site and it says the first sign of Tay-Sachs is an exaggerated startle reflex. Cameron has an exaggerated startle reflex.' I went cold. When she said it, I went cold. I thought, 'Fuck, I'm a carrier.' It hadn't even occurred to me. I said, 'I think we should get her tested and get you tested, so you feel better.' "

Tim looks startled. "Oh my God," he says. He's never heard Charlie's side of those first horrible hours.

"What's interesting," Charlie goes on, "is that I didn't call Tim about my fear for my daughter until Blyth was tested. So I went through the first ten days of waiting for Blyth's results—"

"By yourself," Tim interjects, sounding sorry.

"—not talking to anybody because I had decided, Everyone is

struggling with Hayden. I'm not going to add to their worries. I thought, This will be a drama-queen move if I mention it. It will suddenly be about me and Blyth, and it shouldn't be about me and Blyth. It's about Hayden and Tim and Ali."

The waiting period for Blyth's test results were rough. "That was a really bad ten days," Charlie says. "But it wasn't ridiculously bad, because the genetics counselor we saw had said to Blyth, 'Statistically it is so improbable that all four of you would be carriers. There's just no way Cameron has Tay-Sachs, but I'll just indulge you anyway and get you tested.' "

But the unimaginable scenario unfolded before their eyes. Blyth was a carrier, too.

"When Charlie called and said, 'Blyth is a carrier and they're testing Cameron,' I almost went crazy," Tim recalls. "I remember my partner at work, Jason, was trying literally to make sure I didn't lose it. I was *that* emotional. All of a sudden it was almost as if I was getting a sense of what this looked like from the outside—what people were seeing in terms of what we were going through. It seemed *much* more terrible, more horrible. I think I almost went crazy when I got that phone call. All of a sudden I was running around One Hundredth Street and the East River Drive, screaming. I could not believe that this was going to happen. I literally could not believe it."

Charlie looks stunned. "I never heard that story."

Cameron's test came back positive. She had Tay-Sachs, too; double death sentences for two cousins whose fathers couldn't be closer.

Blyth said her first reaction was, *Of course*. "It made total sense to me," she says. "Ever since Cameron was diagnosed, I've always said that the coincidence was connected to their 'twin thing.' Because it's so inexplicable otherwise. I mean, it makes sense that they're both carriers: They're identical twins; they have the same genetic makeup. It is *possible* that their wives are both carriers—that is *possible*. But statistically, it's like one in—I don't even know the math on it. And therefore the 'why' of it to me is fatelike, mystical;

this was always going to be their thing. They needed to be there for each other."

"Tim's and my mutation is a random mutation," Charlie explains. "It was a mutation they'd never seen. The Genome Project maps this thing, and our case is a unique spot on the seventeenth chromosome."

"If the letters are switched," says Tim, helping to explain, "or if there's a missing code, it will happen. And ours happens on a stretch of that code where they've never seen it happen before. So it's literally completely random and unique."

"It turns out that Blyth's grandmother was Jewish," Charlie says.

She hadn't known that?

"She hadn't."

Nova, the science series on public television, did a segment on the Lords' case for their genetics special, *Cracking the Code of Life*, which aired in 2002. The correspondent, Robert Krulwich, calls their situation "an unbelievably bad roll of the genetic dice." Poignant home videos of Hayden as a vibrant blond baby with long eyelashes give way to pictures of him lolling in his baby seat, listless in his father's arms, eyes rolling up in his head, clearly losing his connection to the world. Tim cries on the program as he says:

"I remember the last time Hayden laughed. I took a trip with him out to pick up a suit because we were going to a wedding that night, and we came back and it was really windy, and he just loves to feel the wind, and so we had a great time. We came back and I propped him up right here on the couch and I was sitting next to him and he just kind of threw his head back and laughed, like, you know, 'What a fun trip,' you know? And that's the last time he was able to laugh."

The footage of Charlie and Tim sitting on a bed, each holding their adorable, limp children in their arms, is shattering. The twin fathers just keep massaging their babies' tiny feet, kissing their cheeks, over and over again, as if to will them to reanimate. Tim says on-camera, "Charlie and I are incredibly close and have been all our lives. And when I think about him and Blyth having to go through this, it just seems really cruel. It just seems too much."

Charlie says now, "I had really geared up in the three weeks after Hayden's diagnosis to be Tim's rock. I had a book that I bought that was designed to help figure out how to be a real source of support for Tim. So when we got *our* diagnosis, the first thing I thought of was, How am I going to play that role and also go through this myself?" He looks at his brother and says, "When Cameron was diagnosed, the second thing I thought—after obviously thinking about Cameron—was that I was sorry that I wasn't going to be as available to you as I wanted to be."

"I had the exact same feeling," Tim admits. "First it was too painful to think that you were going to have to go through what I knew *we* were going to have to go through. That just seemed like too much. It was like that whole thing we talked about earlier: wanting very much for you not to feel something that bad. And then the second part of it was like, 'How am I going to be able to support you and how are you going to be able to support me when we're both having to deal with this?' "

Hayden was eighteen months when he was diagnosed. Cameron was six months. "This child was thriving up until that time," Charlie recounts. "The symptoms for Tay-Sachs don't kick in till about eight months old."

Hayden lived a little over a year more, and died in December 2000, when he was two years, eight months old. Cameron lived for eighteen months after her diagnosis, and died just a week past her second birthday, in May 2001.

"There's a lot of very difficult stuff that goes on at the end," Tim says quietly. "It's terrible. It's terrible what happens to them. There were some people you couldn't describe it to—it was too horrifying. But I could share it with Charlie, and it was important that we did."

"We made a lot of our key decisions together," Charlie says.

Tim clarifies: "Our decisions about how to take care of the children. Because the decisions are so hard. . . . The two critical junctures are about whether or not you insert a feeding tube, because essentially you pump food into them. And what we'd come to is that, when they couldn't eat anymore, I think intuitively that was going to be—"

"That they were ready," Charlie says, finishing Tim's sentence.

"Our belief ended up being that that was going to be their way of saying they were ready to go," Tim continues. "And then later on, what happens, which we hadn't expected, is that they get new things like pneumonia and other complications, and then there's the decision whether there's one complication that you finally don't treat with antibiotics; you sort of allow that also to be a moment that they choose. For both of the children, there was a moment where they didn't eat anymore, and a moment when they were sick. And it was very much about doing our best, as everybody does in those situations, trying to imagine that you're really listening to their choice. End of life is something that society is tremendously poor at, and so we were able to share decisions about how we were going to handle the end of their lives."

Alison underscores they were all in sync on a philosophical approach. "I think we all decided intuitively that we would go in the general area of nonintervention," she says. "Because the basic decision path is: Are you going to use all of the medical tools available to you to prolong a life that is ultimately not sustainable, or are you going to use medical tools and intervention to increase levels of comfort and help ease the transition into death? And we all knew that we would be in that latter category. I don't know how you know that, but we just knew that."

"We helped each other," Tim says. "It was pretty unbelievable." He takes a breath. "Charlie was there for the entire last week of Hayden's life."

"That was extremely important," Charlie asserts. "Because it took away my fear of the end of Cameron's life. So there was a profound way in which Tim and Hayden were a remarkable foundation for us and what we would go through after them."

Blyth says the symmetry was a solace. "I remember being so incredibly grateful that they were there with us," she says.

I ask if she was able to lean on her brother-in-law, Tim, as well as her husband. "Oh, tremendously," she replies. "He and Alison were amazing—"

She's suddenly overcome and can't continue. "They were so generous," she says finally, through tears. "Tim has a beautiful relationship with my children, especially Taylor, whom he's known longer, who is the eldest grandchild; he just swept in and was so amazing with her. During the last week of Cameron's life, he was up in Boston the whole time, keeping Taylor occupied. He knew exactly what needed to happen, that Charlie and I needed to be free to focus on Cameron."

Charlie echoes Blyth in his interview. "Tim's ability to be there for Taylor was one of the most remarkable things I'll ever see in my life."

Alison says she missed her niece's final days because she and her daughter, Annie, were staying at her parents' apartment in Boston at the time. "I don't know what happened when Cameron died," she says. "I wasn't there. Our son, Hayden, died very peacefully. We took him into our room, which we had almost never done, and Annie was in there—we were all in there together—and he basically took a huge breath and didn't breathe again. That last week was horrific from the standpoint of watching him go. It was not easy. But it was very gradual and very peaceful. I don't know what happened with Cameron, but it was not like that. It was a struggle. That's what I know. Tim has never spoken to me about it. He left the morning after she died and drove back to New York to see our therapist because he was so upset. So I don't really know what happened."

I ask her why she never asked Tim about it. "I don't want to know, actually," she admits. "Because it's done and it happened and it's over. I know enough about what it might have been, just in terms of how someone might struggle against dying and what can happen." She pauses. "I don't want to know about it."

She says the four of them, as a group, don't talk about it today. "It's referenced, but I don't really talk about it with barely anybody.

I'm not the person 'Talking' about it with a capital *T*. Tim and Charlie do. On their birthday, if they can be in New York, they'll go to Green-Wood, where we have a family plot, and they'll hang out there and read poetry and write in their journals. Then they'll go have a big boozy lunch together."

In my living room, Tim suddenly gets emotional. "You know, the thing about my son, Hayden, dying first"—he falters—"was that I realized I hadn't really gotten to know Charlie's daughter Cameron. And at first that was really difficult for me"—he addresses Charlie—"because you got to know"—he can't say the name for a moment—"Hayden. But I did get to know Cameron the last few months, and that was very important to me. And her death was actually the hardest part of the whole thing for me, oddly enough."

"Was it really?" Charlie asks genuinely.

"Yes," Tim admits. "I don't know why. Her death was the thing that completely ripped me apart."

Tim asks Charlie's permission to talk about it.

"Can I describe it actually?" he says.

"Yes," Charlie replies.

"I know *you* should be the one to describe it, but I want to, because I think it's very important," Tim continues. "This is an amazing thing: Even though they're ravaged at this point in their lives, there's obviously a spirit. If you've been through something like this, I think you would know what I'm talking about. We were so concerned about Taylor [Charlie's older daughter] that we took her away that day. And we took her away much of the day before. We took her to the park. And her sister Cameron hadn't seen her all day. She had basically stopped breathing a couple of times, right?"

"Five or six times," Charlie affirms.

"Five or six times over the course of the afternoon. Charlie and Blyth were with her. And then she would come back. It was very hard. And it was exhausting. And everybody couldn't figure out why she wouldn't let go. We were asking each other, 'Why isn't she letting go?'

And then we realized that Taylor hadn't been in to see her, and maybe Cameron was waiting for that. And so then Taylor went in to say good night."

Tim has tears on his face.

"And Cameron died ten minutes later."

Tim and Charlie represent to me the paradigm of a twinship that managed to expand over the years—to include friends and spouses— in a way that appears unforced, and without modulating the brothers' intensity. That's not to suggest their foursome is flawless—there have been strains and spats. But overall, they've built an intimate universe that salutes each person's importance in it. Which is probably why Blyth said she doesn't spend a lot of time measuring her bond to her husband against his with Tim.

"I have a reverence for their twinness," she says. "I'm like, 'Whatever that needs to be, you get to have that.' Because I can't even imagine what they have. That's cool as hell. Their relationship preceded me by twenty years. So I have a reverence and a deep respect for it. Now, there have been times, like when Tim's son, Hayden, was dying and Charlie was focused on Hayden's being sick and being about to die, and he had to be in New York over and over again, and I was eight months pregnant with my third child and I had my three-and-a-half-year-old, Taylor, and my one-and-a-half-year-old terminally ill daughter, Cameron, having seizures, and I was managing at home—sometimes I was like, Hello!? But then I would realize, Of course he has to be down there with Tim."

Blyth takes a heavy breath. "My issues with relation to the Charlie-Tim thing were never that I felt that I was being locked out by Tim, but more that my husband's intensity of focus was not on me at that moment. And yet I respected it. I had moments of feeling sorry for myself, but I realized, This is not a competitive thing, Blyth; it's just that now's the time for his focus to be on Tim and Tim's dying baby. That's where his focus belongs. It doesn't belong on you right now. Get over yourself. That's the way I would describe it. Because I'm not the twin here."

"We don't actually talk about our marriages very much," Charlie says. "This was the one time we leaned on each other for that."

I ask whether it was indeed a big strain on their relationships.

"We dodged some bullets," Charlie replies. "And maybe it's because we've chosen well in terms of being with women who have similar basic values. Not only did Tim and I have ultimately very similar feelings about life and death but our spouses did, too."

"I also remember a walk that the four of us took that Thanksgiving weekend," Tim says. "We had just found out that Cameron had Tay-Sachs—so it was three weeks after Hayden had been diagnosed and three days after Cameron had been diagnosed—and the four of us were walking around Boston together, and feeling this weird sense of 'Thank God we have each other. I wish this wasn't a club I had to belong to, but I have a club.'"

11 ME AND MY SHADOW:
EXPLORING DOUBLENESS

Stay, stand apart. I know not which is which.
—*The Comedy of Errors*, William Shakespeare

I rented an office to write this book—a street-level room in a chiropractor's office on Fifth Avenue, with a picture window overlooking Central Park. There were times where I felt like performance art: *Live Twin Typing*. Pedestrians who know Robin would happen by, gape, wave tentatively, or look generally confused.

One day, Robin forwarded me the following e-mail from an acquaintance of hers: "**Subject:** Are you working in a building on 5th avenue in the 70's today?"

It isn't unusual for me to be mistaken for Robin on a weekly basis in Manhattan (no exaggeration), and this means I'm regularly reminded that I'm someone's double. What does it mean to be a copy of another person, for there to be two of you, for you to impersonate or replicate someone else just by existing?

Physical likeness is what most people focus on when they encounter identical twins, but doubleness manifests itself more ambiguously from inside the twinship. It gives some twins a kick and enervates others. It can make you feel proud or shy. It can also muddy your clarity of self. When you look like someone, spend all your early years with them, are assumed to resemble them, and are compared to them, you have an ingrained sense of being not just one, but two.

The title of this book is no accident: I found that unpacking twinship means exposing the tension between being one and the same. I've tried to explore what it takes ultimately to forge individuality, but I also set out to examine sameness, because it's integral to every twinship and how it is perceived.

Author/neurologist Oliver Sacks opened a 1986 book review in the *New York Times* as follows:

> We assume we are all individuals, autonomous, unique—and this assumption is suddenly tested, even shattered, when we meet twins. It is not just the biological rarity and extraordinariness of identical twins that so impress the imagination. It is the exact, the uncanny, doubling of a human being, a doubling (we may see, or imagine, or fear) which may extend to the innermost, most secret depths of the soul. There is always a shock—of interest, surprise, pleasure . . . and consternation—on encountering twins. We gaze from one to the other: identical faces, expressions, voices, movements, mannerisms—and feel a mixed sense, a double sense, of both marvel and outrage (this is reflected in some cultures, which sometimes revere twins and sometimes destroy them).

Hillel Schwartz affirms in his book *Culture of the Copy* that whether replicas are considered a blessing or a hex, freakish or adorable, varies by culture. Some civilizations have been spooked by twins; others have venerated them. At one time, Nigerians killed their twins, then did an about-face and exalted pairs as near deities. Brazilians thought multiple births were a product of adultery; sometimes the mother was executed. Hindus thought twins protected them from bad weather. On some Pacific islands, it was thought that opposite-sex fetuses had had an incestuous relationship in the womb.

Today, Schwartz points out, society attaches great importance to copies and the idea that replication is verification. We require two signatures, make duplicate documents for security in case the original is lost, or to prove the original exists. "Think of a backup drive on your computer," Schwartz says. "Well, how does that play out with *living* copies? Is one twin there as a security for the other twin? For example, if one twin needs a bone-marrow transplant, his or her twin is a perfect match. It's a wonderful security to have a twin."

That idea appeals to me. Robin is my backup copy. My hard drive. She's proof that I exist, my documentation. She shares my blood-type, is my marrow match, my stunt double. I auditioned for her once when she got sick (and lost the part). We can use each other's passports in a pinch. On a mundane level, it reminds me how easily I walk past her doorman—he just nods when I walk by, never questions why I'm entering a home that isn't mine. The larger idea of my twin as insurance resonates for me because I have so often experienced her as a refuge, my protection, and also the verification of me.

Schwartz says nontwins' judgment about whether twinship is enviable or disconcerting depends on how we feel about the notion of counterfeit and the fear of being tricked. The anxiety of not knowing what's really genuine can color a person's response to a twin. I've experienced this when one of our relatives sees me at an extended family event and hesitates before calling me by name, or when a stranger looks stricken after hugging me on the street before realizing I'm not Robin, the person she knows. Just as someone might worry whether the designer bag they buy on eBay is the real thing or a fake, there's a wariness about being duped or embarrassed when people aren't sure which twin they're talking to.

And there's an unease on a twin's part, too: Maybe this person doesn't really know it's me. I often greet someone by adding, "I'm Abby," and they'll usually reply indignantly, "I *know*!" But it's my way of removing the anxiety of doubleness in that situation—the uncertainty of identity.

Some twins are still tickled by—or at least accustomed to—the "who is who" scrutiny. I'm aware that I do enjoy the quirks of being Robin's replica, making people's heads turn when we walk into a restaurant, knowing people confer on us a kind of intimacy and intuition about each other that indeed I know we have; we are our own secret society. But for other twins, it exposes a deeper disquiet: the idea that they might be transposable: not one and the same, but just the same. There's a silent exasperation: "Don't you know me by now?"

Schwartz speaks frankly about the ambivalence of sameness. "One aspect of how we all think about twins is our fear of identicals, fear of copies; our fear of losing our own identity in another. And the twins themselves express both of these, right? Loss of identity in the other, and on the other hand, this great complementarity. Both of those are there."

And yet, it has to be acknowledged that there's power in doubleness. There's impact. You stand out; you're remembered. It's that "star power" that Joan Friedman said was so insidious, but can also feel like a steroid. When I was growing up, my twinship conferred something extra, something fizzy, unique. Francine Klagsbrun thinks the glut of doubles today mutes the spotlight. "It used to be that twins were almost magical," she tells me. "In some ways that made it harder to be twins, because people were always watching, but in some ways it was easier, because either way they were *stars*; they were the center of the world. Today there are so many more twins around, it's just not unusual. I think that changes the equation to some extent. They don't grow up feeling so special." It's a true oxymoron: Being a copy of someone made me unique. With the novelty reduced, maybe twins today miss out on that jolt of originality. But conversely, maybe they'll be better for the normalcy.

I would say that Robin and I are definitely less similar now than we once were. Our alikeness persists mostly in our faces. It makes me wonder what it means to me to be a *copy* of Robin today. How are we still replicas?

What I find most moving is that our identical DNA makes her children and mine not just cousins but half siblings. (Or as Nancy Segal puts it in her book *Entwined Lives*, "Identical twin parents are equally related to their own children and to their twin's children.") There's a potency in that, as if our twin connection is sealed in our sons' and daughters' bodies.

But at the same time, I know that Robin's kids never see me as a replacement for her; when they sleep over at my house and I tuck them in, they miss their mom and I'm no substitute. They know our voices, our different scents. As memorable as it was to hear Kathy Giusti describe her sister, Karen, as a ready understudy if she succumbs to cancer, parents definitely cannot be copied, no matter how much we look or act alike. Robin's children will marvel sometimes, saying, "Mommy says the exact same thing!" or "Mom makes the same expression!" But they've never mistaken us.

Doug and Mike Starn, identical twins who are forty-seven when I meet them, have focused their life's work—photography and collage—almost entirely on what they describe as "questions about our distinctness." Their art sums up the conundrum of twinship: how we are both particular and alike. The Starn brothers, who shot to prominence at the age of twenty-four, when they were hits at the 1987 Whitney Biennial, work together virtually every day in their scruffy, vast studio in Red Hook, Brooklyn. (Their most public work is on view inside the rebuilt World Trade Center subway station, renamed South Ferry Terminal.) Every image or diptych of theirs is a collaboration—dual authorship over a lifetime.

On the morning of our interview, both are dressed with similar inattention—Doug in loose jeans, Mike in a faded T-shirt and laceless sneakers. Mike's long salt-and-pepper hair is shorter than his brother's, but otherwise they're hard to tell apart. Both five seven, they have the same slim build and slouchy posture, same goatees and sleepy eyes. I notice Doug's voice is a little softer, which is an almost meaningless distinction, since both Starns speak *so* quietly.

Though they admit that early in their careers they used their twinship to get noticed, billing themselves as the Starn Twins, now they hate the moniker. And yet their art, even by their own admission, has *everything* to do with their twinness, and their photographic projects revolve around images of doubleness, mirroring, or repetition.

On the day I visit, Mike surveys their framed and unframed work—large rectangles and squares, which seem to deserve a more pristine space than the crowded walls and dirty floor strewn with cables, nails, and bubble wrap. "Everything you see here—nothing is individual," he explains. "Everything is made up of pieces; everything is sectioned. And that is something we can't help; we just do it."

It's no accident that their subway installation is titled *See It Split, See It Change*.

"One of the major themes that drives us," Doug says, "is: *the same but different*. Parts within parts . . . this is who we are."

It's also how they work, how they speak. Everything is seamlessly cooperative, with no clear ownership of a collage they create or a sentence they utter—the doubleness is their system, and it's effective for them. "When we're out shooting," Doug says, "and it's been this way since we first started, back when we were thirteen years old, we have one camera that we share and we trade it back and forth. We don't usually know who took what picture."

"Or how we decided what to photograph," Mike adds. "It's constant talking between each other."

Any conflict between them erupts solely from the "art making," as they put it.

"Because we get so passionate about something," Mike explains.

"If here's an individual viewpoint that the other one is not picking up on," Doug interjects, "we argue. There was a time when I had to leave the studio for a few hours while Mike continued to work on a piece we'd started, and when I came back, I didn't like it at all; I hated what he had done. And then after we got through our fight, we sort of started working backward and then ended up at the same place anyway. . . . So we basically know, even if I do some work that he didn't do, he'll look at it and say, 'Yeah, that's actually what I would do, too.' "

Doug points to the wall-size study of moths, titled *Attracted to Light*. The insects were photographed at night, fluttering around the porch of one of the Starns' homes in Putnam County, New York. (The brothers have country houses minutes from each other.) "You can see that serial image there. It's a moth, just replicated—I forget how many times—140 times or something. Each one is the same image, but each print is different because of the chemical process we used."

"That is . . . us," continues Mike. "We both start out as that same negative, but then what happens to us makes us each unique."

Their snowflake series is a jewel-like example of this persistent theme: similarity and uniqueness. The Starns took photographs of snowflakes as they fell, then magnified them so massively that the clarified details look too luminous to be real. Many of the snowflakes are in pairs, and Doug explains that often it's the same snowflake printed differently. "In all of our work, there's a common thread that has to do with how we look at ourselves."

"The snowflakes are about the individual," Mike says. "The unique individual. And yet they all are the same."

The symbolism may be too obvious to restate, but standing in their Brooklyn laboratory it hits me how many twins return to this refrain of being one and yet not one: We're particular, we're analogous; we're singular, we're similar; we're an original and a copy, solitary and combined. We're alone, but we never are.

Whatever the conflicting forces may be, twinship, Doug acknowledges, is usually the organizing principle of a twin's life. "It permeates it," Doug says. "That's all."

"It's an interesting thing to think about," Mike says. "Who would I be if he never existed? I can't imagine."

Though they don't come across as sentimental guys (when I ask if they ever tell each other "I love you," they both immediately answer no), the Starns do buy into the notion that their unshakable union can be traced to the womb.

"Years ago, we photographed some Siamese twins in a formalde-hyde jar," Doug tells me.

"At the Harvard medical museum," Mike adds.

"And it was really shocking," Doug says, "because these babies were holding hands. And that really sort of was important to us, to recognize how far and deep this is."

12 BUT FOR HER

"If not for her, I wouldn't be here."

Helen Rapaport declares this in a heavy Yiddish accent, looking over at her identical twin sister, Pearl Pufeles.

The two eighty-six-year-olds are sitting side by side in a Chicago hospital lounge on a patterned sofa. Helen is wearing a green floor-length hospital gown and medical bracelet—unexpectedly, she was kept overnight for some cardiac tests, so our interview has to take place here. She is frustrated that we're not meeting in her home in Buffalo Grove, as planned. "I cooked all day yesterday," she says ruefully.

"She made kugel," offers Pearl, who is dressed in a purple ensemble—purple polyester pants, purple top with flower appliqué on the left shoulder—and cream-colored orthopedic sneakers.

Both twins fold their hands in front of them when they talk. They don't look nearly as identical now as they do in the black-and-white pictures from their youth; in those, they are indistinguishable, wearing identical outfits well into their twenties. What remains similar about them today is their thinning hair, their drooping eyelids—which give their faces a soft kindness that reminds me of my late grandma Esther—and the blue numbers tattooed on their arms: Helen is 5080; Pearl is 5079.

I thought I'd have to ease gingerly into their memories of Dr. Josef Mengele—the monstrous Nazi doctor who experimented on twins in Auschwitz. But they start talking about him right away.

"You've heard about him," Pearl says. "He was the one who called out when we got off of the train." She refers to the cattle car that transported prisoners to the camps. "He called out, *'Zwillinge aus-treten,'* which means 'Twins, step out.' And we were pushed aside. I don't know, there were about seventy sets of twins."

"More," Helen corrects her. "More."

In his 1986 book, *The Nazi Doctors*, Robert Jay Lifton describes how Mengele, who had a Ph.D. in genetics, "embodied the selections process" for many survivors, who remember him always at "the ramp" when the transports arrived. ". . . He frequently went to the ramp when not selecting in order to see that twins were being collected and saved for him," Lifton writes. "Mengele could exploit the unique opportunity Auschwitz provided for quick and absolute availability of large numbers of these precious research subjects."

"They took the twins to a different barracks," Pearl continues. "And we didn't know what was waiting for us."

"We didn't know first if we should *tell* him we were twins," Helen recalls.

"We didn't know what they were going to do with us," Pearl repeats.

"But we were so identical, they would have known anyway," Helen explains. "So Pearl said, 'Let's just step out. Whatever will be with one will be with the other.' So that's how we wound up in the barracks with other twins."

They had been herded, at the age of twenty-three, from their home in Czechoslovakia, along with their father, Isaac Herskovic—"a top tailor," Pearl says—and a brother, Morris, an older sister, Miriam, and Miriam's husband and three children. (Their mother, Hannah, had died years earlier of a stroke, and their four other siblings were already in other parts of the world by the time the war began.)

The train journey was gruesome. "Terrible." Helen shakes her head. "They piled us up; I don't know how many. There was no air, no water."

"And kids crying," Pearl adds. "There was no food."

"It was locked," Helen continues. "No washroom, nothing. A pail in one end and a pail in the other. You have to relieve yourself in front of the whole car. It was degrading, terribly."

"My sister had an onion," Pearl recalls. "And she passed it around to have a lick. Just a lick. And her kids cried and cried."

"Miriam said, 'I only want to live as long as I have food for the children,' " Helen adds.

"And she went right away," Pearl says flatly, meaning Miriam was killed almost as soon as she arrived at the concentration camp. "The ones who they pushed to the left," Helen explains, "they were doomed. Straight to the crematorium."

"They gassed them," Pearl says.

"They gave them a towel," Helen chimes in, "and a soap to make believe they were going for a shower, and then when they were inside—"

"—instead of water," Pearl interjects.

"—the Zyclon gas came down." Helen's hands are in a fist against her belly.

"That's how my father and my sister and her children died," Pearl says. "We never saw them anymore."

The twins didn't understand their relatives' fate at first.

Pearl: "There were women in the barracks from Poland."

Helen: "They had been already years there."

Pearl: "They told us."

Helen: "We asked, 'When will we be reunited with our loved ones?' And she said—"

Helen starts to weep.

Pearl: "They took us by our hand and opened the barracks door—"

Helen: "—and showed us the chimneys. We were a couple feet away from the crematoriums. 'There is where they are,' they said."

Pearl: " 'You will never see them again.' And we started crying."

Helen: "We didn't believe it; we said, 'How is that possible?' They told us, 'No, you won't see them.' The Polish people were already there like four or five years; they knew how everything worked. So we cried and cried and hugged. And that was it."

After a week or so in the barracks, the Herskovic twins received a grisly assignment.

"They needed some workers to volunteer," Pearl recalls. "And Helen and I said, 'Well, maybe if we get out of the barracks, we'll see our brother. Let's volunteer wherever they are taking us.' "

"So we volunteered," Helen continues. "Two SS men came with dogs and brought two pails and some disinfectant, and they took us to a big warehouse, and we thought we were going to do some work. And then they opened the door and we almost fainted. Oh my God."

"There was a mountain of bodies," Pearl recounts. "Dead bodies. We almost fainted, both. Because we never saw dead people before. In the Jewish religion, they didn't display dead bodies; always the casket was closed."

"So one—the SS man with the dogs—he said, 'Oh, you'll get used to it,' " Helen says.

"We'll see it in our minds until we die," Pearl says quietly. "Just a big, big mountain. And our job was to first pile them—the Germans were very correct with making everything perfect. So when they dumped the bodies out after they were gassed, they scattered. It wasn't a neat mountain."

The young women were told to make a neat stack of corpses. "We had to lift them onto the pile," Helen explains, "wash the floor where the bodies had been, then pile them back on the clean side and wash the other. And the worst thing was that we saw children." She starts to weep again.

"Because we were looking," Pearl remembers. "Thinking, Maybe we'll see our nieces."

"The mouths open," Helen recounts, "and blood was still coming. They must have been gassed a few hours before."

"That was Mengele who was doing the selections," Pearl recalls. "He was waving his wand—whatever you call it. To the right, you still have a chance of living. To the left, all the elderly, the sick, the little ones, they all went to the left and those were taken straight with the towels."

I ask Pearl to describe Mengele, and her eyes light up. "He was the most handsomest—"

"Like Clark Gable," Helen interjects.

"He was tall and the most handsome guy," Pearl continues. "He should have been an actor or something and not killed Jews. His boots—they were so shiny that instead of a mirror, you could have used his boots."

The boots clearly made an impression. "They were cleaned like three times a day," Helen goes on. "And he changed always his uniforms. He was the most handsomest guy. I don't think Clark Gable was as handsome as he was."

"No," Pearl says definitively. "Walking around with a little— what is it called? Swagger?"

"Even the prisoners," Helen says. "Some of them fell in love with him."

The twins cleaned the warehouse for twelve days. "Then Mengele needed us for his experiments," Pearl says.

"Toward the end, you didn't know it was bodies anymore," Helen says dully. "I said to Pearl, 'Pretend it's a sack of potatoes. Or a sack of onions.' To this day, if we go shopping and we want to pick out some oranges . . ." She pauses. "To this day, sometimes if I pick up an orange and I see it sliding, I'm right back in Auschwitz. Or potatoes or pumpkins. Anything that's on a pile. You can't help it."

They keep focusing on the fact that at least they had each other. "We had to do the job," Pearl says. "But we were together. We were always together."

Did they talk to each other a lot while they worked?

"We were quiet," Helen replies.

Their memories of the Nazi doctor are incredibly benign. "Mengele wasn't beating us or killing us," Pearl says. "He was kind to us. And how could you hate him, when he was so handsome?"

He took their medical history and measured them meticulously. "We were sitting like Pearl and I are now, and he was in the middle," Helen recounts. "We were always nude."

"No clothes," Pearl confirms.

"Because he measured us," Helen explains.

"Every single thing," Pearl adds.

"Even our hair was counted," Helen marvels. "The eyelashes. He was measuring Pearl; then he came to me, and vice versa. Everything was written down."

Mengele left the injections to his nurses. The sisters don't know what the needles contained, but they do remember blood being drawn constantly. "They were taking our blood every single day," Pearl says, "and so Helen asked one of the nurses, 'How much blood can they take?' And she said, 'Endless. You have plenty blood.'"

"'You always make more,'" Pearl recalls the nurse explaining.

"One nurse was taking blood from one way; the other was injecting us with monstrosities that we don't know." Helen shakes her head. "To this days. And we never will find out, because all the records are gone."

But Mengele himself was never cruel to them?

"Never," they say in unison.

They said he was almost fatherly. "We knew he's not going to harm us. We knew it."

"Because he was so handsome," Pearl says. "You forgot about anything."

"He was like an angel," Helen adds.

"We were like friends with him," Pearl says. "Really."

"He was very smart," Helen says. "People were falling in love with him; I'm not kidding."

Their report is consistent with those of other twin survivors who said Mengele was their protector as much as their persecutor. The twins weren't treated any better than other prisoners in terms of being fed or clothed, but they were rarely outwardly harmed—in order to keep their bodies intact for comparisons—and they were allowed to keep their hair (so Mengele could measure and analyze it), which preserved a shred of humanity. Mengele prized the twins as case studies for investigating genetics; some say it was to understand how to engineer a master race with ideal traits; others say it was to devise a way to mass-produce twins to repopulate Germany. His laboratory had to be spotless, and his assistants were often Jewish prisoners.

Lifton writes that, by all accounts, Mengele was a "Dr. Jekyll and Mr. Hyde" figure, who one minute was offering children sweets and a ride in his car, and the next minute driving those same kids to the crematorium. He was known to give a pat on the head but also to inject twins' eyeballs, cut off a twin's testicles, or kill one twin immediately after the other twin died, in order to contrast autopsies. "They wanted to compare if the insides were as identical as the outside," Helen explains. Lifton describes how Mengele injected twins with chloroform to stop their hearts, and one incident when Mengele shot two of his "favorite" twin boys—eight years old—in the neck and autopsied them on the spot, in order to resolve a dispute with other doctors as to whether they carried tuberculosis. (They didn't.) In one infamous operation, Mengele is said to have sewed two Gypsy twins together to create conjoined twins.

Helen says she was "sick for years" after the war, but doctors were stymied as to the cause, and they kept sending her to psychiatrists. "They all think, if you're a survivor, there must be something wrong with your mind," Helen says. "But I knew it was something drastically wrong with me. It wasn't my head." Finally one doctor deduced that she had TB in the bladder. "He calls me up on a Monday morning; I'll always remember the day. He says, 'Helen, I finally know what's wrong with you and you're not crazy.' I started crying."

After the sisters had spent a year in Auschwitz, in January 1945, it became clear that the Germans were losing the war. "The Russians were approaching and the Americans from the other side," Helen recounts. "The Nazis evacuated the camps. They didn't want no evidence. But they left hundreds of people in beds who couldn't walk. Whoever was able to walk, they chased out. And we were in that death march that lasted from January to—when were we liberated?"

"May," Pearl replies.

"April," Helen corrects her.

"When they took us for the march," Pearl goes on, "it was our birthday: January eighteenth."

"I said to Pearl, 'We never will forget this day.' "

They marched in frigid temperatures. "There was no food, no water, nothing," says Pearl, describing the march. "So wherever we were walking, the snow disappeared."

"Because we ate up all the snow," Helen explains. "We slept in sties and warehouses. No taking baths, no changing clothes. We were walking around like crazy people."

Pearl says some of the German onlookers threw bread when their ragged convoy passed by. "When a prisoner ran toward the people that were throwing bread," Helen says, "the SS shoot them right on the spot."

They actually saw that happen?

"All the time," Pearl replies.

"That was daily," Helen states. "In that march, people were laying like flies all over. A lot of people couldn't take all that walking. I don't know, to this day, how I made it. I couldn't tell you. It was just—I don't know—God was pushing me."

"You said, 'Let me lay down here,' " Pearl reminds Helen.

"Because I was very sick," Helen says. "And I didn't want to go on. I didn't have shoes. My feet were wrapped in rags. No clothes. And we were freezing. And I just wanted to give up. I couldn't walk anymore." She looks at Pearl. "So she dragged me."

"If you can picture a skeleton," Pearl tells me. "She was a skin-colored skeleton. And so many people were lying dead on the road;

we were hungry and she couldn't walk. And she said, 'Just put me down here—' "

" 'Let me die,' " Helen recounts.

" 'And if you survive,' " Pearl continues, repeating her sister's words to her, " 'you'll tell the world what happened to us.' "

Helen picks up the story: "Pearl said to me, 'You cannot die. Because if you die, I'll die.' "

"So I told her," Pearl continues, " 'Put your arms around my neck.' I couldn't carry her; I was skinny, too."

"So she dragged me," Helen says.

"She was holding on to me." Pearl's voice breaks. "And we survived." She leans over to kiss her sister. It's a little awkward to do over the tape recorder I've placed between them, but she doesn't let it get in her way, planting a little wrinkled pucker on Helen's cheek. Helen kisses her right back.

Sitting with these two, I am aware of one overriding thought: Twinship need not be layered or loaded. It can be simple. Every bleak day that these sisters survived the camps, they reminded themselves, *At least we are together.* And in a world of unimaginable horror, that was enough. More than enough: It kept them alive.

"We survived together," Pearl goes on with wet eyes. "So we have two of us. We were never separated. Even when Mengele worked on us. We were always together. So we're lucky."

ROBIN: *I remember us talking on the phone the night before*
I went on my honeymoon and you were sad.
ABIGAIL: *What did I say?*
ROBIN: *You said it was like I was going off without you.*

Robin's wedding, in January 1993, was one of those magical weekends. Guests stayed at the rustic Mohonk Mountain House in New
Paltz, New York, where our parents had taken me, Robin, and my
brother, David, so many times during our childhood; the snow had
fallen fresh and thick, and twinkling icicles hung from every tree as if
some cosmic wedding planner had ordered them up just for the occasion. After the ceremony, Robin and Edward looked incandescent,
everyone mobbed the dance floor, and I sang my toast with the
band—a spoof on Billy Joel's song about Brenda and Eddie.

It didn't occur to me to feel sorry for myself that night; Robin's
happiness was intrinsically mine, too. I'd hosted her bridal shower,
tried on endless black bikinis in order to buy her the perfect one for
her honeymoon, and made her a mixed tape of the songs most evoca-
tive of our twenty-seven years—everything from "Rubber Ducky" to
"Chariots of Fire." I felt like the world was right, and of course, as her

twin and maid of honor, I felt indispensable. But as the evening unfolded, I began to discern a whiff of pity when friends and family congratulated me. They looked worried for Abigail. *One twin is flying the nest. How will the other handle it?* I felt them scrutinizing my bridal ministrations for glimpses of hidden despair; I noticed them notice I was not just lacking my own fiancé but entirely boyfriend-less at the ball. A few asked me if I was "okay."

I was honestly fine. I loved the man Robin was marrying and had always wanted her to launch first. All our lives, she'd preceded me in every milestone except walking: She rode the city bus by herself first, went abroad first, had the first boyfriend. She seemed to prefer the role of older sister, and I ceded it to her. Conversely, I felt protective of Robin—as if her contentment was more important for the balance of our friendship; somewhere in my mind, I felt I could better handle being the single, adrift twin, so I wanted her settled. I wanted her to have the first wedding. If she was taken care of, I could relax. Thus, I was unambiguously buoyant on her big day.

It was the night *after* that I crashed.

I remember where I was sitting: in my blue-and-white-checked armchair in my one-bedroom walk-up apartment on Columbus Avenue and Sixty-ninth Street, in my pajamas, trying not to cry on the phone with her as she said good-bye before her honeymoon departure. It finally hit me that something was over.

What flew into my head was that famous line from Carson McCullers's 1946 novel, *The Member of the Wedding,* when the young spark plug of a girl, Frankie Adams, fantasizes about a future life with her brother and his fiancée: "They are the *we* of me," she says. But the sentiment rang differently for me: The bride and groom were not "the we of me"; Robin was. My lifelong "we" was flying off to Martinique the next morning, on to a new partnership. I was left holding the "we."

It just so happens that I met my future husband one month later on a perfect blind date. But that happy ending doesn't change what shifted permanently for my twinness: the feeling that I was losing Robin. It wasn't that Edward took her away; it's that, on a deeper level, she was leaving *us*—our little compact duo, which had been my organizing principle and home base for twenty-seven years. And she was ready to go; I didn't sense any second thoughts on her part. Robin's post–wedding night ranked as one of many moments over the next decade—some momentous, some mundane—that have signaled to me a dilution, or muting, of our partnership.

Why is it that I sentimentalize my twinship at age forty-three? Usually we sentimentalize something we've lost; but I still have Robin. We talk daily, make lunch plans, borrow clothes, go to shows together. She's still essential to my equanimity, my confessor and adviser; I feel a kind of blissful ease when we steal an unexpected afternoon to go shopping, when we share a Corona while cooking together in the summer, or when we grab ten minutes to talk before she takes her kids home from a play date at my apartment. Her support is typified perhaps by the fact that she never once asked me not to write this book. In fact she kept emphasizing that it would be pointless if it wasn't honest. She read it not just as a sister but as an editor whose opinion she knows I require; and she was beyond generous about the end result, despite her misgivings.

But something isn't the same anymore; we both know it, and writing this book didn't change it. We don't make sure to schedule a regular meal, we only double-date with our husbands once a year, we aren't physically affectionate, we skirt certain topics, and we dodge conflict. I know I should chalk it up to separate lives, separate families, but after a twinship like ours, separate isn't simple—at least not for me. I don't so much *need* Robin as miss her. There's a gnawing absence from the person with whom I used to feel most present. Robin and I once had the ultimate intimacy. And I want it back.

When we were a few years out of college, Robin and I went to Greece together. It was the only vacation we ever took, just the two of us. (I don't count the American Jewish Congress tour to Israel, when my parents chose the senior tour by mistake and we traipsed around the Holy Land with a group of doting grandparents.) For this adventure, Robin and I chucked our usual exacting preparation and decided to travel where the impulse took us—from Athens to the islands of Mykonos, Naxos, and Santorini. We stayed in small white rooms wedged into cliffs overlooking azure water, ate the freshest tomato and feta salads, tried ouzo, and rode donkeys. We met cute Australians and held on to their waists on rented mopeds as we rode to cafés that sat on the sand.

But the moment I remember most vividly was lying on my back next to Robin on the sunbaked deck of a ferry. We were warm and brown from insufficient sunblock, aware that we were absolutely untethered and unaccounted for, but entirely safe side by side. We were anchored, even if we were God knows where in the middle of the ocean. On my Walkman, the Roches sisters were singing "Love Radiates Around." I insisted Robin listen to it after I did; the melody somehow glistened like the water around us, and the lyrics roused a sense of unshakable well-being. Sisters were harmonizing in my ears. To me, at least, it was our anthem.

> *My heart may break and it might fall*
> *She is mine and I am hers through seasons all . . .*
> *Her love is true music*
> *And it radiates around*

Robin left, Abigail right

❋ ❋

ACKNOWLEDGMENTS

Thanks (alphabetically) to so many people who offered advice, support, and twins:

Ronnie Abrams, Ricardo Ainslie, Laura Baker, Liora Baor, Soma Golden Behr, Isaac Blickstein, Dorret Boomsma, Thomas Bouchard, Stephanie Bowen, Angela Buchdahl, Antoinette Delruelle, Todd Doughty, Rachel Dretzin, Andrea Dunlop, Susan Edelstein, Deb Forese, Debbie and Tammy Freeman, Adam Freifeld, Joan Friedman, Debra and Lisa Ganz, Nancy Goodman, Gerald and Larry Gordon, Alan Hager, Aaron Harnick, Jane Harnick, Aileen and Gregory Hoffman, Sharon Jordan, Donald and Louis Keith, Erica Keswin, Billy Kingsland, Edward Klaris, Lorin Klaris, Deborah Copaken Kogan, Paul and George Kogan, Jill Krementz, Itamar Kubovy, Harry Lander, Belinda and Gretchen Langner, Miranda Levenstein, Jaclyn Levin, Suzanne Braun Levine, Tom Levine, Adam Liebowitz, Thomas Mack, Nicole Marcus, Nick Martin, Jessica McCarthy, Eric Nestler, Fern O'Neill, Neil Newman, Eileen Pearlman, Elizabeth Pector, Lisa and Richard Plepler, Lynn Povich, Anna Quindlen, Michael Ravitch, Liz Rosen, Martine Rubenstein, Ira Sachs, Hillel Schwartz, Brooke Sebold, Nancy Segal, R. Allen Shoaf, Annie Silberman, Joshua Steiner, Richard Stolley, Paris Stulbach, Alexandra Styron, David Teplica, Richard Todd, Eric Vilain, Burton Visotzky,

Pamela Weinberg, David Wolpe, John Wood, Hanya Yaragihara, Donna Zaccaro.

To David Kuhn, upon whose judgment I have become wholly dependent.

To Deb Futter, whose confidence made both my books happen and to whom I'll always be indebted.

To my remarkable editor, Kris Puopolo, for knowing this book as well as I do, and for great perception, wisdom, and new friendship.

To Dani Shapiro, for the kind of listening that leads to clarity.

To Marcia DeSanctis, for stunning constancy.

To my in-laws, Phyllis and Milton Shapiro, for their cheerleading and for giving me the best balcony in Fort Lauderdale on which to finish this.

To Mom, for her editor's eye, for carrying Robin and me when we made her enormous, and for all her love.

To Dad, for his unflagging faith and model fatherhood.

To my brother, David, the true optimist in the family, who weathered the whole Twin Thing with wit and warmth.

To Robin, for the smartest edits, for endless patience, and, most of all, for her blessing.

To my daughter, Molly, ten, for her canny suggestions and incomparable good-night kisses.

To Benjamin, twelve, who reminds me daily of what really matters.

To Dave, who makes me want to be better than I am, guides me more than he knows, and whose love is found in the quietest places.

NOTES

❖ ❖

EPIGRAPH

VII "I wouldn't be myself without her.": Allen Shawn, *Wish I Could Be There: Notes from a Phobic Life* (New York: Viking Penguin, 2007), p. 242.

INTRODUCTION

10 "Fraternal twins are not as close": Nancy L. Segal, Ph.D., *Entwined Lives* (New York: Penguin Group, 2000), p. 101.

1. THE MECCA: TWINSBURG

13 Twinsburg was named: http://www.mytwinsburg.com/site.cfm/about-twinsburg.cfm.

13 in the year I attended: author's interview with Sandy Miller, cofounder of Twins Days, September 2006.

GEE WHIZ

28 a British married couple: "Unknowing Twins Married," at http://www.cnn.com/2008/WORLD/europe/01/11/twins.married/index.html.

28 Lech and Jaroslaw Kaczynski: "Polish President's Twin to Be PM," BBC News, July 8, 2006, at http://news.bbc.co.uk/2/hi/europe/5161446.stm.

28 a tracking dog can find: S. Craig Roberts et al., "Body Odor Similarity in Noncohabiting Twins," *Chemical Senses* 30, no. 8: 651–656.

28 biracial British couple: Lucy Laing, "Black and White Twins," *Daily Mail*, March 2, 2006.

28 Elvis Presley's twin: Pamela Clark Keogh, *Elvis Presley: The Man, the Life, the Legend* (New York: Atria, 2004), p. 56.

28 Identical twins Mike and Bob Bryan: Tom Weir, "Chest-Bumping Bryan Brothers Always a Twosome on, off Court," *USA Today*, June 22, 2008.

28 German twins Oskar and Jack: Nancy L. Segal, *Indivisible by Two: Lives of Extraordinary Twins* (Cambridge: Harvard University Press, 2005), p. 120.

29   Mothers of twin pandas: Nancy L. Segal, "Parenting Twin Pandas," *Twin Research* 5, vol. 4: 314.

29   Minnesota becomes the first state to pass legislation: www.twinslaw.org

29   Identical twin sisters meet identical twin brothers: "Identical Twins Marry, Give Birth to Identical Twins," at Telegraph.co.uk.

29   Becky and Birdie Jo Hoaks: Jason George, "The Incredible True-Life (Mis)Adventures of the Hoaks Sisters," *Chicago Tribune*, May 10, 2007.

29   Massachusetts boasts the highest twin rate: Julie Suratt, "Double Trouble," *Boston Magazine*, June 2008, p. 1.

29   Twins from Erie, Pennsylvania: WPXI, Pittsburgh, April 24, 2007, at http://www.wpxi.com/health/13016039/detail.html.

29   "telepathy art": http://www.nyas.org/snc/calendarDetail.asp?eventID=11492&date= 4/11/2008%206:30:00%20PM.

30   Twin stars Mary-Kate and Ashley Olsen: http://www.oprah.com/slideshow/oprahshow/20081015_tows_olsentwins.

30   ten sets of twins: Jennifer Stagg, "Ten Twins Born in Just One Month at SLC Hospital," KUTV2, Salt Lake City, June 5, 2008.

30   Identical twins Dan and Walter Christ: Kathleen Daminger, "Seeing Double," *Lancaster New Era*, March 1, 2007.

30   Pop-rock duo Tegan and Sara: Colin Davenish, "Tegan and Sara Go Pop," rollingstone.com, September 14, 2004.

30   identical twins separated at birth: Nancy L. Segal, *Entwined Lives: Twins and What They Tell Us About Human Behavior* (New York: Dutton, 1999), p. 118.

30   twin brothers are killed on their bicycles: http://news.bbc.co.uk/2/hi/europe/1858721.stm.

2. EMBRYO TO END ZONE: TIKI AND RONDE BARBER

31   Tiki Barber, retired running back: http://hubpages.com/hub/All-Time_NFL_Rushing_Leaders_by_TeamNFC; see also http://en.wikipedia.org/wiki/Tiki_Barber

33   In 2005, Ronde became the first cornerback: http://www.buccaneers.com/team/playerdetail.aspx?player=Barber, Ronde,20; see also http://en.wikipedia.org/wiki/Ronde_Barber

38   Tiki was paid more than Ronde: Geraldine Fabrikant, "Talking Money With: Tiki and Ronde Barber; Atop Their Game, Ahead of the Market," *New York Times*, March 9, 2003.

3. IDENTICALS: A LOVE STORY

47   "Each is the other's soul": Karl Jay Shapiro, "The Twins," in *Person, Place and Thing* (New York: Reynal & Hitchcock, 1942), p. 27.

48   opened the first Twins Restaurant in 1994: *People*, December 12, 1994.

55   "wish to return to a symbiotic relationship": Ricardo Ainslie, *The*

Psychology of Twinship (Northvale, New Jersey: Jason Aronson, Inc., 1997), p. 137.

56   "There seems to be a feeling that the recognition of differences": ibid., p. 169.

60   "a degree of anxiety associated with": ibid., p. 65.

61   "While twins can engage in their own 'chumship' ": Michael Rothman, "The 'Self-Twin' System" (unpublished paper, Derner Institute, Adelphi University, 1999), p. 26.

69   "An identical twin may be the best source": Nancy L. Segal, *Entwined Lives: Twins and What They Tell Us About Human Behavior* (New York: Dutton, 1999), p. 101.

71   The pioneering research came from German obstetrician Birgit Arabin: author's interviews with Dr. Nicholas Martin, Dr. Isaac Blickstein, and Dr. Louis Keith. See also Birgit Arabin et al., "The onset of inter-human contacts: longitudinal ultrasound observations in early twin pregnancies," *Ultrasound in Obstetrics & Gynecology* 8, no. 3 (1996): 166–173; Birgit Arabin et al., "Registration of fetal behaviour in multiple pregnancy," *Journal of Perinatal Medicine* 21, no. 4 (1993): 285–294; Birgit Arabin et al., "Fetal behavior in multiple pregnancy: methodologic, clinical, and scientific aspects." *Geburtshilfe und Frauenheil Kunde* 51, no. 11 (1991): 869–875.

72   Child psychotherapist Alessandra Piontelli had done similar studies: author's interviews with Dr. Isaac Blickstein, Dr. Louis Keith, and Dr. Michael Rothman.

4. YOU DEPLETE ME: COMPETITION

81   "Competition and issues of power are embedded in the twin relation-ship": Michael Rothman, "The 'Self-Twin' System" (paper delivered, Derner Institute, Adelphi University), 1999.

82   "Commentators describe the two struggling for primogeniture": Hillel Schwartz, *The Culture of the Copy: Striking Likenesses, Unreasonable Facsimiles* (New York: Zone Books, 1998), p. 389 n.22.

82   The Yoruba believe that the older twin: Fernand Leroy et al., "Yoruba Customs and Beliefs Pertaining to Twins," *Twin Research* 5, no. 2 (2002): 132–136.

82   The Yoruba give every second-born twin: ibid.

88   "The fact that each twin might have different areas of talent": Ricardo Ainslie, *The Psychology of Twinship* (Northvale, New Jersey: Jason Aronson, Inc., 1997), p. 170.

88   "a whopping 84 percent": Francine Klagsbrun, *Mixed Feelings: Love, Hate, Rivalry and Reconciliation Among Brothers and Sisters* (New York: Bantam, 1992), p. 14.

88   "Parental favoritism": ibid., p. 259.

88   "Twins are not favored equally in the womb": Rothman, "The 'Self-Twin' System," p. 15.

92 psychoanalyst Dr. Susan Davison: ibid., p. 20. See also Susan Davison, "Mother, Other and Self—Love and Rivalry for Twins in Their First Year of Life," *International Review of Psycho-Analysis* 19 (1992): 359–374.

93 "Both the rivalry and the closeness may be fueled by the same thing": Klagsbrun, *Mixed Feelings*, p. 84.

93 "There is one side of you": Lawrence Wright, *Twins: And What They Tell Us About Who We Are* (New York: John Wiley, 1997), p. 159.

93 A news story several years later: *New York Journal-American,* 1947.

96 "competition can also be a source of differentiation": Ainslie, *The Psychology of Twinship,* p. 163.

98 "What you could be walks right next to you": Caroline Paul, *Fighting Fire* (New York: St. Martin's Press, 1998), p. 7.

5. RISKY BUSINESS: THE SHOALS OF BIRTHING TWINS

105 "not being able to have a baby": Chistine Gorman, "The Limits of Science," Time.com, April 15, 2002.

107 twin births in the United States: Joyce A. Martin et al. "Births: Final Data for 2006," *National Vital Statistics Reports* 57, no. 7 (January 7, 2009), p. 2.

107 Between 1980 and 1995, the number of triplets ballooned: ibid.

107 one in thirty-one births is a twin: ibid.

108 From 25 to 35 percent of IVF pregnancies produce multiple fetuses: Gorman, "The Limits of Science."

108 an estimated three million–plus IVF children in the world today: "History of IVF in the UK," Human Fertilisation and Embryology Authority, March 2, 2009, at http://www.hfea.gov.uk/en/1737.html; "Three Million Babies Born After Fertility Treatment," *Red Orbit,* June 21, 2006, at http://www.redorbit.com/news/health/545282/three_million_babies_born _after_fertility_treatment/index.html; Rebecca Tuhus-Dubrow, "ART in America," *The Nation,* November 8, 2007, at http://www.thenation.com/ doc/20071126/tuhus-dubrow.

108 Natural twins will happen only one or two times in a hundred births: Gilles Pison et al., "Frequency of Twin Births in Developed Countries," *Australian Academic Press* 9, no. 2 (2006): 250–260, at http://www. atypon-link.com/AAP/doi/abs/10.1375/twin.9.2.250.

108 Fraternal twins can run in families: Pamela Prindle Fierro, "If I Have Twins in My Family, Will I Have Twins?" at http://multiples.about.com/ od/pregnancy/a/familytwin_2.htm; P. Lichtenstein et al., "Twin births to mothers who are twins: a registry based study," *British Medical Journal* 312, 7035 (1996): 879–881, at http://www.pubmedcentral.nih.gov/ articlerender.fcgi?artid=2350609.

108 Neonatal death is five times higher for twins than for singletons: Audrey C. Sandbank, *Twin and Triplet Psychology: A Professional Guide to Working with Multiples* (London: Routledge, 1999), p. 157.

108   For triplets, the chance of infant death is eleven times higher than for single babies: http://www.nature.com/jp/journal/v23/n5/full/7210950a.html.

108   50 percent of all twins are premature: http://www.nature.com/jp/journal/v23/n5/full/7210950a.html.

108   90 percent of triplets: http://www.nature.com/jp/journal/v23/n5/full/7210950a.html. See also http://www.npr.org/templates/story/story.php?storyId=101027985.

108   twins who are small for their gestational age: author's interview with Dr. Avner Hershlag, December 9, 2009; "Liza Mundy: Multiple Births 'Changing Our World,' " February 23, 2009, at http://www.npr.org/templates/story/story.php?storyId=101027985; Centers for Disease Control and Prevention, press release, "National Birth Defects Prevention Study Shows Assisted Reproductive Technology Is Associated with an Increased Risk of Certain Birth Defects," November 17, 2008, at http://www.cdc.gov/media/pressrel/2008/r081117.htm.

108   A twin is four times more likely to be born with cerebral palsy: Isaac Blickstein, M.D., "Do multiple gestations raise the risk of cerebral palsy?" *Clinics in Perinatology* 31 (2004): 395–408; author's interview with Isaac Blickstein, June 8, 2007.

110   twins born as a result of fertility treatment: Michele Hansen, et al., "Twins born following assisted reproductive technology: perinatal outcome and admission to hospital," *Human Reproduction*, published online (May 20, 2009): http://humrep.oxfordjournals.org/cgi/reprint/dep173.

110   The crude summary of how IVF works: American Pregnancy Association, "In Vitro Fertilization: IVF," May 2007, at http://www.american pregnancy.org/infertility/ivf.html; author's interviews with fertility specialists Dr. Avner Hershlag, December 9, 2008, and Dr. James Grifo, December 9, 2008.

116   the UK and several European countries have: Human Fertilisation and Embryology Authority, "Multiple Births and Single Embryo Transfer Review," February 2009, at http://www.hfea.gov.uk/en/483.html.

120   In 2008, the American Society of Reproductive Medicine recommended: American Society for Reproductive Medicine, "Guidelines on Number of Embryos Transferred," November 2008, at http://www.asrm.org/Media/Practice/Guidelines_on_number_of_embryos .pdf.

6. TWIN SHOCK 101

130   she lists twenty modern myths about twins: Eileen M. Pearlman and Jill Alison Ganon, *Raising Twins: What Parents Want to Know (And What Twins Want to Tell Them)* (New York: HarperCollins, 2000), p. 68.

130   Spillman's 1991 study: Isaac Blickstein, Louis G. Keith, and Donald M.

Keith, eds., *Multiple Pregnancy: Epidemiology, Gestation and Perinatal Outcome*, 2d ed. (Abingdon, England: Taylor & Francis, 2005), p. 490.

130 "It is known that mothers of preterm twins": ibid., p. 788.

136 " 'Twin shock' can overwhelm the best-prepared mother": ibid., p. 489.

137 "parents are reluctant to separate their twins": ibid., p. 788.

139 "Several mothers have plainly said": Dorothy Burlingham, *Twins: A Study of Three Pairs of Identical Twins* (London: Imago Publishing Company, 1952), p. 13.

140 "Labels or personality styles are assigned to each twin": Michael Rothman, "The 'Self-Twin' System" (master's thesis, Derner Institute, Adelphi University, 1999), p. 24.

7. MAKING THE BREAK: SEPARATION

146 "The 'pushing away' and 'holding on' . . .": Ricardo Ainslie, *The Psychology of Twinship* (Northvale, New Jersey: Jason Aronson, Inc., 1997), p. 107.

147 won the National Poetry Slam championship: http://www.aifestival.org/index2.php?menu=5&sub=2&id=363.

151 "On the one hand, some of these twins articulate an ideal fantasy of twinship": Ainslie, *The Psychology of Twinship*, p. 141.

154 "One striking feature in many twinships": ibid., p. 128.

155 "With identical twins, the similarity in looks": Dorothy Burlingham, *Twins: A Study of Three Pairs of Identical Twins* (London: Imago Publishing Company, 1952), p. 16.

158 "What was Narcissus mourning?": Dale Ortmeyer, "The We-Self of Identical Twins," *Journal of Contemporary Psychoanalysis* 6, no. 2 (Spring 1970): p. 128.

159 "You could view the twins": Diane Setterfield, *The Thirteenth Tale* (New York: Washington Square Press, 2006), p. 178.

162 *Red Without Blue:* A documentary directed by Brooke Sebold, Benita Sills, and Todd Sills, Sundance Channel, 2007; see www.redwithout-blue.com.

8. AND THEN THERE WAS ONE

169 "So when I looked into a mirror": Chris Adrian, "Stab," in *A Better Angel: Stories* (New York: Farrar, Straus and Giroux, 2008), p. 59.

171 "The separation of twins is no ordinary separation": Diane Setterfield, *The Thirteenth Tale* (New York: Washington Square Press, 2006), p. 183.

172 the *New York Times* ran an article about her search: Jane Gross, "A Nation Challenged: The Families; For Twins, a Loss Doubled and a Missing Half," *New York Times,* November 24, 2001.

172 Twinless Twins: www.twinlesstwins.org.

172 some eighty people attended the Twinless Twins gathering in Toronto: Katie Rook, "Only One of Me Now," *National Post,* July 11, 2008.

175   higher initial "grief intensity ratings": Nancy L. Segal and S. L. Ream, "Decrease in grief intensity for deceased twin and non-twin relatives: an evolutionary perspective," *Personality and Individual Differences* 25 (1998): 317–325. See also http://www.ncbi.nlm.nih.gov/pubmed/8436394.

175   "We are born alone": Allen Shawn, *Wish I Could Be There: Notes from a Phobic Life* (New York: Viking Penguin, 2007), p. 218.

180   losing a twin is "profound": Joan Woodward, *The Lone Twin: Understanding Twin Bereavement and Loss* (London and New York: Free Association Books Limited, 1998), p. 3.

180   those twins who described their loss as "severe": ibid.

181   "He can't possibly remember": Kim Edwards, *The Memory Keeper's Daughter* (New York: Viking, 2005), p. 116.

181   "Until about twenty years ago": A. M. Hayton, ed., *Untwinned: Perspectives on the Death of a Twin Before Birth* (St. Albans, England: Wren Publications, 2007), p. 1.

182   "The potential exists that such an undiscoverable twin *might* be hidden": Kay Cassill, *Twins: Nature's Amazing Mystery* (New York: Atheneum, 1982), p. 60.

183   psychological profile of a surviving twin: http://www.altheahayton.com/wombtwin/.

188   cover image for Wally Lamb's best-seller: Wally Lamb, *I Know This Much Is True* (New York: HarperCollins, 1998).

191   the highest rate of fraternal-twin births in the world: http://emedicine.medscape.com/article/977234-overview.

192   statue called ibeji: Fernand Leroy et al., "Yoruba Customs and Beliefs Pertaining to Twins," *Twin Research* 5, no. 2 (2002): 132–136.

192   "Twins-child, please do not leave me": George Chemeche, ed., *Ibeji: The Cult of Yoruba Twins* (Milan: Five Continent Editions, 2003), p. 44.

9. SPLITTING THE DIFFERENCE: WHEN IDENTICAL TWINS DIFFER

195   "The study of twins is about the best natural experiment": interview with Dr. Nick Martin, *Australian Broadcasting, 1997*, at https://genepi.qimr.edu.au/general/articles/quantum.html.

195   "I just feel so guilty": http://www.thisislondon.co.uk/news/article-23493726-details/Identical+twin+sisters+face+ultimate+heartbreak+after+one+is+diagnosed+with+terminal+cancer/article.do. See also http://www.mirror.co.uk/news/top-stories/2008/06/28/girl-lives-on-in-twin-after-cancer-death-115875-20624119/.

196   multiple myeloma: www.multiplemyeloma.org.

201   one 2006 experiment: author's interview with Dr. Eric J. Nestler, October 22, 2008. See also Vaishnav Krishnan et al., "Molecular Adaptations Underlying Susceptibility and Resistance to Social Defeat in Brain Reward Regions," *Cell,* 131(2), no. 2 (2007): 391–404.

202   called a similar 2005 report "startling": Bob Weinhold, "Epigenetics: The

Science of Change," *Environmental Health Perspectives* 114, no. 3 (2006): p. 5.

202   "how adversity might reach inside the brain": Peter Kramer, "Scarred DNA and How It Might Heal," at http://blogs.psychologytoday.com/blog/in-practice/ 200805/scarred-dna-and-how-it-might-heal.

202   One rat study in 2004: Ian C. G. Weaver et al., "Epigenetic programming by maternal behavior," *Nature Neuroscience* 7, no. 8 (2004): 847–854; Christen Brownlee, "Nurture Takes the Spotlight: Decoding the Environment's Role in Development and Disease," at Sciencenews.org.; e-mail from Dr. Moshe Szyf, October 18, 2008.

203   a research group led by Manel Esteller: Mario F. Fraga et al., "Epigenetic differences arise during the lifetime of monozygotic twins," *PNAS: Proceedings of the National Academy of Sciences of the United States of America* 102, no. 30 (2005): 10604–10609. See also Rick Weiss, "Twin Data Highlight Genetic Changes," *Washington Post,* July 5, 2005.

205   the studies in the early 1990s: J. Michael Bailey and Richard C. Pillard, M.D., "A Genetic Study of Male Sexual Orientation," *Archives of General Psychiatry* 48, no. 12: 1089–1096; "Gay Men in Twin Study," *New York Times,* December 17, 1991.

206   one that made use of the Australian database of twins: J. Michael Bailey et al., "Genetic and Environmental Influences on Sexual Orientation and Its Correlates in an Australian Twin Sample," *Journal of Personality and Social Psychology* 78, no. 3 (2000): 524–536.

209   Their DNA isn't as alike: C. Bruder et al., "Phenotypically Concordant and Discordant Monozygotic Twins Display Different DNA Copy-Number-Variation Profiles," *The American Journal of Human Genetics* 82, no. 3: 763–771. See also "Identical Twins Not As Identical As Believed," *ScienceDaily,* February 20, 2008.

209   "When we started this study": Anahad O'Connor, "The Claim: Identical Twins Have Identical DNA," *New York Times,* March 11, 2008.

210   Studies of twins reared apart: Nancy L. Segal, *Entwined Lives: Twins and What They Tell Us About Human Behavior* (New York: Dutton, 1999), pp. 116–151. See also http://www.psych.umn.edu/people/faculty/bouchard.htm.

210   "every measured behavioral trait": ibid., p. 150.

211   "Children's achievements might still be the same": ibid., p. 57.

211   "The bottom line is that living together does not make people in a family alike": ibid., p. 76.

211   "Twins threaten us": Lawrence Wright, *Twins: And What They Tell Us About Who We Are* (New York: John Wiley, 1997), p. 144.

213   "Experiences in childhood and adolescent peer groups modify children's personalities": Judith Rich Harris, *The Nurture Assumption: Why Children Turn Out the Way They Do* (New York: Simon & Schuster, 1998), p. 359.

213   1999 Pulitzer finalist: http://www.pulitzer.org/bycat/General+Nonfiction.

213 "If the example of parents were important": Malcolm Gladwell, "Do Parents Matter?" *The New Yorker,* August 17, 1998, p. 3.

214 "The child's parents and siblings": e-mail from Judith Rich Harris, October 27, 2008.

THE RESULTS ARE IN: TWIN STUDIES

215 Aggression: James J. Hudziak et al., "A twin study of inattentive, aggressive, and anxious/depressed behaviors," *Journal of the American Academy of Child and Adolescent Psychiatry* 39 (2000): 469–476.

215 Alcohol dependence among adolescents: author's interview with Dr. Danielle Dick at the International Twins Conference, June 2007, Ghent, Belgium. Dick, a member of the Department of Psychiatry and Psychology at Washington University, St. Louis, studies the impact of genes on alcohol use and related behaviors..

215 Alcoholism: author's interview with Dr. Nick Martin, winter 2007. Martin, who heads the genetic epidemiology laboratory at Queensland Institute of Medical Research, was recently elected to the Australian Academy of Science for his contributions to the genetics of human behavior and complex diseases. See also http://www.qimr.edu.au/research/labs/nickm/index.html#staff: "Alcohol consumption is associated with many medical and social variables. With support from both NHMRC and three large grants from the U.S. National Institute of Alcoholism and Alcohol Abuse, 5,000 pairs of twins plus their relatives—23,000 subjects in all—have been surveyed, and we have conducted telephone interviews with over 11,000 twins and 4,000 of their spouses. Genetic factors account for about two thirds of the susceptibility to alcoholism in both women and men in Australia. Now we are obtaining blood samples from these twins with a view to identifying particular genes predisposing to drinking problems. A major finding this past year is that the alcohol dehydrogenase gene complex on chromosome 4 has a significant effect on risk of alcoholism."

215 Alcohol use: author's interview with Dr. Dick, June 2007.

215 Allergies: http://www.ncbi.nlm.nih.gov/pubmed/10887305.

215 Alzheimer's: http://news.bbc.co.uk/1/hi/health/4686806.stm.

215 Anorexia: http://www.washingtontimes.com/news/2006/mar/07/20060307-124606-2610r/. See also T. Wade et al., "The structure of disordered eating in a twin community sample," *International Journal of Eating Disorders* 19 (1996): 63–71.

215 Antisocial behavior with psychopathic tendencies (lack of empathy, remorse): http://personalitydisorders.suite101.com/article.cfm/antisocial_children.

215 Anxiety: James J. Hudziak et al. "A twin study of inattentive, aggressive, and anxious /depressed behaviors," *Journal of the American Academy of Child and Adolescent Psychiatry* 39 (2000): 469–476.

215 Attention deficit disorder: http://www.pslgroup.com/dg/F3356.htm;

author's interview with the late Dr. Richard Todd, Winter 2007. Todd was the director of the division of child and adolescent psychiatry at the Washington University School of Medicine, St. Louis.

216   Attitudes toward sex and religion: http://www.apa.org/monitor/apr04/beliefs.html.

216   Autism: Jim Dryden, "Autism's Genetic Structure Offers Insights," *Record* 29, no. 33 (2005) (quotes John N. Constantino, M.D., associate professor of psychiatry and of pediatrics, Washington University, St. Louis), at http://record.wustl.edu/news/page/normal/5290.html.

216   Back pain: http://www.sciencedaily.com/releases/2008/04/080408160636.htm.

216   Baldness: http://www.nature.com/jid/journal/v121/n6/full/5602102a.html.

216   Bipolar disorder: http://www.nimh.nih.gov/health/publications/bipolar-disorder/complete-index.shtml. See also Nancy L. Segal, *Entwined Lives: Twins and What They Tell Us About Human Behavior* (New York: Dutton, 1999), p. 87.

216   Cholesterol: author's interview with Dr. Dorret Boomsma, winter 2007. Boomsma is a behavioral geneticist and professor of biological psychology at the Vrije Universiteit, Amsterdam, the Netherlands.

216   Cocaine abuse: http://www.pubmedcentral.nih.gov/picrender.fcgi?artid=1305731&blobtype=pdf.

216   Cognitive abilities: http://www.psych.umn.edu/courses/spring05/mcguem/psy8935/koeppen2003.pdf.

216   Communication: http://biomed.gerontologyjournals.org/cgi/reprint/58/6/M566.

216   Criminality: Laura A. Baker et al., "Behavioral Genetics: The Science of Antisocial Behavior," *Law and Contemporary Problems*, nos. 1–2 (2006): 7–46.

216   Depression: http://www.counsellingconnection.com/index.php/2008/07/16/aetiology-of-depression/.

216   Extroversion: Robert Plomin, *Development, Genetics, and Psychology* (Hillsdale, New Jersey: Lawrence Erlbaum Associates, 1986), p. 281.

216   Happiness: http://news.bbc.co.uk/go/pr/fr/-/1/hi/health/7278853.stm.

217   IQ: Dr. Nancy Segal cites the finding that "identical twins are nearly as alike in IQ as the same person tested twice." See Nancy L. Segal, *Entwined Lives: Twins and What They Tell Us About Human Behavior* (New York: Dutton, 1999), pp. 49–51.

217   Job choice: Nancy L. Segal, "Career of Your Dreams, Career of Your Genes," *Psychology Today*, September/October 1999, at http://www.psychologytoday.com/articles/pto-19990901-000038.html.

217 Job salaries: Hal R. Varian, "Economic Scene; Ask not what you can do for marriage; ask what marriage can do for your bottom line," *New York Times,* July 29, 2004.

217 Left-handedness: C. E. Boklage, "The Biology of Human Twinning: A Needed Change of Perspective," in *Multiple Pregnancy, Epidemiology, Gestation and Perinatal Outcome,* 2d ed. Isaac Blickstein, Louis G. Keith, and Donald M. Keith, eds. (Abingdon, England: Taylor & Francis, 2005), pp. 260–261. See also Michael Corballis, Chris McManus, and Michael Peters, *Twin Lateralisation: Biology and Psychology* (London: Psychology Press, 1999), p. 266.

217 Loneliness: "Heredity May Be the Reason Some People Feel Lonely," *Science Daily,* at http://www.sciencedaily.com/releases/2005/11/051110222344.htm. See also Dorret I. Boomsma et al., "Genetic and Environmental Contributors to Loneliness in Adults: The Netherlands Twin Register Study," *Behavior Genetics* 35, no. 6 (2005): p. 1.

217 Menopause: Amanda Gardner, "Twin Sisters at High Risk for Early Menopause," *HealthDay News,* October 25, 2006, at Healthywoman.org.

217 Moliness: http://www.qimr.edu.au/research/labs/nickm/index.html.

217 Multiple sclerosis: author's interview with Dr. Thomas Mack, who specializes in studies on MS at the Norris Cancer Center, USC.

217 Nearsightedness: "Strong Evidence for a Genetic Marker for Nearsightedness," *Science Daily,* at http://www.sciencedaily.com/releases/2008/06/080602120910.htm.

217 Obesity: http://news.smashits.com/264005/Lifestyle-can-change-gene-activity-cause-insulin-resistance.htm.

217 Phobias: David H. Barlow, *Anxiety and Its Disorders* (New York: Guilford Press, 2004), p. 187.

217 Sleep patterns: Nathaniel F. Watson et al., "Genetic and Environmental Influences on Insomnia, Daytime Sleepiness, and Obesity in Twins," *SLEEP* 29, no. 5 (2006): 645.

218 Sleepwalking: Christer Hublin, et al. "Prevalence and genetics of sleepwalking: a population-based study," *Neurology* 48, no. 1 (1997):177–181.

218 Smoking: http://www.abc.net.au/catalyst/stories/s1408939.htm.

218 Social life: http://www.msnbc.msn.com/id/25192829/. See also Takeo Fujiwara et al., "Social Capital and Health: A Study of Adult Twins in the U.S.," *American Journal of Preventive Medicine* 35, no. 2 (2008): 139–144.

218 Stuttering: S. Felsenfeld et al., "A Study of the Genetic and Environmental Etiology of Stuttering in a Selected Twin Sample," *Behavior Genetics* 30, no. 5 (2000): 359–366.

218 Voting behavior: Charles Q. Choi, "The Genetics of Politics," *Scientific American,* October 2007.

10. CRUEL DNA: THE LORDS

227   Tay-Sachs disease:
http://kidshealth.org/parent/medical/genetic/tay_sachs.html.
genetics special, *Cracking the Code of Life:*
http://www.pbs.org/wgbh/nova/genome/program.html#03.

11. ME AND MY SHADOW: EXPLORING DOUBLENESS

238   "We assume we are all individuals": Oliver Sacks, "Bound Together in Fantasy and Crime," a review of *The Silent Twins,* by Marjorie Wallace, *New York Times,* October 19, 1986.

238   Nigerians killed their twins: Hillel Schwartz, *The Culture of the Copy: Striking Likenesses, Unreasonable Facsimiles* (New York: Zone Books, 1999), p. 22.

238   Brazilians thought multiple births were a product of adultery: E. A. Stewart, "The Comparative Constitution of Twinship: Strategies and Paradoxes," *Twin Research* 3 (2000): 142–147.

239   On some Pacific islands, it was thought that opposite-sex fetuses had had an incestuous relationship in the womb: S. Errington, "Incestuous Twins and the House Societies in Insular Southeast Asia," *Cult Anthropol* 2, no. 4 (1987): 403–444.

241   "Identical twin parents are equally related to their own children": Nancy L. Segal, *Entwined Lives: Twins and What They Tell Us About Human Behavior* (New York: Dutton, 1999), p. 17.

12. BUT FOR HER

246   "embodied the selections process" for many survivors: Robert Jay Lifton, *The Nazi Doctors: Medical Killing and the Psychology of Genocide* (New York: Basic Books, 1986), p. 342.

246   ". . . He frequently went to the ramp when not selecting in order to see that twins were being collected and saved for him": ibid.

251   Mengele was a "Dr. Jekyll and Mr. Hyde" figure: ibid., p. 355.

251   kill one twin immediately after the other twin died: ibid., p. 353.

251   Lifton describes how Mengele injected twins with chloroform to stop their hearts: ibid., pp. 350–351.

251   Mengele is said to have sewed two Gypsy twins together to create conjoined twins: Rabbi Joseph Telushkin, *Jewish Literacy* (New York: William Morrow, 1991), p. 393.

EPILOGUE

257   "My heart may break": "Love Radiates Around," by Mark Johnson, *Another World* album, 1985.

BIBLIOGRAPHY

* *

Adrian, Chris. *A Better Angel: Stories*. New York: Farrar, Straus and Giroux, 2008.

Ainslie, Ricardo. *The Psychology of Twinship*. Northvale, New Jersey: Jason Aronson, Inc., 1997.

Bailey, J. Michael, and Richard C. Pillard, M.D. "A Genetic Study of Male Sexual Orientation." *Archives of General Psychiatry* 48, no. 12 (1991): 1089–1096.

Bailey, J. Michael et al. "Genetic and Environmental Influences on Sexual Orientation and Its Correlates in an Australian Twin Sample." *Journal of Personality and Social Psychology* 78, no. 3 (2000): 524–536.

Blickstein, Isaac, Louis G. Keith, and Donald M. Keith, eds. *Multiple Pregnancy: Epidemiology, Gestation and Perinatal Outcome*. 2nd ed. Abingdon, England: Taylor & Francis, 2005.

Brandt, Raymond William. *Twin Loss: A Book for Survivor Twins*. Leo, Indiana: Twinsworld Publishing Co., 2001.

Burlingham, Dorothy. *Twins: A Study of Three Pairs of Identical Twins*. London: Imago Publishing Company, 1952.

Burton-Phillips, Elizabeth. *Mum, Can You Lend Me Twenty Quid?: What Drugs Did to My Family*. London: Portrait, 2007.

Cassill, Kay. *Twins: Nature's Amazing Mystery*. New York: Atheneum, 1982.

Chemeche, George, ed. *Ibeji: The Cult of Yoruba Twins*. Milan: Five Continent Editions, 2003.

Courlander, Harold. *Tales of Yoruba Gods and Heroes*. New York: Original Publications, 1973.

Davison, Susan. "Mother, Other and Self—Love and Rivalry for Twins in their First Year of Life." *International Review of Psycho-Analysis* 19 (1992): 359–374.

Friedman, Joan. *Emotionally Healthy Twins: A New Philosophy for Parenting Two Unique Children*. Philadelphia: Da Capo Press, 2008.

Gedda, Luigi. *Twins in History and Science*. Springfield, Illinois: Charles C. Thomas, 1961.

Harris, Judith Rich. *The Nurture Assumption: Why Children Turn Out the Way They Do*. New York: Simon & Schuster, 1998.

———. *No Two Alike: Human Nature and Human Individuality*. New York: W. W. Norton, 2006.

Hayton, Althea, ed. *Untwinned: Perspectives on the Death of a Twin Before Birth*. St. Albans, England: Wren Publications, 2007.

Klagsbrun, Francine. *Mixed Feelings: Love, Hate, Rivalry and Reconciliation Among Brothers and Sisters*. New York: Bantam, 1992.

Leroy, Fernand et al. "Yoruba Customs and Beliefs Pertaining to Twins." *Twin Research* 5, no. 2 (2002): 132–136.

Lifton, Robert Jay. *The Nazi Doctors: Medical Killing and the Psychology of Genocide*. New York: Basic Books, 1986.

Martin, Joyce A. et al. "Births: Final Data for 2005." *National Vital Statistics Reports* 56, no. 6 (2007).

Noble, Elizabeth. *Primal Connections: How our Experiences from Conception to Birth Influence Our Emotions, Behavior and Health*. New York: Simon & Schuster, 1993.

Noble, Elizabeth et al. *Having Twins and More: A Parent's Guide to Multiple Pregnancy, Birth, and Early Childhood*. 3d ed. New York: Houghton Mifflin, 2003.

Ortmeyer, Dale. "The We-Self of Identical Twins." *Journal of Contemporary Psychoanalysis* 6, no. 2 (1970): 126–139.

Paul, Caroline. *Fighting Fire*. New York: St. Martin's Press, 1998.

Pearlman, Eileen M., and Jill Alison Ganon. *Raising Twins: What Parents Want to Know (And What Twins Want To Tell Them)*. New York: HarperCollins, 2000.

Piontelli, Alessandra. *From Fetus to Child: An Observational and Psychoanalytic Story*. London: Routledge, 1992.

Rothman, Michael. "The 'Self-Twin' System" (unpublished paper, Derner Institute, Adelphi University). A version was presented at the meeting of the Division of Psychoanalysis, American Psychological Association, New York City, April 15, 1999.

Setterfield, Diane. *The Thirteenth Tale*. New York: Washington Square Press, 2006.

Sandbank, Audrey C., ed. *Twin and Triplet Psychology: A Professional Guide to Working with Multiples*. London: Routledge, 1999.

Schwartz, Hillel. *The Culture of the Copy: Striking Likenesses, Unreasonable Facsimiles*. New York: Zone Books, 1998.

Segal, Nancy L. *Entwined Lives: Twins and What They Tell Us About Human Behavior*. New York: Dutton, 1999.

———. *Indivisible by Two: Lives of Extraordinary Twins*. Cambridge: Harvard University Press, 2005.

Shawn, Allen. *Wish I Could Be There: Notes from a Phobic Life*. New York: Viking Penguin, 2007.

Torrey, E. Fuller, M.D., et al. *Schizophrenia and Manic-Depressive Disorder: The Biological Roots of Mental Illness as Revealed by the Landmark Study of Identical Twins*. New York: Basic Books, 1994.

Woodward, Joan. *The Lone Twin: Understanding Twin Bereavement and Loss*. London & New York: Free Association Books Limited, 1998.

Wright, Lawrence. *Twins: And What They Tell Us About Who We Are*. New York: John Wiley, 1997.

Printed in the United States
by Baker & Taylor Publisher Services